EDEXCEL
A LEVEL
HISTORY

ActiveBook included

Paper 3:

Poverty, public health and the state in Britain, c1780–1939

Rosemary Rees
Series editor: Rosemary Rees

ALWAYS LEARNING

PEARSON

Published by Pearson Education Limited, 80 Strand, London, WC2R 0RL

www.pearsonschoolsandfecolleges.co.uk

Copies of official specifications for all Edexcel qualifications may be found on the website: www.edexcel.com

Text © Pearson Education Limited 2016

Designed by Elizabeth Arnoux for Pearson

Typeset and illustrated by Phoenix Photosetting, Chatham, Kent

Produced by Out of House Publishing

Original illustrations © Pearson Education Limited 2016

Cover design by Malena Wilson-Max for Pearson

Cover photo © akg-images Ltd: Imagno

The rights of Rosemary Rees to be identified as author of this work have been asserted by her in accordance with the Copyright, Designs and Patents Act 1988.

First published 2016

19 18 17 16

10 9 8 7 6 5 4 3 2

British Library Cataloguing in Publication Data

A catalogue record for this book is available from the British Library

ISBN 978 1 447 985419

Printed in the UK by CPI

Websites

Pearson Education Limited is not responsible for the content of any external internet sites. It is essential for tutors to preview each website before using it in class so as to ensure that the URL is still accurate, relevant and appropriate. We suggest that tutors bookmark useful websites and consider enabling students to access them through the school/college intranet.

A note from the publisher

In order to ensure that this resource offers high-quality support for the associated Pearson qualification, it has been through a review process by the awarding body. This process confirms that this resource fully covers the teaching and learning content of the specification or part of a specification at which it is aimed. It also confirms that it demonstrates an appropriate balance between the development of subject skills, knowledge and understanding, in addition to preparation for assessment.

Endorsement does not cover any guidance on assessment activities or processes (e.g. practice questions or advice on how to answer assessment questions) included in the resource, nor does it prescribe any particular approach to the teaching or delivery of a related course.

While the publishers have made every attempt to ensure that advice on the qualification and its assessment is accurate, the official specification and associated assessment guidance materials are the only authoritative source of information and should always be referred to for definitive guidance.

Pearson examiners have not contributed to any sections in this resource relevant to examination papers for which they have responsibility.

Examiners will not use endorsed resources as a source of material for any assessment set by Pearson.

Endorsement of a resource does not mean that the resource is required to achieve this Pearson qualification, nor does it mean that it is the only suitable material available to support the qualification, and any resource lists produced by the awarding body shall include this and other appropriate resources.

Contents

How to use this book

STRUCTURE

This book covers Paper 3, Option 34.2: Poverty, public health and the state in Britain, c1780–1939, of the Edexcel A Level qualification.

You will also need to study a Paper 1 and a Paper 2 option and produce coursework in order to complete your qualification. All Paper 1/2 options are covered by other textbooks in this series.

EXAM SUPPORT

The examined assessment for Paper 3 requires you to answer questions from three sections. Throughout this book there are exam-style questions in all three section styles for you to practise your examination skills.

Section A contains a compulsory question that will assess your source analysis and evaluation skills.

A Level Exam-Style Question Section A

Study Source 1 before you answer this question.

Assess the value of the source for revealing the attitude to paupers of those administering the old Poor Law, and the importance of settlement.

Explain your answer, using the source, the information given about it and your own knowledge about the historical context. (20 marks)

Tip
Consider the ways in which the magistrates and overseers are acting towards the Pyman family, and the importance of settlement as it related to the poor rates.

Section B contains a choice of essay questions that will look at your understanding of the studied period in depth.

A Level Exam-Style Question Section B

'The workhouse system in the years 1834–47 failed to uphold the principle of less eligibility.' How far do you agree with this statement? (20 marks)

Tip
Consider the ways in which the principle of less eligibility was met and the ways in which it could not be, and was not, met before reaching a judgement.

Section C will again give you a choice of essay questions but these will assess your understanding of the period in breadth.

A Level Exam-Style Question Section C

To what extent was the work of John Snow in discovering how cholera was transmitted the key turning point in public health reform in the years 1780–1939? (20 marks)

Tip
Think about what changed and what stayed the same as a result of Snow's discovery, and then consider at least two other possible turning points within the time period in order to judge whether Snow's was 'key'. These might be, for example, the work of Edward Jenner, Joseph Bazalgette or one of the Public Health Acts. Make sure that what you write covers the whole period of 1780–1939.

The Preparing for your exams sections at the end of this book contains sample answers of different standards, with comments on how they could be improved.

FEATURES
Extend your knowledge

These features contain additional information that will help you gain a deeper understanding of the topic. This could be a short biography of an important person, extra background information about an event, an alternative interpretation, or even a research idea that you could follow up. Information in these boxes is not essential to your exam success, but still provides insights of value.

EXTEND YOUR KNOWLEDGE

Sir John Simon (1816–1904)
Born in London, John Simon received his medical training by first being apprenticed to a surgeon at St Thomas' Hospital, and then completed his formal medical studies at King's College, London. Between 1840 and 1847, he worked as a surgeon at King's College Hospital, and later lectured in pathology. A founder member of the Health of Towns Association in 1844, in 1848 Simon became medical officer of health for the City of London and Chief Medical Officer for Health to the Privy Council in 1858. Like Chadwick, he was initially a firm supporter of the miasma theory of the spread of disease but, unlike Chadwick, he changed his mind as evidence supporting the germ theory gradually became available. Simon helped transform the issue of public health from a political matter to one founded in scientific investigation and analysis, and his detailed reports helped bring about both the Sanitary Act 1866 and the Public Health Act 1875. He stepped down from office in 1876, and in 1887 received a knighthood for his contribution to public health.

Knowledge check activities

These activities are designed to check that you have understood the material that you have just studied. They might also ask you questions about the sources and extracts in the section to check that you have studied and analysed them thoroughly.

> ### ACTIVITY
> #### KNOWLEDGE CHECK
>
> **Henry Mayhew**
>
> 1 How helpful do you find Henry Mayhew's classification of the labouring poor?
>
> 2 Compare Mayhew's classification to the simpler one of dividing the poor into 'deserving' and 'undeserving'. Which classification would a Poor Law officer find a) easier and b) fairer when administering poor relief?
>
> 3 Read Source 11. In what ways could the female shirt-maker described by Mayhew be helped by any of the agencies described in this section?
>
> 4 To what extent did Henry Mayhew challenge the prevailing orthodoxy relating to the poor?

Summary activities

At the end of each chapter, you will find summary activities. These are tasks designed to help you think about the key topic you have just studied as a whole. They may involve selecting and organising key information or analysing how things changed over time. You might want to keep your answers to these questions safe – they are handy for revision.

> ### ACTIVITY
> #### SUMMARY
>
> **Social reform, 1880–1914**
>
> 1 To what extent did Booth and Rowntree challenge contemporary beliefs about the causes and extent of poverty?
>
> 2 How revolutionary was the Liberal government's social reform programme?
>
> 3 What was the impact of the Liberal reforms on the Poor Law?
>
> 4 Read Extracts 3 and 4.
>
>   a) To what extent do the authors Birch and Fraser disagree about Liberal achievements by 1914?
>
>   b) With which author do you agree, and why?

Thinking Historically activities

These activities are found throughout the book, and are designed to develop your understanding of history, especially around the key concepts of evidence, interpretations, causation and change. Each activity is designed to challenge a conceptual barrier that might be holding you back. This is linked to a map of conceptual barriers developed by experts. You can look up the map and find out which barrier each activity challenges by downloading the progression map from this website: www.pearsonschools.co.uk/historyprogressionsapproach.

progression map reference

> ### THINKING HISTORICALLY   Evidence (6c)
>
> **Comparing and evaluating historians' arguments**
>
> Source 12 and Extract 4 are two historians' accounts about the effects of the Depression.
>
> 1 Compare the two accounts above and identify factual statements or claims that they both agree upon. Make a list of these points.
>
> 2 Look carefully at how the historians use language. Do they both use equally cautious language in making their claims or is one more confident and assertive than the other? Is one, or both, of the historians over-claiming?
>
> 3 Historians select evidence in order to make their arguments. Look back in this chapter and find evidence to support the arguments of each historian.
>
> 4 Are both of the historical accounts equally credible or are there reasons to prefer one account more than the other?

Getting the most from your online ActiveBook

This book comes with three years' access to ActiveBook* – an online, digital version of your textbook. Follow the instructions printed on the inside front cover to start using your ActiveBook.

Your ActiveBook is the perfect way to personalise your learning as you progress through your A Level History course. You can:

- access your content online, anytime, anywhere
- use the inbuilt highlighting and annotation tools to personalise the content and make it really relevant to you.

Highlight tool – use this to pick out key terms or topics so you are ready and prepared for revision.

Annotations tool – use this to add your own notes, for example links to your wider reading, such as websites or other files. Or, make a note to remind yourself about work that you need to do.

*For new purchases only. If the access code has already been revealed, it may no longer be valid. If you have bought this textbook secondhand, the code may already have been used by the first owner of the book.

Introduction
A Level History

WHY HISTORY MATTERS

History is about people and people are complex, fascinating, frustrating and a whole lot of other things besides. This is why history is probably the most comprehensive and certainly one of the most intriguing subjects there is. History can also be inspiring and alarming, heartening and disturbing, a story of progress and civilisation and of catastrophe and inhumanity.

History's importance goes beyond the subject's intrinsic interest and appeal. Our beliefs and actions, our cultures, institutions and ways of living, our languages and means of making sense of ourselves are all shaped by the past. If we want to fully understand ourselves now, and to understand our possible futures, we have no alternative but to think about history.

History is a discipline as well as a subject matter. Making sense of the past develops qualities of mind that are valuable to anyone who wants to seek the truth and think clearly and intelligently about the most interesting and challenging intellectual problem of all: other people. Learning history is learning a powerful way of knowing.

WHAT IS HISTORY?

History is a way of constructing knowledge about the world through research, interpretation, argument and debate.

Building historical knowledge involves identifying the traces of the past that exist in the present – in people's memories, in old documents, photographs and other remains, and in objects and artefacts ranging from bullets and lipsticks, to field systems and cities. Historians interrogate these traces and *ask questions* that transform traces into *sources of evidence* for knowledge claims about the past.

Historians aim to understand what happened in the past by *explaining why* things happened as they did. Explaining why involves trying to understand past people and their beliefs, intentions and actions. It also involves explaining the causes and evaluating the effects of large-scale changes in the past and exploring relationships between what people aimed to do, the contexts that shaped what was possible and the outcomes and consequences of actions.

Historians also aim to *understand change* in the past. People, states of affairs, ideas, movements and civilisations come into being in time, grow, develop, and ultimately decline and disappear. Historians aim to identify and compare change and continuity in the past, to measure the rate at which things change and to identify the types of change that take place. Change can be slow or sudden. It can also be understood as progressive or regressive – leading to the improvement or worsening of a situation or state of affairs. How things change and whether changes are changes for the better are two key issues that historians frequently debate.

Figure 1 Fragment of a black granite statue possibly portraying the Roman politician Mark Antony.

Debate is the essence of history. Historians write arguments to support their knowledge claims and historians argue with each other to test and evaluate interpretations of the past. Historical knowledge itself changes and develops. On the one hand, new sources of knowledge and new methods of research cause *historical interpretations* to change. On the other hand, the questions that historians ask change with time and new questions produce new answers. Although the past is dead and gone, the interpretation of the past has a past, present and future.

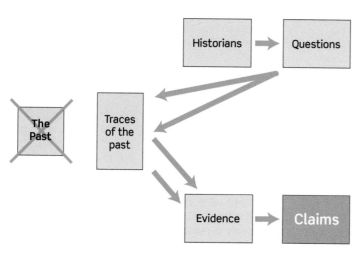

Figure 2 Constructing knowledge about the past.

THE CHALLENGES OF LEARNING HISTORY

Like all other Advanced Level subjects, A Level history is difficult – that is why it is called 'advanced'. Your Advanced Level studies will build on knowledge and understanding of history that you developed at GCSE and at Key Stage 3 – ideas like 'historical sources', 'historical evidence' and 'cause', for example. You will need to do a lot of reading and writing to progress in history. Most importantly, you will need to do a lot of thinking, and thinking about your thinking. This book aims to support you in developing both your knowledge and your understanding.

History is challenging in many ways. On the one hand, it is challenging to build up the range and depth of knowledge that you need to understand the past at an advanced level. Learning about the past involves mastering new and unfamiliar concepts arising from the past itself (such as the Inquisition, Laudianism, *Volksgemeinschaft*) and building up levels of knowledge that are both detailed and well organised. This book covers the key content of the topics that you are studying for your examination and provides a number of features to help you build and organise what you know – for example, diagrams, timelines and definitions of key terms. You will need to help yourself too, of course, adding to your knowledge through further reading, building on the foundations provided by this book.

Another challenge is to develop understandings of the discipline of history. You will have to learn to think historically about evidence, cause, change and interpretations and also to write historically, in a way that develops clear and supported argument.

Historians think with evidence in ways that differ from how we often think in everyday life. In history, as Figure 2 shows, we cannot go and 'see for ourselves' because the past no longer exists. Neither can we normally rely on 'credible witnesses' to tell us 'the truth' about 'what happened'. People in the past did not write down 'the truth' for our benefit. They often had clear agendas when creating the traces that remain and, as often as not, did not themselves know 'the truth' about complex historical events.

A root of the word 'history' is the Latin word *historia*, one of whose meanings is 'enquiry' or 'finding out'. Learning history means learning to ask questions and interrogate traces, and then to reason about what the new knowledge you have gained means. This book draws on historical scholarship for its narrative and contents. It also draws on research on the nature of historical thinking and on the challenges that learning history can present for students. Throughout the book you will find 'Thinking Historically' activities designed to support the development of your thinking.

You will also find – as you would expect given the nature of history – that the book is full of questions. This book aims to help you build your understandings of the content, contexts and concepts that you will need to advance both your historical knowledge and your historical understanding, and to lay strong foundations for the future development of both.

Dr Arthur Chapman
Institute of Education
University College London

Poverty, public health and the state in Britain, c1780–1939

SOURCE 1

Applicants for Admission to a Casual Ward painted by Sir Luke Fildes in 1874. He was a popular illustrator of social issues, who believed in the power of visual images to change public opinion. In this painting, the destitute are queuing to obtain a ticket that would give them basic temporary, overnight accommodation in a casual ward.

The men, women and children in Sir Luke Fildes' painting are clearly desperately poor. They have nowhere to live, are almost certainly cold and hungry and will be vulnerable to all the diseases normally associated with poverty: cholera and tuberculosis, typhoid and diphtheria, scarlet fever and measles. They are living close to the edge. Yet this image was painted towards the end of the 19th century, when the 'old' Poor Law had been swept away and replaced with a supposedly streamlined, efficient, universal system of dealing with poverty – the Poor Law Amendment Act of 1834. Had something gone horribly wrong?

The poor, paupers and pauperism

To be poor was not necessarily to be a **pauper**, but all paupers were, by definition, poor. Paupers were all those people who could not support themselves and their families at a level generally acceptable to society, and so were given **relief**. This relief could be 'outdoor' and come in the form of food, clothing or grants of money from the pauper's **parish**, enabling the pauper to

KEY TERMS

Pauper
A person in receipt of poor relief.

Relief
Support given to paupers to enable them to maintain a basic standard of living. This relief could be 'outdoor' (provided in their own homes) or 'indoor' (provided in a poorhouse or workhouse).

1601 – Poor Law establishes parish as the unit for administering poor relief — 1601

1819 – Sturges-Bourne Act empowers parishes to distinguish between 'deserving' and 'undeserving' poor — 1819

1834 – Poor Law Amendment Act passed; Poor Law Commission set up to oversee its implementation — 1834

1845–46 – Andover Workhouse scandal — 1845–46

1848 – Public Health Act (permissive)
Second cholera epidemic: 62,000 die — 1848

1853 – Vaccination Act
Third cholera epidemic kills 20,000; John Snow states cholera is a water-borne disease — 1853

1871 – Local Government Board takes on responsibility for administration of Poor Law — 1871

1903 – Letchworth Garden City founded
Government Inter-Departmental Committee set up — 1903

1909 – Old Age Pensions Act
Trade Boards Act
Labour Exchanges Act — 1909

1929 – Wall Street Crash — 1929

1936 – Jarrow march
Public Health Act — 1936

1796	**1796 –** Edward Jenner's first cowpox vaccination
1831	**1831 –** Central Board of Health and local boards of health set up. First cholera epidemic: 31,000 die
1837–8	**1837-8 –** *Oliver Twist* by Charles Dickens published
1847	**1847 –** Poor Law Board replaces Poor Law Commission
1849	**1849 –** Henry Mayhew's *London Labour and the London Poor* published
1865	**1865 –** Joseph Bazalgette's sewerage system for London opens
1875	**1875 –** Public Health Act (compulsory)
1906	**1906 –** Education (Provision of Meals) Act
1911	**1911 –** National Insurance Act
1934	**1934 –** Special Areas Act Unemployment Act
1939	**1939 –** Second World War breaks out

stay in his or her own home and be supported there. Relief could, on the other hand, be 'indoor', whereby paupers were given support only if they entered a parish poorhouse or workhouse. Whether or not individuals received indoor or outdoor relief depended very much on their own circumstances – whether, for example, they were forced to ask for relief because they were old and infirm, sick or simply unable to find work – and on the attitude of parish officials to the giving of relief and to those who received it.

> **KEY TERM**
>
> Parish
> An area served by a vicar and a parish church; Acts of Parliament from the 16th century used the parish as an area for secular administration.

Thousands of families drifted in and out of pauperism. The death of the main wage earner could plunge a whole family into long-term pauperism, from which it could only be retrieved by, say, remarriage or the older children becoming wage earners. In a similar way, for a family existing at or around subsistence level with little or no money put aside for emergencies, the illness of the main wage earner, or more generalised crises like an economic depression, could force a family to ask for short-term relief. It was, indeed, the volatile nature of the economy itself that created poverty for many thousands of people. A rapidly increasing population, coupled with an economy that was moving fast from a pre-mechanical one to an industrialised one, created huge fluctuations in job opportunities and wages over which people had no control. In short, the labour market was, at times, chaotic and this in itself created pauperism.

What was the connection between poverty and public health?

Poverty and pauperism affected the most vulnerable members of society: those who had few saleable skills and less education, who were at the mercy of market forces, the vagaries of employers and their own health. A poor diet, lack of sufficient clean clothing, or even a change of clothing at all, and crowded, often dirty accommodation created conditions in which disease flourished.

Poor families were prone to infection. Influenza, measles and scarlet fever were all killers in the 19th century. Diphtheria, tuberculosis and typhus were common. However, improving the health of the community, particularly the health of the poor, posed huge problems. There had to be appropriate technical skill and knowledge of sanitary engineering and there had to be appropriate medical knowledge about the causes of disease. Above all, there had to be willingness on the part of the public, local authorities and parliament to legislate and conform to that legislation. This latter requirement was going to be particularly tricky where the well-to-do had paid for their own private arrangements for sewage removal and a clean water supply, and were going to be asked to pay again to help the poor have similar arrangements for free.

The provision of public health that would inevitably favour the poorer members of society was to be no easy task in a Britain wedded, in the early years of this period, to the doctrine of **laissez-faire**. The theme that links the issues of poverty and public health is how and why individuals and governments responded to pressure for change, and the ways in which this period saw a growth in the responsibilities assumed by the state.

> **KEY TERM**
>
> Laissez-faire
> Literally 'let be' or 'leave alone', this is the belief that the government should interfere as little as possible in the affairs of its people.

3.1 The impetus for public health reforms

KEY QUESTIONS

- Why did reforms to public health become such a pressing issue from c1780?
- To what extent did attitudes to public health reforms change in the years 1780–1939?

INTRODUCTION

Poverty and pauperism affected the most vulnerable members of society: those who had few saleable skills and less education, who were at the mercy of market forces and the vagaries of employers. Disease, on the other hand, was no respecter of persons. Maria Woolf, wife of a struggling law clerk, died from cholera in 1849 when she was 32 years old and eight months pregnant; her unborn child died too. Her husband George survived the cholera only to die from tuberculosis two years later. Prince Albert, husband to Queen Victoria, died from typhoid on 14 December 1861 aged 42. Their daughter Alice died from diphtheria in 1878, when she was 35 years old; she was buried with her four-year-old daughter, Marie, who had died from the same disease a few weeks before her mother. All of these diseases were related to poor public health. If the prevalence and spread of such diseases was to be controlled, effective public health was essential.

Improving the health of the community has always posed problems for those intent on developing public health provision. There has to be appropriate technical skill and knowledge of sanitary engineering; there has to be appropriate medical knowledge about the cause and prevention of disease; and there has to be willingness on the part of the public, local authorities and parliament to legislate and carry through and uphold that legislation.

WHY DID REFORMS TO PUBLIC HEALTH BECOME SUCH A PRESSING ISSUE FROM c1780?

KEY TERM

Bubonic plague
A highly infectious epidemic disease that was carried by fleas that lived on rats, and transmitted to people via flea bites.

In pre-industrial Britain, there were few pressing public health problems. True, there were no drains or sewerage systems, no clean piped water and no effective measures to prevent the spread of disease. From time to time, edicts and directives were issued by government and town councils regarding, for example, the removal of waste from the streets and the emptying of privies. There were periodic outbreaks, too, of **bubonic plague**. While there was some concentration of people in fairly crowded conditions in London and some provincial towns, the vast majority of people lived, thinly spread, in rural areas. There was certainly no perceived need for anything like a national public health system.

1802 – Lambeth Waterworks replaces wooden pipes with cast iron pipes

1829 – Chelsea Waterworks Company installs sand filtration system to purify Thames' water

1830 – Election of Whig government

1831 – Temporary Board of Health set up
Cholera epidemic kills 31,000

1842 – Chadwick's *Report on the Sanitary Condition of the Labouring Population of Great Britain* is published
John Roe invents system of flushing gates to control flow of sewage through sewers

| 1800 | 1820 | 1825 | 1830 | 1835 | 1840 | 1845 |

1822 – Southwark Water Company extracts water from the River Thames using steam pumps

1832 – Street riots protesting against cholera
Temporary Cholera Acts give local authorities the power to enforce measures and fund them from the poor rates
Parliamentary Reform Act passed

1844 – Friedrich Engels' *The Condition of the Working Class in England* is published
Report of the Royal Commission into the Sanitary Condition of Large Towns and Populous Districts is published
Health of Towns Association founded

Public health problems caused by the Industrial Revolution

Enormous, cataclysmic change was to come with industrialisation that began in England in the late 18th century. Between 1781 and 1871, the population of Britain grew from approximately 13 million to over 31 million, and by 1939 to nearly 48 million, with the most rapid period of growth being between 1811 and 1841. It was a population that was not only growing, but was on the move. Industrialisation had created work in factories, mills and foundries and people flocked into the rapidly growing towns and cities to take advantage of the new job opportunities. The sudden influx of people forced many to crowd together, living in substandard housing with little by way of clean water or adequate sanitation. This had the potential to become a public health catastrophe.

The impact of a rising, mobile population

The overall population increase in Britain was most rapid in the years between 1811 and 1841. This was due almost entirely to the consequences of industrialisation.

The death rate fell due to:

- the medical industry producing the vaccine that prevented smallpox killing so many people

- the agricultural industry producing food that was better in quantity and quality

- the chemical industry producing soap that was cheap and readily available, enabling people to keep themselves and their clothes cleaner than before

- the textile industry producing cotton cloth that was cheap to buy and easy to wash and so help people to keep clean.

The birth rate rose because:

- fewer people dying when young meant that more people survived into their twenties and thirties to have babies

- more babies living to adulthood meant that their generation, too, would have more children, and so on through following generations.

The marriage rate rose because:

- in rural areas, farmers employed fewer live-in servants. It was therefore easier for men and women agricultural labourers to begin life together on their own and so they married earlier

- in industrial areas, unskilled workers were replacing skilled craftsmen who had to work a seven-year apprenticeship. Therefore, industrial workers could marry as soon as they had a job or even if they didn't have one

- earlier marriages, in the days before contraception, meant more babies.

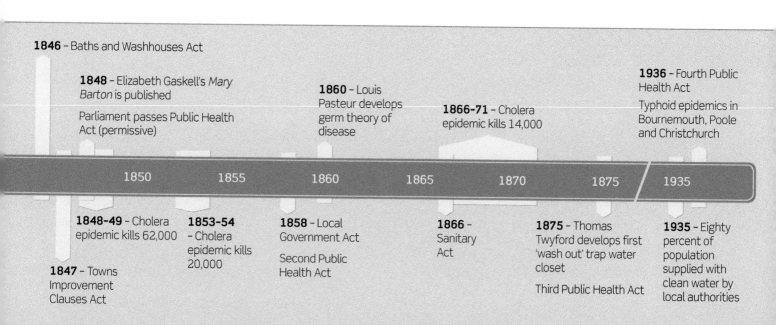

1846 – Baths and Washhouses Act

1848 – Elizabeth Gaskell's *Mary Barton* is published

Parliament passes Public Health Act (permissive)

1860 – Louis Pasteur develops germ theory of disease

1866–71 – Cholera epidemic kills 14,000

1936 – Fourth Public Health Act

Typhoid epidemics in Bournemouth, Poole and Christchurch

1850   1855   1860   1865   1870   1875   1935

1848–49 – Cholera epidemic kills 62,000

1853–54 – Cholera epidemic kills 20,000

1858 – Local Government Act

Second Public Health Act

1866 – Sanitary Act

1875 – Thomas Twyford develops first 'wash out' trap water closet

Third Public Health Act

1935 – Eighty percent of population supplied with clean water by local authorities

1847 – Towns Improvement Clauses Act

It was not just the size of the population that changed; the distribution changed, too. In 1801, around 33 percent of the population lived in towns. This had increased to 50 percent in 1851 and 72 percent in 1891. By 1900, four out of every five British citizens were urban dwellers. The steady and relentless growth conceals the even more dramatic, and differential, growth of individual towns, as is shown in Figure 1.1. Official national censuses were held every ten years from 1841, and were estimated, sometimes by contemporaries and later by historical statisticians, for earlier years. It was not uncommon, in the 19th century, for industrial centres to show an increase in their population of one-third at each count.

Civil registration of births, deaths and marriages – introduced in 1837 – revealed a young, fertile and actively reproducing population in most urban centres. Urban birth rates were continually above death rates and so natural increase, from the 1840s, added to the increase from internal migration. However, these global rates, too, conceal as much as they inform. In Manchester in the 1840s, for example, 57 percent of babies died before their fifth birthday. Epidemics of cholera, smallpox and scarlet fever, for example, were recorded and their rate and geographical distribution were analysed by statisticians and used by those pushing for reform in public health.

> ### KEY TERM
>
> **Civil registration**
> Before 1837, vicars were required to keep registers of baptisms, marriages and burials that had occurred in their parishes. A mobile population and the growth of nonconformity meant that these registers became increasingly unreliable. In recognition of the need for accurate records for voting and taxation purposes, for example, parliament legislated for compulsory civil registration that was administered by the Poor Law unions. This began on 1 July 1837, and certificates of births, marriages and deaths were issued as legal documents.

> ### EXTEND YOUR KNOWLEDGE
>
> **William Farr (1807–83)**
> A qualified doctor, William Farr, started a medical practice in Fitzroy Square, London, in 1833. Farr was fascinated by medical statistics, and was appointed chief statistician to the newly set up Office of the Registrar General, a post he held until 1879. From 1 July 1837, all births, deaths and marriages in England and Wales had to be registered there. By insisting that doctors registered the cause, and not simply the fact, of the death, Farr was able to produce statistics that were invaluable to public health reformers. He used his position to advocate public health reform, drawing attention to the wide variations in mortality between different areas of the country. Farr had been a supporter of the miasma theory of disease (see page 17), but the 1866 cholera outbreak finally convinced him that cholera had to be water-borne.

It was not so much the fact of urban growth that created public health problems, but the rate of urban growth. The fast pace of this growth created almost insuperable problems and daunting challenges insofar as public health was concerned.

SOURCE
1

The death certificate of Maria Woolf, dated 18 June 1849.

CERTIFIED COPY OF AN ENTRY OF DEATH

Given at the **GENERAL REGISTER OFFICE, SOMERSET HOUSE, LONDON.**

The fee for this certificate is 8s. 0d. When application is made by post a handling fee is payable in addition.

Application Number..... PAS...925.4/.../.71.

REGISTRATION DISTRICT   West London

1849. **DEATH** in the Sub-district of   West London   in the   City of London.

No.	When and where died	Name and surname	Sex	Age	Occupation	Cause of death	Signature, description, and residence of informant	When registered	Signature of registrar
	1	2	3	4	5	6	7	8	9
100	Eighteenth June 1849 106 Shoe Lane St. Brides	Maria Woolf	Female	32 years.	Wife of George Woolf Accountant	Diarrhoea 8 days Cholera 4 days Premature Labour 32 hours Exhaustion. Certified.	G. Woolf Present at the Death 106 Shoe Lane London.	Nineteenth June 1849	William Nason Registrar

CERTIFIED to be a true copy of an entry in the certified copy of a Register of Deaths in the District above mentioned.
Given at the GENERAL REGISTER OFFICE, SOMERSET HOUSE, LONDON, under the Seal of the said Office, the   17ᵗʰ   day of   March   19 7!

DA 571745

This certificate is issued in pursuance of the Births and Deaths Registration Act 1953. Section 34 provides that any certified copy of an entry purporting to be sealed or stamped with the seal of the General Register Office shall be received as evidence of the birth or death to which it relates without any further or other proof of the entry, and no certified copy purporting to have been given in the said Office shall be of any force or effect unless it is sealed or stamped as aforesaid.
CAUTION.—Any person who (1) falsifies any of the particulars on this certificate, or (2) uses a falsified certificate as true, knowing it to be false, is liable to prosecution.

	Pre-1801	1831	1841	1851	1861	1871
London	775	1,685	1,948	2,362	2,804	3,254
Birmingham	42	144	183	233	296	344
Bradford	4	44	67	104	106	146
Brighton	3	41	47	66	78	90
Bristol	55	104	124	137	154	183
Cardiff	-	6	10	18	33	40
Edinburgh	85	162	166	194	203	242
Glasgow	62	202	275	345	420	522
Leeds	24	123	152	172	207	259
Leicester	13	41	53	61	68	95
Liverpool	35	202	286	376	444	493
Manchester	30	182	235	303	339	351
Newcastle	33	54	70	88	109	128
Norwich	39	61	62	68	75	80
Sheffield	27	92	111	135	185	240
Swansea	4	15	20	25	33	43
York	13	26	29	36	40	44

Figure 1.1 The population of some British towns and cities (in thousands).

ACTIVITY
KNOWLEDGE CHECK
Population growth and distribution

1 Look at Source 1. What questions would you need to ask of the source that would lead you to an understanding of the state of public health in the City of London at that time?

2 How far did the civil registration of births, marriages and deaths help to drive public health reforms?

3 Look at Figure 1.1.

   a) Which towns would you expect to experience the greatest challenges with regard to public health problems?

   b) How would you explain the differences in growth rates shown here?

4 a) Look back to the section: 'The impact of a rising, mobile population'. Use the Information to construct a spider diagram or flow chart to show how changes in death, marriage and birth rates were linked.

   b) What, in your view, was the most important factor that brought about change? Explain your answer.

The impact on people's living conditions
Public health is closely connected to people's living conditions. The influx of thousands and thousands of people into small market towns and cathedral cities that had the fortune, or misfortune, to have one or more industries located there had a catastrophic effect on the existing housing and sanitation provision. This, in turn, led to the explosion of what the Victorians called 'filth diseases', such as typhoid, diphtheria, tuberculosis, scarlet fever and, most dreaded of all, cholera. Other 19th-century killers, such as measles and whooping cough, became endemic.

Housing
Bad housing was nothing new and it certainly was not a product uniquely of the Industrial Revolution. There had been slums in medieval London and, throughout the centuries, agricultural labourers had lived in conditions that were frequently no better than those of the animals they tended. What was unique about the Industrial Revolution was that it resulted in widespread, dense overcrowding. Urban communities responded, first, by using up and adapting existing 'vacant' living space and, second, by building new dwellings. Cellars and attics were filled with working people and their families, and were also used as workplaces.

13

SOURCE 2

From Friedrich Engels *The Condition of the Working Class in England,* published in 1844. Engels was a German philosopher and journalist who, together with Karl Marx, wrote the Communist Manifesto in 1848. He worked in Manchester (1842–44) in his father's cotton mill.

First, there is the old town of Manchester. Here the streets, even the better ones, are narrow and winding, as Todd Street, Long Millgate, Withy Grove and Shude Hill, the houses dirty, old and tumble-down, and the construction of the side streets utterly horrible. Going from the Old Church to Long Millgate, there is a row of old-fashioned houses at the right, of which not one has kept its original level; these are remnants of the old pre-manufacturing Manchester, whose former inhabitants have moved with their descendants into better-built districts. Here, [back in the old town] one is in a working-men's quarter for even the shops and beer houses hardly take the trouble to exhibit a trifling degree of cleanliness. But all this is as nothing compared to the courts and lanes that lie behind, to which access can be gained only through covered passages, in which no two human beings can pass at the same time. Every scrap of space left by the old way of building has been filled up and patched over until not a foot of land is left further to be occupied.

Engels not only created a vivid impression of housing in industrial Manchester, but also revealed a new development. Prior to the Industrial Revolution, rich, poor and those in-between lived in close proximity to each other in Britain's towns and cities. In industrialising Britain, the absence of affordable public transport meant that industrial workers had to be housed close to the mills and factories in which they worked. The middle classes moved out, beyond the pollution and smut-laden pall that covered the industrialising cities.

SOURCE 3

A plan of eight houses to be built in Holme Top Street, Little Horton, Bradford, dated 1852.

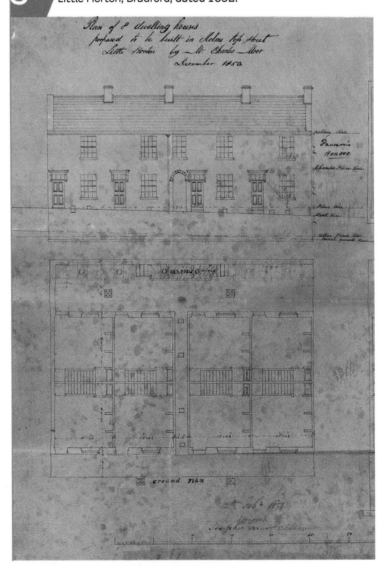

Most of the housing for those moving to live and work in the fast-growing cities had to be newly built. These new homes varied wildly in style: rows of industrial cottages were common in the North, back-to-back houses in parts of industrial Lancashire and Yorkshire, enclosed courtyards in Birmingham and vast tenements in Glasgow. They varied also in standard. Many were poorly built, with floors being nothing more than bare boards over beaten earth. Others were planned carefully, but the most careful planner could not legislate for the number of families that would occupy a house designed for one.

Sanitation

It was the lack of services to a house rather than the house itself that caused problems, no matter how overcrowded it was with occupants. Most housing in the first half of the 19th century lacked drainage, sewerage and a regular water supply.

Lavatories (or privies) were usually outside, in the courtyards and alleys, and emptied into cesspits. Human waste collected in these cesspits that were, from time to time, cleaned out by '**night-soil men**'. They piled what they had collected in huge dunghills and then sold it on to local farmers at a price per tonne. Some houses (as in Source 3) had their own privies. These were ash privies where, instead of flushing, the users covered the contents with ash. Some middle-class houses had flushing lavatories, but these flushed either into a cesspit in the cellar or into a closed sewer. These, as with the ash privies, had to be physically emptied.

Water was needed for washing, cooking and drinking; not only was water in short supply but it was expensive. Its supply, too, was controlled by vested interests in the form of private water companies. Water companies sometimes took their water from deep, natural underground reservoirs and springs, but more usually from local rivers. The middle classes had water piped to their houses and, because the supply was frequently irregular and uncertain, stored it in huge cisterns so that they could, quite literally, have water on tap. The poorer areas of towns and cities had to make do with standpipes, and the inhabitants queued with buckets and saucepans to buy what they could afford when the water company turned on the supply. People too poor to buy water, or to buy enough water for their needs, either didn't bother or took what they could from local wells and streams.

KEY TERM

Night-soil men
People who collected human waste, usually at night.

SOURCE

Jacob's Island, Bermondsey, on the south side of the River Thames, London, drawn in 1810. It illustrates the nub of the problem: the wooden shacks are privies emptying into the stream. The stream provides water for those living in the houses.

OLD HOUSES IN LONDON STREET, DOCKHEAD, ABOUT 1810.

EXTRACT

1 From Peter Mathias *The First Industrial Nation,* published in 1969.

The new urban environment, affecting a steadily rising proportion of the nation, brought problems of discipline in living, of social controls, just as much as factory employment brought the problem of discipline and regularity in work. Industrialists solved their problems – often harshly – more efficiently than local government, police and public administration solved theirs.

Some attributes of rural life proved lethal when translated into high-density urban housing in the absence of strict local government regulations – sanitation being a clear example. The context of urban life proved socially more lethal than the context of work. Environmental decline was, and remains, the most intense social problem resulting from industrialisation. Not until the second half of the nineteenth century was the general administrative basis for effective social controls in towns successfully evolved. With lagging public provision and public initiative, encouraged by the anti-interventionist philosophy prevailing at Westminster – even the absence of a national education system – great scope remained for the spontaneous evolution of appropriate social values by social elites.

ACTIVITY
KNOWLEDGE CHECK

Housing and sanitation

1 What public health problems would arise because of the rapid growth of towns?

2 In your group, discuss which problems would be the easiest to solve.

3 Consider Sources 3 and 4. How far would the public health problems illustrated by Source 4 have been solved by the houses illustrated in Source 3?

4 Read Extract 1. What point is the author making about public health?

The impact of epidemics on the health of the nation

The connection between dirt and disease had been appreciated for hundreds of years, but what was not known was just what that connection was. That had to wait until 1867, when Louis Pasteur developed his germ theory of disease. In the first half of the 19th century, overcrowding and lack of sanitation and clean water meant that disease was rampant and life expectancy of the working classes was low for the following reasons.

- People living in overcrowded, unsanitary conditions and without easy access to a supply of clean water housed body lice, which spread typhus fever, from which many died. There were typhus epidemics in 1837 and 1839; an outbreak in 1847 killed 10,000 people in north-west England alone.

- Influenza, scarlet fever, tuberculosis (often called the white plague) and measles were endemic and were often killers.

- Typhoid and diarrhoea were common.

- Cholera hit Britain in four massive epidemics: 1831–32, 1848–49, 1853–54 and 1866. The first epidemic killed 31,000 and the second 62,000.

EXTEND YOUR KNOWLEDGE

Typhus
Typhus is caused by the rickettsia bacteria and it cannot live for long outside living cells. The bacterium is transmitted to humans by parasites such as ticks and fleas.

The first stage of typhus consists of 'flu-like symptoms': fever, headaches and chills lasting about two weeks. Five to nine days after having been infected, a rash develops on the body that spreads to the arms and legs and will eventually cover the whole body. The brain may become inflamed and, if this happens, coma and death will probably follow.

Increasing understanding about the causes of disease

Public health is about the prevention of disease and about the spread of disease in the community. It is not about curing disease, which is the function of medicine. Nevertheless, the two are connected. The causes of disease have to be understood before effective cures can be developed. If the causes of specific diseases (especially those diseases the Victorians regarded as 'dirty') are understood, then the spread of those diseases within a community can be reduced to a minimum or eliminated altogether. In the 19th century, there were two main theories about what caused disease. The first was the miasma theory; this was replaced, though not all at once and not by everyone, by the germ theory of disease. These two theories had a profound effect on public health in the years 1830–75.

The miasma theory of disease

People had understood for hundreds of years that there was a link between dirt and disease, but they were unsure as to just what that link was. In the 19th century, the most popular explanation was 'miasma', or bad air. This was an old theory, developed first in the Middle Ages. Diseases, it was believed, were caused by the presence, in the air, of a miasma. A miasma was a kind of poisonous gas in which, so it was said, were suspended minute particles of decaying matter that couldn't be seen by the naked eye. It was characterised by a foul smell. So, the theory went, if you were breathing in a miasma, you were going to get ill because the miasma carried disease. Diseases were spread because the poisonous gases were carried from person to person and place to place on the air.

It was a neat theory, and made a lot of sense to people who were trying to improve public health in the 19th century. Industrialisation and the rapid growth of towns had created many filthy, foul-smelling areas in most cities. It was these areas in which disease was rampant, epidemics common and death rates high. So the answer was clear: clean them up, improve housing and sanitation, and public health would automatically improve.

The germ theory of disease

Scientists became very interested in decaying matter and in the maggots and flies that lived on and in it. The development of microscopes (principally by Joseph Lister, who in 1830 built a microscope that could magnify 1,000 times without distortion) enabled them to observe micro-organisms in rotting material that were much, much smaller than the flies and maggots. Where did these micro-organisms come from? There were two ideas: that the decaying material created the micro-organisms, and that micro-organisms in the air were attracted to the decaying material.

Which theory was correct?

In 1860, a French scientist, Louis Pasteur, conducted a series of experiments proving that micro-organisms existed in the air and were not created by the decaying material. It was a small step from this to his germ theory. He discovered that a disease in silkworms was caused by a particular micro-organism. If micro-organisms could cause a disease in silkworms, surely different micro-organisms could cause diseases in people? And he was right. Germs could, and did, cause disease in humans. Not everyone believed him and many influential people were slow to let go of the miasma theory. It was left to a German doctor, Robert Koch, to prove this once and for all, and in the 1880s and 1890s he and his team identified the germs that caused most of the killer diseases of the 19th century.

The cholera epidemic, 1832

The cholera epidemics, more than endemic diseases like typhoid and tuberculosis, had a profound effect upon the public and the legislators that was out of all proportion to their statistical importance. This was for two main reasons:

- the high percentage of fatalities (40–60 percent) among those contracting the disease

- the speed with which cholera could strike.

Cholera-phobia riots

The fear that cholera engendered was palpable. There were 30 recorded 'cholera-phobia' riots in towns and cities throughout Britain. Principally affected were Birmingham, Bristol, Edinburgh, Exeter, Glasgow, Leeds, Liverpool, London, Manchester and Sheffield.

The Liverpool riots were worse than those that happened anywhere else in Britain, and some of those were pretty bad. Between 29 May and 8 June 1832, eight major street riots occurred, with minor disturbances as well. The rioters were not protesting against the disease (which would not have been too sensible); rather, they were rioting against the local medical men. It was a generally held belief that cholera victims were being taken to the local hospital where they died, doubtless murdered by the doctors in order to provide bodies for dissection. There was some basis for this belief. In 1826, 33 bodies had been found on the Liverpool docks, ready to be shipped to Scotland for dissection. Two years later, a local surgeon, William Gill, was tried and found guilty of running a grave-robbing system in order to provide bodies for dissection. The riots ended abruptly, largely because of pleas from the local Catholic clergy and a well-respected local doctor, James Collins.

In Exeter, the authorities had instituted regulations for the disposal of cholera-infected corpses and their clothing and bedding. People rioted, and even attacked gravediggers, because they objected to the burial of cholera victims in local graveyards.

It seems clear that cholera riots were not directed at the authorities for failing to contain the epidemic, but arose because of specific fears that medical students were stealing bodies for their anatomy classes; doctors were murdering cholera victims; victims were being buried in unconsecrated ground and that victims were being buried hastily, possibly before they were dead, and without proper religious ceremony.

The rioting should be seen in the context of the general political and social unrest prevalent at the time. In the years 1831–32, pressure amongst people and politicians for the reform of parliament was intense. Meetings urging reform were held in all major towns and cities, accompanied by marches and, frequently, rioting. Parliament was reformed, governments were not overturned and the fabric of society held firm.

How did the government react to the cholera outbreak?

Central government had done nothing about the endemic fevers and 'dirty' diseases that were common among all classes in all large towns, and which claimed the lives of thousands more people than cholera. Cholera, however, was different. It was deadly, it was swift – and it was capable of engendering fear in a way that typhoid and tuberculosis could not. The government had to take action.

In 1831, realising that cholera was fast approaching the shores of Britain, the government sent two medical commissioners to St Petersburg in Russia, where there had been an outbreak, to assess the situation. Their report, coupled with general alarm among government officials, resulted in a temporary **Board of Health** being quickly set up. It consisted of the president and four fellows of the Royal College of Physicians, the superintendent-general of quarantine, the director-general of the Army Medical Department, the medical commissioner of the Victualling Office and two civil servants.

The Board of Health advised local government areas to set up their own boards of health, which would be in a position to deal with problems at grass-roots level. It suggested that these local boards of health should include one or more magistrates, a clergyman, some 'substantial householders' and one or more medical men. These local boards of health appointed district inspectors to report on the food, clothing and bedding of the poor, the ventilation of their dwellings, the number of people per room, the ways in which they kept clean and their behaviour. It also issued advice.

- Houses were to be whitewashed and limed and all infected furniture and clothing was to be fumigated.
- People with cholera were to be put into strict quarantine.
- Food and flannel clothing were to be distributed to the poor.
- Temporary fever hospitals were to be set up.

In the absence of any knowledge about the causes of cholera, the Board of Health was understandably a trifle hazy about what people should do once they had caught the disease. It suggested a variety of remedies, amongst them rubs of castor oil and laudanum, plasters of mustard, peppermint and hot turpentine, bleeding by leeches and warm baths. This sort of advice could do no harm and maybe would do some good. What was important is that here central government was, for the first time, officially recognising that cleanliness, adequate clothing and food are necessary factors in public health. Later, Edwin Chadwick was to change the emphasis to water supply and sewerage.

A number of cities were sufficiently frightened by the advance of cholera to set up their own boards of health, as suggested by the central board. There were inspectors who did submit reports to their local board, and local boards sent returns to the central board noting the cases of cholera in their area and deaths from the disease. However, this tended to be information gathering, not disease prevention or cure. Some areas set up cholera hospitals and other areas tried to institute a quarantine regime, but in the absence of firm knowledge and understanding as to what caused cholera, any measures tended to be rather hit or miss affairs.

Almost immediately, legality became a problem. What legal right did the boards have to insist that people co-operate with them? Could individuals be compelled to have their houses limed? Could children be separated from parents and sent to fever hospitals? In 1832, temporary 'Cholera Acts' were passed to allow local authorities to enforce some measures and to finance them from the poor rates. Even so, and despite people's fear of cholera, local action was haphazard. Local boards were only temporary, and, once the first cholera epidemic had died down, they were disbanded.

> **KEY TERM**
>
> Board of Health
> A central, London-based organisation set up in 1831 as a temporary measure to collate information and disseminate advice in relation to the cholera epidemic. It was made permanent by the Public Health Act 1848 (see page 30) and merged into the Local Government Board in 1871 (see page 115).

SOURCE 5

From the *Report of the Leeds Board of Health* by Dr Robert Baker, district surgeon, published in 1833.

On 26th [May 1832] the first case of CHOLERA occurred in the Blue Bell Fold, a small, dirty cul-de-sac containing about 20 houses inhabited by poor families on the North side of the river in an angle between it and an offensive beck or streamlet which conveys the refuse water from numerous mills and dye-houses. The income of one family of eight persons, of whom four died in succession at the very start of the disease, had not averaged more than twelve shillings per week for the four preceding months.

The disease ran through Blue Bell Fold, spread with considerable rapidity, became general in the beginning of July, was at its height in August and the Board of Health ceased to have reports from its district surgeons on 12 November.

Amid a population of 76,000 persons, not more than 14 streets have sewers. Most [of the streets] are unsewered, undrained, unpaved, built on clayey soil and broken up by vehicles of every description. The only wonder is that diseases of this pestilential nature do not oftener and more fatally prevail. The disease has prevailed in those parts of the town where there is a deficiency, and often an entire lack, of sewerage, draining and paving. In three parallel streets, for a population of 386 persons, there are but two single privies.

From the privies in the Boot and Shoe yard, which do not appear to have been thoroughly cleansed for the last thirty years, 70 carts of manure were removed by order of the commissioners.

In a town like Leeds where in so many parts it teems with human life and where the operatives are congregated together in small and narrow streets, little attention is paid by the owners of cottage property to their cleanliness and ventilation. With broken panes in every window frame, and filth and vermin in every nook. With the walls unwhitewashed for years, black with the smoke of foul chimneys, without water, with sacking for bed clothing, with floors unwashed from year to year, while without, there are streets elevated a foot, sometimes two, above the level of the causeway, by the accumulation of years, and stagnant puddles here and there, with their foetid exhalations, causeways broken and dangerous.

Can we wonder that such places are hotbeds of disease, or that it obtains, upon constitutions thus liberally disposed to receive it, and forms the mortality which Leeds exhibits. Adult life exposed to such miasmata, gives way. How much more then infant life, when ushered into, and attempted to be reared in, such obnoxious atmospheres. On the moral habits similar effects are produced. An inattention on the part of the local authorities to the state of the streets diminishes year by year the respectability of their occupiers. None dwell in such localities but those to whom nearness to employment is absolutely essential.

A cure for cholera?

The problem with cholera was that it was silent, deadly and had no known cause or cure. Thousands of people tried avoidance rather than attempt prevention or a cure, although plenty of 'cures' were on offer. For those unwilling – or unable – to flee there was a host of remedies and preventatives from which to choose.

- The contagionist theory suggested that cholera was spread by contact with cholera victims. Eminently sensible, it met with considerable opposition. If true, it meant that houses, streets or even whole cities had to be put into quarantine. Opponents pointed to the potential loss of trade and consequent increase in poverty and unemployment. They argued that not everyone in the same household fell ill with cholera and so the theory could not be true.

- The miasmic theory (see page 17) suggested that cholera was spread by a 'miasma of filth' that was breathed in from infected air. At least the actions based on this theory – the removal of heaps of excrement, for example – were steps in the right direction. The connecting of sewers to rivers and other water courses, however, was not.

- In 1831, *The Lancet*, a journal written by doctors for doctors, reported that a community of Jews in Wiesniz had kept themselves free from cholera by rubbing themselves with an ointment made from wine, vinegar, camphor, mustard, pepper, garlic and the crushed bodies of beetles.

- Patent medicines grew and multiplied in number, as did their claims. The most well known were Moxon's Effervescent Universal Mixture, Daffey's Elixir and Morrison the Hygienist's Genuine Vegetable Universal Mixture. All claimed to cure cholera, and, because many who took them undoubtedly did survive, they had a great following of those who believed in their curative properties.

- Prayer was recommended by all the main Christian churches. Cholera, many believed, was God's punishment for lax and immoral behaviour. Repent and all would be well. As with patent medicines, many of those who prayed for themselves survived, as did those for whom they prayed: prayer, the arguments went, was proven to be efficacious.

Until there was acceptable scientific proof that cholera was a water-borne disease, and preventative measures could be taken, survival was very much a hit or miss affair. Some 15 years after the 1832 epidemic, cholera again swept the country with the same effect: local boards of health were set up, and then disbanded once the danger was deemed to have passed. It was the third visitation of cholera in the early 1850s that was to become a turning point in understanding the disease. This is explored in Chapter 2.

EXTEND YOUR KNOWLEDGE

Cholera

Cholera is caught by swallowing water or food that has been infected by the cholera *vibrio*, a minute bacillus. This bacillus can live for up to a fortnight in water, and up to a week in meat, milk or cheese. It is most often spread by water contaminated by the excrement of cholera victims, or by flies that have fed on the excrement.

The first stage of cholera consists of violent, explosive diarrhoea and vomiting. Often the body loses several pints of fluid in a few minutes. Dehydration causes the patient to become shrunken and shrivelled. The second stage of cholera begins with acute pain in the fingers and toes. This spreads to the limbs and chest, and is often accompanied by stomach cramps. The patient's features collapse and the skin turns black and blue. By now, the patient is breathing with difficulty. If this stage is survived, collapse follows. This stage can last from between a couple of hours to a week or more. The patient lies unmoving, with eyes turned up. Although conscious, the patient doesn't appear to hear or understand what is said and only occasionally replies in a feeble whisper. Coma and death soon follow.

ACTIVITY
KNOWLEDGE CHECK

The 1832 cholera epidemic

1 Cholera was just one of the many epidemics that hit 19th-century England. Why did it generate more fear than any of the other epidemics?

2 Were the cholera riots in Liverpool and Exeter in 1832 the result of ignorance or fear?

3 Read Source 5.

  a) What does Dr Baker imply about the causes of cholera?

  b) What evidence does he cite to support his opinion?

  c) Why was this not enough to stop further epidemics breaking out?

4 a) How did central government react to the outbreak of cholera?

  b) Which of their actions were likely to prove effective?

Reports on the state of towns

The 19th century was a time of investigating and reporting, of collecting and collating information. Many reports were local and went no further than the local town hall; others found their way to central organisations, such as the Board of Health. Some reports were the result of the enquiries of select commissions, set up for specific enquiries by parliament; others were generated by bodies such as the Poor Law Commission (see page 90).

The moral and physical condition of the working classes of Manchester, 1832

It was the 1832 cholera epidemic (see page 17) that brought Manchester's Dr James Kay to the attention of those in authority. Cholera hit the city on 17 May 1832, and a board of health was set up, with Kay as its secretary, to co-ordinate the work of the city's 14 district boards. Kay personally visited each area to investigate conditions there, and what he found formed the basis of his report.

SOURCE

6   Part of the report *The Moral and Physical Condition of the Working Classes Employed in the Cotton Manufacture in Manchester* compiled by Dr James Kay in 1832.

The state of the streets powerfully affects the health of their inhabitants. Sporadic cases of typhus chiefly appear in those which are narrow, ill ventilated, unpaved, or which contain heaps of refuse, or stagnant pools. The confined air and noxious exhalations, which abound in such places, depress the health of the people, and on this account contagious diseases are also most rapidly propagated there. The houses are unclean and ill provided with furniture. An air of discomfort, if not of squalid and loathsome wretchedness pervades them. They are often dilapidated, badly drained, damp; and the habits of their tenants are gross – they are ill fed, ill-clothed, and uneconomical – at once both spendthrifts and destitute – denying themselves the comforts of life in order that they may wallow in the unrestrained licence of animal appetites. An intimate connection subsists, among the poor, between the cleanliness of the street and that of the house and the person. Uneconomical habits, and dissipation are almost inseparably allied; and they are so frequently connected with uncleanliness, that we cannot consider their concomitance as altogether accidental. When the health is depressed by the concurrence of these causes, contagious diseases spread with a fatal malignancy among the population subjected to their influence. The records of the Fever Hospital of Manchester prove that typhus prevails almost exclusively in such areas.

The object of the author is simply to offer to the public an example of what he conceives to be too generally the state of the working classes, throughout the kingdom, and to illustrate by specific instances, evils everywhere requiring the immediate interference of legislative authority.

Kay's report was one of the first detailed reports on the condition of a specific group of working people. He was one of the first people to demonstrate the connection between dirt and disease and, as well as demonstrating that dirt and diet affected the health of working people, James Kay threw into the equation (as did most 19th-century writers) the moral condition of the poor. The implication here, of course, was that 'dirty' living led to 'dirty' habits, and this proved to be a powerful motivational force for would-be reformers. This report was important, not simply for the information it contained, but because it set the scene for later investigations.

James Kay-Shuttleworth (1804–77)

James Kay qualified in medicine in 1827 and rapidly developed a reputation as a well-respected doctor in Manchester. He became aware of the suffering of the poor and as a consequence became involved in sanitary and educational reform. As a result of treating people who lived in the slum areas of the city during the cholera outbreak of 1832, he wrote *The Moral and Physical Condition of the Working Classes Employed in the Cotton Manufacture in Manchester*. In 1835, he was appointed Poor Law Commissioner for the eastern counties and London. Four years later, he was appointed secretary to the Privy Council's Committee on Education, where he worked hard to establish a public system of elementary education, supervised by a national body of inspectors. In 1840, Kay founded England's first teacher-training college in Battersea. His wife was Janet Shuttleworth, daughter and heiress to the wealthy Robert Shuttleworth of Gawthorpe Hall, near Burnley in Lancashire. Because of this Kay added 'Shuttleworth' to his name. He died in 1877, having been a leading member of the Lancashire Liberal Party, but failing in his attempt to become a Liberal MP.

Report on the Sanitary Condition of the Labouring Population of Great Britain, 1842

This report started as a smaller piece of work, focused on London, requested by the Poor Law commissioners and carried out under the direction of the commission's secretary, Edwin Chadwick (see Chapter 4). In 1839, Sir James Graham, the home secretary, prompted by the bishop of London in the House of Lords, asked that the enquiry be extended to cover the prevalence of disease among the labouring classes throughout the whole country, and not just London. The complete report was to be submitted by the beginning of the 1842 session of parliament. Chadwick's report was in three volumes: two volumes of local reports from all over Britain, based on questionnaires sent to all local boards of guardians, and a third volume containing his own conclusions and proposals for the way forward. Almost immediately he hit a problem. The Poor Law commissioners refused to allow it to be published in its original form because it criticised the water companies, the medical profession and local administration. It named names, too. Eventually, in July 1842, Chadwick had the whole report published under his own name and at his own expense.

SOURCE

7   From Edwin Chadwick's *Report on the Sanitary Condition of the Labouring Population of Great Britain*, published in 1842.

The annual loss of life from filth and bad ventilation are greater than the loss from death or wounds in any wars in which the country has been engaged in modern times.

The various forms of epidemic, endemic and other diseases caused, or aggravated, or propagated chiefly amongst the labouring classes by atmospheric impurities produced by decomposing animal and vegetable substances, by damp and filth, and close and overcrowded dwellings prevail amongst the population in every part of the kingdom. That such disease, wherever its attacks are frequent, is always found in connection with the physical circumstances above specified, and that where those circumstances are removed by drainage, proper cleansing, better ventilation, and other means of diminishing atmospheric impurity, the frequency and intensity of such disease is abated; and where the removal of the noxious agencies appears to be complete, such disease almost entirely disappears...

Of the 43,000 cases of widowhood, and the 112,000 cases of destitute orphans relieved by the poor rates in England and Wales alone, it appears that the greatest proportion of deaths of the heads of families occurred as a result of the above specified and other removable causes.

The primary and most important measures, and at the same time, the most practicable, and within the recognised province of public administration, are drainage, the removal of all refuse from habitations, streets and roads.

The chief obstacles to the immediate removal of decomposing refuse in towns and habitations have been the expense and annoyance of the labour and cartage required

This expense may be reduced to one-twentieth or to one-thirtieth, by the use of water and removal by improved and cheaper sewers and drains.

For all these purposes, as well as for domestic use, better supplies of water are absolutely necessary.

Chadwick's report was a significant document. In it, he:

- attacked the inadequacy of existing water supplies, drainage and sewerage systems
- linked public health and the Poor Law
- pointed the finger at vested interests that stood in the way of improvement
- stressed the connection between these vested interests, overcrowding, epidemics and death.

It was the latter point that had the greatest impact. Chadwick had demonstrated, beyond reasonable doubt, that there was a connection between disease and the environment.

What was the reaction to Chadwick's report?

The reaction to Chadwick's report ranged from anger to wholehearted acceptance, passing through disbelief and derision on the way. The home secretary, Sir James Graham, was reluctant to act on the findings and conclusions of what was, officially at least, a purely private and largely personal report. He set up a Royal Commission on the Health of Towns with the purpose, not of questioning Chadwick's findings or even his conclusions, but to investigate more fully the legislative and financial side of his recommendations. Chadwick, meanwhile, busied himself, at Graham's request, with a report on burial practices and with giving official and unofficial briefings to the members of the Royal Commission.

EXTRACT

From Anthony Wohl *Endangered Lives,* published in 1983.

> Public opinion was first widely awakened to the need for remedial measures in 1842, when Chadwick published his remarkable, one is tempted to say epic *Report on the Sanitary Condition of the Labouring Population of Great Britain.* Drawing upon the evidence gathered by approximately 1,000 Poor Law Medical Officers of Health, Chadwick skilfully wove the most lurid details and evocative descriptions, damning statistics and damaging examples into a masterpiece of protest literature. The Report, which covered 372 pages of text and another 85 of appendices, powerfully portrayed the inadequacy of existing systems of sewerage, water supply and drainage, and stressed the connection between these and overcrowding on the one hand, and epidemic diseases on the other. Playing down the broader underlying issue of poverty as a root cause of much ill-health, Chadwick stressed the environmental, miasmic causes of disease and resultant pauperism, and maintained that these causes could be removed.

Report of the Royal Commission into the Sanitary Condition of Large Towns and Populous Districts, 1844

This report was generated as a result of Chadwick's *Report on the Sanitary Condition of the Labouring Population of Great Britain.* Members of the Royal Commission into the Health of Towns were drawn from those who could be expected to know something about the subject they were investigating. Led by the Duke of Buccleuch, they included a geologist, a chemist, an expert on land drainage who was also a cotton mill manager and at least two engineers. Questionnaires were sent to the 50 towns with the highest annual death rates, and the returns studied by the commissioners themselves who also made official visits to the worst areas.

When the first report was published in 1844, it upheld Chadwick's findings. Of the 50 towns investigated, 42 were found to have bad drainage and 30 poor water supplies. The second report in 1845 contained proposals for future legislation, and included a long memorandum from Chadwick explaining the recommendations on sewerage, drainage and water supply. It recommended that:

- central government be given extensive powers to inspect and supervise local sanitary work
- local sanitary districts be set up, with authority over drainage, sewerage, paving and water supplies
- local sanitary districts be given powers to raise money for sanitary schemes through local rates.

Report of the Bradford Woolcombers Sanatory Committee, 1845

Urban communities responded to the pressures of increasing populations as a result of the Industrial Revolution, first, by using up and adapting existing 'vacant' living space, and, second, by building new dwellings. Cellars and attics were filled with working people and their families, and were also used as workplaces. An example of this can be found in the West Yorkshire town of Bradford, which was dominated by the production of woollen cloth. In the 1840s, there were more than 10,000 **woolcombers** living and working in their own dwellings. Conditions were appalling; the average age of death of a woolcomber was 14 years, two months. In 1845, the Bradford woolcombers formed a Protective Society and appointed their own 'Sanatory Committee' to report on their living conditions.

SOURCE

8 From the *Report of the Bradford Woolcombers Sanatory Committee,* published in 1845.

NELSON COURT

A great many woolcombers reside in this court. It is a perfect nuisance. There are a number of cellars in it utterly unfit for human dwellings. No drainage whatever. The Visitors [those compiling the Report] cannot find words to express their horror of the filth, stench and misery which abounds in this locality, and were unable to bear the overpowering effluvia [smell] which emanates from a common sewer which runs beneath the houses. Were this to be fully described, the Committee might subject themselves to the charge of exaggeration. We trust that some of those in affluent circumstances will visit these abodes of misery and disease.

HOLGATE SQUARE

A miserable hole, surrounded by buildings on all sides. This place resembles a deep pit – no chance of ventilation; a number of men and women work in the cellars near charcoal fires, seven feet below the surface.

BACK ADELAIDE STREET

The visitors give a heart-rending description of this neighbourhood – extreme destitution and suffering appears to be the result of their crowded and unhealthy dwellings. Very damp – no ventilation – privy ten feet three inches from the door – three persons work and sleep in this filthy yard and confined cellar, five feet three inches below the surface.

MARY GATE

Upper apartment contains three charcoal stoves, at which six persons work – there are two beds in the same room in which four persons sleep – bad smell – very hot.

The way was open for the government to act. It did so, tentatively, in 1848 (see page 30).

ACTIVITY
KNOWLEDGE CHECK

Reports on the state of towns

1 Read Source 6. How does James Kay make the connection between dirt and disease?

2 James Kay's *Report on the Moral and Physical Condition of the Working Classes Employed in the Cotton Manufacture in Manchester* (Source 6) was written in 1832; Friedrich Engels' description of Manchester (Source 2) was written 12 years later. How far are the findings of Source 6 supported by Source 2?

3 Read Source 7. What connection does Chadwick make between dirt and disease? Is it the same connection as that made by James Kay?

4 Why was Chadwick's report so controversial?

5 Using your knowledge of the period, explain what obstacles might prevent the implementation of Chadwick's recommendations?

6 We now know that the miasma theory of disease, in which Chadwick believed, was wrong. Does this mean that his report was unimportant?

7 Anthony Wohl (Extract 2) describes Chadwick's report as 'protest literature'. Do you agree?

8 Does the fact that the Bradford woolcombers commissioned their own report (Source 8) invalidate the report?

Drainage systems and water supplies: technological advance

It was gradually becoming clear, by the mid-19th century, that public health reform was needed, and that this was dependent on the effective removal of sewage and the supply of clean water to people's houses. Investigations, reports and recommendations were one thing; undertaking the change was quite another. This was dependent, not only on the will of parliament and the acceptance of the public, but on the technological knowledge and practical ability to undertake such reforms.

Flushing toilets

Water to flush away human waste, usually into rivers and waterways, had been in intermittent use since Neolithic times. However, it was not until the Industrial Revolution, and the advances in technology that came with it, that the flushing toilet became a feature of many people's lives. An important breakthrough came in 1775, with the invention of the S-trap by Alexander Cummings. This sealed the toilet bowl, preventing foul air coming up from the sewer. It was Joseph Bramah who combined this invention with a float valve system for a cistern to build the first practical, workable, flush toilet.

Growing urbanisation and the growth of a sewerage system, especially in London, enabled George Jennings to establish a business manufacturing toilets (known as water closets) and accompanying sanitary ware. His South-Western Pottery was opened outside Bournemouth in 1856 and, by 1861, was employing 97 men and 18 boys, indicative of the immense popularity of these new water closets, particularly among the middle classes. Jennings was granted a patent in 1852 for his invention of an improved water closet, whereby the pan and water trap were constructed in one piece so that a small amount of water was retained in the pan. Additionally, he improved the construction of valves and drain traps. By the end of the 1850s, building codes required all new-build homes (predominantly for the middle class) to be equipped with a water closet.

It was Thomas William Twyford who, in 1875, developed and sold the first 'wash out' trap water closet that proved immensely popular. Throughout the 1880s, Twyford was granted further patents for his inventions that improved the flushing rim and the outlet. In 1888, he applied for, and was granted, a patent whereby the toilet pan was refilled with a small quantity of clean water. This remained the standard water closet throughout the late 19th and early 20th centuries.

SOURCE

9 An advertisement for sanitary ware, produced in 1884 by the Thomas Twyford company.

THE PERFECTION OF CLEANLINESS, UTILITY, AND SIMPLICITY.

TWYFORD'S "UNITAS,"

COMBINING

W.C. BASIN & TRAP, URINAL & SLOP SINK,

Has the following special advantages:

UNLIKE ordinary W.C. Basins, *it is not enclosed with woodwork*, but is fully exposed, so that no filth, nor anything causing offensive smells, can accumulate or escape detection.

ALL joints and connections *being in sight* any leakage or other defect can be easily detected and remedied.

NO Wood Fittings are required except a hinged seat, which being raised, the Basin can be used as a Urinal or a Slop Sink, the "wetting" so objectionable in Closets having permanent seats being avoided. Free access can thus be had to all parts of the Basin and Trap, so that everything about the Closet can be easily kept clean.

THE Flushing arrangements are so perfect that with a flush of 2 gallons of water it is guaranteed that all the soil and paper will be completely removed from the Basin and through the Trap, the whole of the inside being thoroughly washed, and with the aid of the patent "After Flush" Chamber the full quantity of water required to receive the soil is left in the bottom of the Basin.

MADE WITH OR WITHOUT SLOP TOP IN THREE WAYS.

No. 1. With raised Ornamentation, Oak or Florentine Pattern (White or Ivory).
No. 2. Plain, White or Ivory, or with Printed Pattern.
No. 3. In strong Fire Clay, specially adapted for Factories, Workhouses, Asylums, firmaries, Hospitals, &c., &c.

THOMAS W. TWYFORD,

Manufacturer of all descriptions of Sanitary and Plumbers' Earthenware, and Sole Maker of the "Unitas," "National," "Alliance," and "Crown" Closet Basins,

HANLEY, STAFFORDSHIRE.

Sewerage

Human and industrial waste piled up on land, and rivers offered an easy and cheap solution to the problem of disposal. Rivers moved without the need for the expense of installing and maintaining pumps, and they eventually emptied into the sea; in this sense, they could be seen to be self-cleansing. Faced with public health requirements not to allow piles of filth to accumulate, local authorities were reluctant to move away from the traditional method of disposal. Given the prevalence of the belief in the miasma theory of the spread of disease throughout most of the 19th century, a quick and apparently efficient removal of waste into the river system seemed ideal.

Before the development of a sewer system in the latter part of the 19th century, such sewerage as existed did not carry away waste matter in an effective way. Rough walls, inadequate connections between sewers of different sizes, intermittent volumes of water and inadequate slopes meant solids accumulated and only a heavy storm would flush the sewers clean. A system of flushing gates to control the flow of liquids through the sewers was invented by the engineer John Roe in 1842, whereby cast iron gates were fixed in the sewers and only opened when there was a sufficient accumulation of water-borne sewage behind them to enable the force of water to clear off any deposits. However, it was not until the 1870s and 1880s that these were combined with hydraulic pumps to ensure a constant flow of water through the sewers and make them virtually self-flushing. Construction of an effective sewerage system involved, too, the production of millions of bricks and tonnes of cement, as well as a transport infrastructure to deliver them to where they were needed.

There remained, though, the perennial problem of into what the sewers were to be flushed. Discharging untreated sewage into the natural water system became a problem as more was understood about the transmission of disease, and Chadwick's idea of spraying it onto fields as a fertiliser was not well received. Some cities attempted to treat the sewage before discharge by adding sedimentation systems to their sewers. However, the breakthrough came in 1912 when scientists at Manchester University developed the sewage treatment system of activated sludge, whereby the sewage was biologically treated to make it safe.

Water supply

The provision of water was, like the provision of sewerage, in the hands of private companies for most of the 19th century. Whether or not individual companies took advantage of new technology was very much up to shareholders who, in turn, were guided by the need to make a good profit on their investment. Some companies did invest in modernising, using the latest equipment and taking up-to-date advice. The following examples are taken from the London area.

- In 1802, the Lambeth Waterworks expanded its operations to supply Kennington and replaced its wooden pipes with cast iron ones. Six years later, the West Middlesex Waterworks Company also installed cast iron pipes.

- In 1822, the Southwark Water Company extracted water from the River Thames using steam engines to pump it to a cistern at the top of an 18-metre-high tower. It was collected there before being piped to customers.

- In 1829, the Chelsea Waterworks Company became the first in the country to install a sand filtration system to purify the water taken from the River Thames.

- In 1838, the Grand Junction Waterworks Company built a pumping station near Kew Bridge at Brentford on the River Thames to house three steam pumps. The water was taken from the middle of the river and pumped into filtering reservoirs and a 61-metre-high water tower that used gravity feed to supply the area.

As the century progressed, more and more water companies built reservoirs to enable a reliable supply of water to be pumped to houses. A major problem, insofar as public health was concerned, was that water companies in London and elsewhere extracted drinking water from rivers that were themselves polluted by industrial and faecal waste. Further change had to wait until the knowledge that disease could be water-borne was combined with the science of removing impurities and the will of the people and the government that this should be done.

Water and sanitation

1 The connection between dirt and disease had been well known since medieval times. Why, then, was the supply of clean water and effective sanitation in towns and cities so slow to be realised?

2 'The development and marketing of flush toilets solved the sanitation problems of the growing towns.' Explain how far you agree with this statement.

TO WHAT EXTENT DID ATTITUDES TO PUBLIC HEALTH REFORMS CHANGE IN THE YEARS 1780–1939?

Rarely do attitudes change as the result of a single, cataclysmic event. More often, change in attitudes is the result of a gradual erosion of previously held views. This usually happens because of a growing awareness of the nature of a situation combined with the impact of new discoveries or inventions and the increasing readiness of the authorities to intervene. This was, and is, an organic process. In the years 1780–1939, a growing awareness of the nature of the problems created by poor living conditions, combined with an understanding of the implications of various medical and scientific discoveries, pressurised local and national authorities to intervene. This intervention resulted in a deeper awareness of the need for reform amongst the public, press and parliament, and generated a desire for further change. Throughout, it was a combination of knowledge, understanding and the determination of dedicated individuals that changed attitudes and reformed public health for millions.

Why did attitudes to public health reforms change?

Raising social concerns

Public concern about the health of the working class was raised in a number of ways.

- Housing conditions were reported by writers and journalists. Contemporary novels written by, for example, Charles Dickens (see page 125) and Elizabeth Gaskell, created vivid pen-pictures of working-class living conditions in mid-Victorian Britain. Dickens focused on London, where he had first-hand experience of poverty. His books were enormously successful, reaching a wide readership partly because they were serialised and so more readily accessible than if they had been published in single volumes. Elizabeth Gaskell, married to a Unitarian minister, lived in Manchester and, although not poor herself, witnessed desperate poverty all around her. She wrote movingly of the impact of poor living conditions in her novel *Mary Barton* that was published in 1848. The conditions described by such authors chimed with the findings of the investigative journalist Henry Mayhew (see page 124). Throughout the period, there were novelists who focused on living conditions. For example, Arnold Bennett, at the beginning of the 20th century, wrote a series of novels that had the housing and health of the Staffordshire pottery towns as their backdrop. George Orwell, in his 1937 novel *The Road to Wigan Pier,* documented the bleak living conditions of many working-class people in Yorkshire and Lancashire.

- National and local newspapers reported public health matters, and commented on them, not always favourably (See Source 11 on page 31). Local outbreaks of scarlet fever and typhoid, for example, were reported in local newspapers such as the *Leeds Mercury*, and occasionally connections were made between poor living conditions and disease. It was the national newspapers that had the greatest impact on changing the attitudes of those with the power to bring about change. *The Times* newspaper, for example, headed a campaign for effective sewerage of London as a result of the 'Great Stink' of 1858 (see page 58).

- Artists created paintings and engravings of the rural and urban poor, usually incorporating street scenes and interiors. Whilst some were bought and hung on middle-class walls for their sentimental value – the rural poor usually presented as romantic idylls – those of the urban poor were more disturbing. They attracted the attention of those writing novels about the urban poor and destitute. Dickens, for example, was a great admirer of the work of Sir Luke Fildes, one of whose paintings you can see on page 8.

SOURCE
10 An engraving by Gustav Doré of a London street scene. In 1869, Doré accepted a contract from the publishers Grant & Co. to produce a comprehensive portrait of London. The completed book *London: A Pilgrimage* contained 180 engravings, of which this is one, and was published in 1872. It was a great success.

- Doctors, parishes and county councils improved their record-keeping facilities. This enabled the production of statistical evidence to illustrate, for example, the connection between population density and overcrowding on the one hand, and death and disease on the other.

Percentage of total population overcrowded	Death rates, all causes, per 1,000
15	17.51
15–20	19.51
20–25	20.27
25–30	21.75
30–35	23.92
Over 35	25.07

Figure 1.2 From the report by the Medical Officer for Health, London, in 1892.

Type of accommodation	Death rate per 1,000
One room	32.7
Two rooms	21.3
Three rooms	13.7
Four rooms	11.2

Figure 1.3 Death rates in Glasgow, 1901.

Persons per square mile	Mean death rate, per 1,000
27 districts with an average density of 136	11.63
40 districts with an average density of 1,303	18.53
18 districts with an average density of 4,424	21.56
5 districts with an average density of 7,480	26.54
4 districts with an average density of 55,563	34.82

Figure 1.4 Statistics released by the Registrar-General's Office, 1907.

- There was increasing scientific knowledge and understanding about the causes of water-borne and sanitation-related diseases. This led to increased public awareness about the need for clean water, sewerage and drainage in general and encouraged the emergence of Health and Sanitation Committees to pressurise councils and the government to take action. For example, in 1844 the Health of Towns Association was established. It had a central committee based in London and branches in most provincial towns. Its aim was simple: to carry out a propaganda campaign for public health legislation. Members gave public lectures, published and distributed informative pamphlets and produced a weekly sheet of facts and figures.

- Governments set up Royal Commissions to investigate the living conditions of the poor and authorised a range of investigations during the period. A Royal Commission for Enquiry into the State of Large Towns and Populous Districts, for example, was set up in 1843 and reported in 1844.

Knowledge and understanding of public health issues grew and developed throughout the period as a result of these developments and changing attitudes to the need for public health reform.

ACTIVITY
KNOWLEDGE CHECK

Raising social concerns

1 How reliable is the evidence provided by Charles Dickens, Elizabeth Gaskell and Gustav Doré about the state of public health in 19th-century Britain?

2 What conclusions can be drawn from the statistical tables in Figures 1.2–1.4?

3 Discuss in your group which was the more effective way of raising public concern about public health: novels, illustrations or statistics.

Economic imperatives

Economic imperatives often play a large part in changing people's attitudes. It was the same with regard to public health reform. Factory managers, mill owners, bankers, treasury officials and all those affected by public health issues gradually became aware, not only of the cost of the reforms themselves, but of the cost of not undertaking reform.

- The cost of public health reforms could be calculated against the cost of losing a productive worker to one of the so-called 'dirty' diseases.

- The cost to the nation of the Poor Law, when looked at in terms of maintaining workhouses and paying for relief, was escalating (see Chapter 4, page 106). When local officials set this against the cost of public health reform, many could see a reduction in the poor rate occurring as a result of providing good drains and clean water. Any reduction in rates and taxes would resonate well with voters.

- A major consideration in persuading people of the need for public health reform had to be, not only the overall cost, but also which sections of society would be paying for clean water and drains for all. Inevitably, the initial costs of connecting a house to a water supply and to sewerage systems fell upon the householder. Whilst the informed middle class, generally, paid out for their own comfort and health, it was by no means clear that they should pay for the poor to have similar facilities. Indeed, the landlords of the tenements and lodgings, should they be persuaded to link the properties they were letting out to the new drains and water supplies, would inevitably increase rents to cover costs – and the very poor could not pay. This, in turn, would throw more of the poor into pauperism. There was a way out of this seemingly vicious circle, and that was for local authorities to step in and take over responsibility for the public health of those living within their catchment area. This did happen but it happened slowly as economic and political imperatives altered the minds and attitudes of those in a position to bring about change.

Ultimately, the economic imperative was central to changing attitudes to the provision of public health. The economic benefit derived from a fit workforce was more persuasive than any moral imperative. If the initial investment produced an improved workforce, then, so the persuasive argument went, it was worth the initial outlay. The second Boer War (1899–1902) had a specific impact (see Chapter 6, page 139), as army recruitment showed up the poor physical condition of working men in industrial towns. Gradually, attitudes were changing and this impacted on the role of central government.

ACTIVITY
KNOWLEDGE CHECK

Economic imperatives

1 Set up a debate on the proposition that 'The middle classes should not be expected to pay for the public health of the poor.'

2 How far do you agree that economic considerations were the key driving force behind public health reform?

A Level Exam-Style Question Section C

How far do you agree that the key factor in changing attitudes to public health reform in the years 1780–1939 was the work of novelists and artists?
(20 marks)

Tip
As well as addressing the work of novelists and artists, you will need to identify other factors, such as official reports, that could be seen to change attitudes, and then reach a balanced conclusion as to which of the factors you have identified was the key one.

How far did the role of government grow in the 19th and early 20th centuries?

At the start of the period, in 1780, government involvement in social policy was minimal. Taxes were raised mainly to finance foreign wars and to keep the borders of the country secure. There was a generally held belief that social policy, and this included public health, was the business of parishes. This view was strongly supported by the prevailing ideology of laissez-faire. However, the election of a Whig government in 1830 ended 23 years of Tory government, and raised the hope of many that reforms in different areas of government would be possible. This would involve a move away from laissez-faire.

- The Representation of the People Act 1832 did make some important adjustments to the franchise and to the distribution of seats, allowing for greater representation from the growing industrial towns of the Midlands and the North. It might have been expected that some attention would be paid, after 1832, to the much-needed public health reforms in the areas they represented. However, middle-class representation with a desire to keep rates low meant that sanitary reform was low on MPs' agendas, and there was still the general feeling that public health reforms were the business of local authorities, not parliament.

- The Municipal Corporations Act 1835 ended the system of 'closed' corporations, whereby the same councillors reappointed themselves, year-on-year. Borough councils were to be elected by male ratepayers for a three-year term of office. Councillors elected a mayor and chose aldermen. Furthermore, the Act stated that councils could, if they wished, assume control of paving, sewerage, street cleaning and drainage in their areas. Even so, they still needed a private Act of Parliament to enable them to do so and this was by no means a cheap undertaking. What is important to recognise here is that central government showed little interest in public health. If town councils wanted to tackle the problem, then that was their affair. However, the very fact that councils were to be elected by ratepayers raised the possibility that the more progressive councils would want to focus on public health reforms.

Central government begins to get involved

By the 1840s, it was becoming clear to all but a handful of people that something had to be done to improve public health. One of the main problems lay in who was to do it: national or local government? Should the aim be to set up a national system of public health, or should public health reform be left to local initiatives? A further, but important, problem was whether people could, or should, be compelled to follow directives that were intended to be for their own good. To do this would be to move a very long way from the laissez-faire attitudes that dominated domestic politics in the earlier years of the century.

The 1844 Report of the Royal Commission into the Sanitary Condition of Large Towns and Populous Districts (see page 22) marked a mid-century appraisal of the sanitary condition of Britain. Almost immediately it was followed by some minor legislation designed to hold the situation until a main Public Health Act could be prepared.

- 1846 saw the first of a series of Nuisance Removal Acts. These were designed to enable justices in petty session courts to prosecute those responsible for 'nuisances'. Nuisances were generally defined as being unwholesome houses, accumulations of filth, foul drains and cesspools.

- The Baths and Washhouses Act 1846 enabled local authorities to provide baths and washhouses out of public money.

- In 1847, the Towns Improvement Clauses Act defined the rights of towns to lay water supplies and drainage schemes and to control nuisances. It also legalised the discharge of sewage into rivers and the sea, and allowed its sale for agricultural purposes.

These Acts shared a common characteristic: they only applied if the authorities wanted them to. They were there if any local authority wanted to take advantage of them. Was this to be the shape of things to come? Health of Towns bills were introduced in 1845 and 1847 but were withdrawn; an attempt to introduce a Public Health bill in 1847 was defeated by MPs who became known as the 'Dirty Party'. However, the onset of the 1848 cholera epidemic provided the necessary impetus for a further public health bill to be successful.

The Public Health Act 1848

- A General Board of Health was set up, which reported to parliament. It was based in London. The three original members of the Board were Lord Morpeth (who was behind the unsuccessful 1847 bill and the successful 1848 Act), Lord Shaftesbury and Edwin Chadwick.

- Local authorities were empowered to set up local boards of health. These could be set up where:

  - ten percent of the ratepayers asked for one

  - the death rate was greater than 23 per 1,000.

- Local boards of health were permitted to appoint a medical officer of health and pay his wages out of the rates.

- Local boards of health were to manage sewers and drains, wells and slaughterhouses, refuse and sewerage systems, burial grounds and public baths, recreation areas and public parks.

- Local boards of health could finance projects by levying local rates and buying land.

This Act, however, was **permissive**: it did not apply everywhere to all local authorities throughout the country. This was at once a great strength and a great weakness. It could be argued that its strengths were that, because it applied where local people wanted it, there was little or no opposition to it and so implementation would be relatively smooth. Because it had to apply where conditions were very poor, people were desperate for any remedy and were unlikely to put up any serious opposition, and piecemeal implementation meant that those who were suspicious or wary could see for themselves how the Act worked to improve public health and would push for its introduction in their own towns and cities. If these were the Act's strengths, then its weaknesses could be seen in its lack of universality. It did not, for example, apply to London – which had its own Act in 1848 to establish the Metropolitan Commissioners of Sewers – or the City of London with its own City Sewers Act. Nor did it apply to Scotland; the Act was only enforced where the death rate in a district was more than 23 per 1,000 living (the national average was 21 per 1,000), and only then could the General Board of Health force a local authority to set up a local board of health. Furthermore, although local boards of health set up compulsorily were to have considerable powers over basic public health requirements – drainage, building regulation, nuisance removal and water supply – they were not required to take on wider public health considerations that included such things as parks and baths.

Despite all of its failings, however, the 1848 Public Health Act does demonstrate that the government was prepared to do something. It was prepared to provide a solution for towns and cities trying to fight their way through the morass of private and local legislation to achieve some sort of standard of public health. It was prepared, too, to intervene on behalf of the most vulnerable members of society to nudge their local authorities in the general direction of providing for their care. This first, national public health Act generated both pressure from the public for further reform and confidence in the legislators that they could deliver it.

Why was there continued opposition to public health provision in the 1850s and 1860s?

Opposition to public health reforms was not so much opposition to the reforms themselves as to a variety of issues that were highlighted by the pressure for reform. These issues varied in their importance from place to place and local priorities changed over time. This is why some areas embraced reform wholeheartedly, others dragged their feet and some refused point-blank to have anything to do with it.

- Improvement schemes of any kind cost money. Property owners spent money to have clean water piped to large cisterns in their own houses, and for sewers or cesspits to hold waste from their inside lavatories. They were loath to pay out again, via local taxes, to have similar facilities provided for their neighbours when, they argued, there would be no benefit to themselves.

- Many people felt that government was encroaching on their individual liberties by requiring them to, for example, remove dung heaps from their properties or whitewash a slaughterhouse.

- Vested interests – for example, directors of local water companies – were usually represented in local government and often on local boards of health. They were unlikely to vote for measures that would reduce their company profits.

- The civil engineering problems posed by sewerage and water supply schemes were barely understood by lay people on local boards of health; this caused delay and, occasionally, the implementation of inappropriate systems.

- Chadwick himself – one of the three commissioners on the General Board of Health set up by the Public Health Act 1848 – irritated, annoyed and angered many because of his bullying tactics.

SOURCE

11 From *The Times* newspaper, July 1854.

We prefer to take our chance with cholera and the rest than to be bullied into health. There is nothing a man hates so much as being cleaned against his will, or having his floors swept, his walls whitewashed, his dung heaps cleared away, or his thatch forced to give way to slate, all at the command of a sort of sanitary bombaliff [official]. It is a positive fact that many have died of a good washing. All this shows the extreme tenderness with which the work of purification should advance. Not so, thought Mr Chadwick. New mops wash clean, thought he, and he set to work, everywhere washing and splashing, and twirling and rinsing, and sponging and sopping, and soaping and mopping, till mankind began to fear a deluge of soap and water. Mr Chadwick has very great powers, but it is not so easy to say what they can be applied to. Perhaps a retiring pension, with nothing to do.

ACTIVITY
KNOWLEDGE CHECK

Towards compulsion

1 In your judgement, was the Representation of the People Act 1832 or the Municipal Corporations Act 1835 the more likely to lead to the introduction of public health reform?

2 How far does Source 11 explain why the Public Health Act 1848 was permissive?

3 How convincing do you find the continuing objections, in the 1850s and 1860s, to public health reforms?

The Local Government Act 1858 and the Public Health Act 1858

These two Acts brought about the following changes.

- The General Board of Health was abolished.

- The powers of the General Board of Health were given to a new Local Government Act office.

- A medical department of the Privy Council was set up.

- Local boards of health were given powers to take preventative action and appoint officials.

Why were these two linked Acts of Parliament needed so soon after the Public Health Act 1848? The ten years in-between had shown a gradual acceptance by local authorities of the need for more powerful local public health bodies, but there was considerable hostility towards the General Board of Health and its commissioner Edwin Chadwick. He had to go, and a more acceptable way of centralising and controlling public health provision had to be found. Splitting the powers and functions of the old General Board of Health between the Local Government Act Office and the Privy Council medical department was the solution. It was a clever one, too. One of the main functions of the old General Board of Health had been to approve loans to local authorities for public health projects. This function was continued, although slightly differently. The permission of the Local Government Act Office was needed for all loans that local authorities wanted to raise in order to carry out public works. It was just a short step for the Privy Council medical department to carry out the relevant inspections where public health projects were involved. In other words, it was central government direct (as in the Privy Council) that for the first time became involved in the administration of public health in the localities. In the ten years up to 1868, 568 towns set up boards of health and began implementing public health reforms.

The Sanitary Act 1866

A key mover behind this new Sanitary Act was John Simon. He had been London's first medical officer of health in 1848 and medical officer to the General Board of Health in 1855. In 1858, when the General Board of Health was wound up, he became the first medical officer to the medical department of the Privy Council. Simon worked within the permissive framework set up by the 1848 Act, seeking to persuade local authorities to accept public health systems. As a direct consequence of the sort of advice given by John Simon in his 1865 annual report, in 1866 parliament passed a new Sanitary Act, which brought about the following changes.

- Sanitary powers that had been granted to individual local boards of health under the 1848 Act were made available to all local boards.

- Local authorities were made responsible for the removal of 'nuisances' to public health. If local authorities failed to act, central government could do the work of improvement and charge the local authorities.

- The definition of 'nuisance' was extended to domestic properties and included overcrowding.

- Local authorities were given the power to improve or demolish slum dwellings.

For the first time, compulsion was a significant element of an Act of Parliament dealing with public health. No longer did the state direct and advise local authorities: it could now compel them to act. In this sense, the state was, from this point on, directing public health reform.

EXTEND YOUR KNOWLEDGE

Sir John Simon (1816–1904)

Born in London, John Simon received his medical training by first being apprenticed to a surgeon at St Thomas' Hospital, and then completed his formal medical studies at King's College, London. Between 1840 and 1847, he worked as a surgeon at King's College Hospital, and later lectured in pathology. A founder member of the Health of Towns Association in 1844, in 1848 Simon became medical officer of health for the City of London and Chief Medical Officer for Health to the Privy Council in 1858. Like Chadwick, he was initially a firm supporter of the miasma theory of the spread of disease but, unlike Chadwick, he changed his mind as evidence supporting the germ theory gradually became available. Simon helped transform the issue of public health from a political matter to one founded in scientific investigation and analysis, and his detailed reports helped bring about both the Sanitary Act 1866 and the Public Health Act 1875. He stepped down from office in 1876, and in 1887 received a knighthood for his contribution to public health.

What were the pressures for further change?

- In 1867, the Parliamentary Reform Act effectively gave the vote to working men in towns. Politicians had to pay attention to their problems, which included public health issues.

- There was a third cholera epidemic in 1865–66, in which 20,000 people died.

- In 1865, Louis Pasteur (1822–95) proved conclusively that germs caused disease and were not caused by it.

- In 1869, a Royal Commission on public health was set up, which revealed that conditions in towns were little better than when Chadwick had been masterminding investigations some 30 years earlier.

- In 1871, a Local Government Board was set up. This consolidated the functions of the Local Government Act Office, the Registrar-General's Office, the medical department of the Privy Council and the Poor Law Board. The president was usually a member of the Cabinet.

The Public Health Act 1875

The Public Health Act 1875 was the most comprehensive legislation to date, codifying and consolidating previous laws. It was to remain the foundation of all public health work until 1936. It established the following:

- Every part of the country had to have a public health authority.

- Every public health authority had to have at least one medical officer and one sanitary inspector to ensure that the laws on food adulteration, housing, water supplies and cleansing were enforced.

- Local authorities were given wide powers to lay sewers and drains, build reservoirs, parks, public baths and public conveniences.

The government was now completely committed to the provision of public health for the people it governed. Additionally, the Act was the turning point in the regulation of house building in British cities. By permitting sanitary authorities to make by-laws that controlled building standards and plans, they were able to lay down such things as street widths and the provision of open space.

The Public Health Act 1936

A further Public Health Act in 1936 consolidated a range of previous legislation, and addressed such matters as sanitation, nuisances and offensive trades, baths and washhouses and the prevention and notification of diseases, over all of which local authorities had immediate responsibility. Extended by the Food and Drugs Act 1938, control over slaughterhouses and food adulteration was added to their responsibilities.

Local authorities continued with their essential public health work of ensuring an adequate water supply and efficient sewerage and sanitation. The years 1919–39 saw the virtual completion of the process whereby local authorities took over control of water supplies with all the complex systems of reservoirs, pipelines and treatment centres that this involved. By 1935, 80 percent of the population of England and Wales were supplied with water by the local authorities. This water was, generally, safe, although typhoid epidemics in Bournemouth, Poole and Christchurch in Dorset in 1936 and Croydon in 1937 caused by sewage contamination demonstrated that there was still work to do in this area. However, generally speaking, the provision of a clean water supply with the combination of an efficient sewerage system represented a major, though unspectacular, advance in public health.

EXTRACT

3 From Bernard Harris *The Origins of the British Welfare State: Social Welfare in England and Wales 1800–1945*, published in 2004.

Despite the tremendous expansion in the scope of public health activity, [throughout the nineteenth century] the vast majority of these measures were really concerned with the protection of the community as a whole, rather than the individuals who comprised it. However, during the late-nineteenth and early-twentieth centuries, public health officials became increasingly concerned with what they regarded as the 'personal factors' associated with the spread of disease. This emphasis on the role of personal factors led in the first instance to a growing concentration on the need for health education, particularly in the areas of infant management, food preparation and personal hygiene, but it soon spilled over into a more general campaign for the provision of health services which were aimed directly at particular groups of individuals.

A Level Exam-Style Question Section C

'The Sanitary Act of 1866 was the most significant piece of public health legislation passed by parliament in the years 1780–1939.'

How far do you agree with this statement? (20 marks)

Tip

You will need to consider the significance of the 1866 Act, and in doing this you should suggest criteria with which to judge significance. Then use these criteria to assess other legislation (the 1848, 1875 and 1936 Public Health Acts, for example) before reaching a conclusion.

ACTIVITY
KNOWLEDGE CHECK

Public Health Acts after 1848

1 The Public Health Act 1848 represented a great step forward in central government's involvement in public health matters. Why, then, were further Public Health Acts necessary?

2 In your judgement, which Act of Parliament had the greatest impact on public health: the 1848, 1875 or 1936 Public Health Act?

3 Given that there were Public Health Acts in 1848 and 1875, why was a Sanitary Act necessary in 1866?

4 How far do you agree with the historian Bernard Harris (Extract 3) that the vast majority of 19th-century public health measures were concerned with the protection of the community, rather than individuals?

Conclusion

The early approach of governments to public health was fundamentally negative. Central government was not proactive: it simply provided the powers for others to use, if they so wished. The whole laissez-faire attitude of government was against positive interference. They had plenty of information in the form of reports on the state of towns and, in particular, about the horrendous conditions in which thousands of the poor were living. But action was slow as long as there was a property-owning electorate in control. Improvement only came slowly partly because the growth of towns was not accompanied by a similarly radical change to local government.

There were, however, other concerns involved in the solution of public health problems. Scientific understanding about public health problems was far from clear or accurate. Civil engineering was in its infancy and new techniques had to be invented and trialled. This was particularly the case where the provision of clean water and water-driven sewage were concerned. As public expectations changed from supporting the least government intervention possible to wanting positive government interference in public health matters, the role of central government reflected this and became more and more directive so that public health reforms moved from the permissive to the compulsory. At the same time, the onus for the actual provision of public health shifted to local government, with central government providing the broad framework within which reforms were instigated. The impact of central government on the localities and on individuals is explored in Chapter 2.

KEY TERM

Collectivism
The belief that the state had a primary responsibility for the welfare of its citizens and the improvement in the quality of their lives.

The move of central government from a laissez-faire approach to social policy, especially where it was concerned with public health, to one of direction can be seen as a move from an individualist approach to one of **collectivism**. No longer, by the early years of the 20th century, were public health matters the province of the whim or the philanthropy of individuals; by 1939, collectivism – the belief that the state was responsible for public health provision – had replaced laissez-faire. This had happened because, despite a strong belief in the primacy of laissez-faire in a free society, legislators had to accept that the problems posed by an urban, industrialised society had to involve an extension of the activities of the state. This move from laissez-faire to state intervention was gradual, as has been shown in this chapter. There was not a moment in time when one theory of legislation took over from another. Rather, the move to collectivism was a pragmatic one, a long-drawn-out evolution of a new legislative and administrative practice.

THINKING HISTORICALLY Change (7a)

Convergence and divergence

Legislative change in England, 1780–1939

1832 Representation of the People Act	**1835** Municipal Corporations Act	**1848** Public Health Act	**1867** Parliamentary Reform Act	**1875** Public Health Act

Economic change in England, 1780–1939

1832 Cholera epidemic	**1842** Edwin Chadwick publishes his *Report on the Sanitary Condition of the Labouring Population of Great Britain*	**1844** Engels writes *The Condition of the Working Class in England*	**1851** 50 percent of the population of England and Wales living in urban areas	**1875** Thomas Twyford develops and markets the first wash-out trap water closet

1 a) Draw a timeline across the middle of a landscape piece of A3 paper. Cut out ten small rectangular cards and write the above changes on them. Then place them on the timeline with legislative events above the line and economic below. Make sure there is a lot of space between the changes and the line.

b) Draw a line and write a link between each change within each strand, so that you have four links that join up the changes in the *legislative* part of the timeline and four that join the *economic* changes. You will then have two strands of change: *legislative* and *economic*.

c) Now make as many links as possible across the timeline between legislative change and economic change. Think about how they are affected by one another and think about how things can link across long periods of time.

You should end up with something like this:

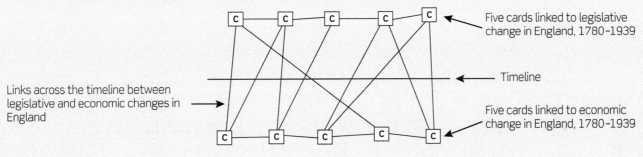

Five cards linked to legislative change in England, 1780–1939

Timeline

Links across the timeline between legislative and economic changes in England

Five cards linked to economic change in England, 1780–1939

Answer the following:

2 How far do different strands of history interact with one another? Illustrate your answer with two well-explained examples.

3 At what point do the two strands of development converge? (In other words, when do the changes have the biggest impact on one another?)

4 How useful are the strands in understanding the move to collectivism?

ACTIVITY SUMMARY

The impetus for public health reforms

1 How far did industrialisation create public health problems?

2 How far do you agree that the 1832 cholera epidemic was the key impetus behind public health reforms in the years 1780–1939?

3 'The significance of discrediting the miasma cause of disease had a minimal impact on public health reform.' How far do you agree with this statement?

WIDER READING

Evans, E.J. *The Forging of the Modern State 1783–1870*, Pearson (1983)

Harris, B. *The Origins of the British Welfare State*, Palgrave Macmillan (2004)

Hill, C.P. *British Economic and Social History 1700–1975*, Edward Arnold (1975)

Mathias, P. *The First Industrial Nation*, Methuen (1969)

Pugh, M. *State and Society 1870–1997*, Arnold (1994)

Stevenson, J. *British Society 1914–45*, Penguin Books (1984)

3.2 Changes in public health

KEY QUESTIONS

- How effective were local initiatives in improving the health of the public, c1780–1939?
- How significant was the work of individuals in improving public health, c1780–1939?

INTRODUCTION

The period 1780–1939 saw a considerable change in attitudes to public health and this change was reflected in parliamentary legislation. Parliamentary legislation was, at first, tentative, with permissive Acts that could be accessed should local authorities wish to do so. By the early years of the 20th century, as described in Chapter 1, governments had become fully committed to public health and Acts of Parliament dealing with public health were compulsory. Clean water and effective sanitation were no longer optional.

However, central government could legislate for public health, but it was in the localities that this central legislation was implemented. When central legislation was permissive, a local council could decide to spend money on civic buildings rather than on drains; a health board hastily assembled in times of epidemic could be disbanded when the danger was seen to have passed. Even when Public Health Acts became compulsory, they still had to be implemented by local councils – and this was done with varying degrees of enthusiasm.

It was during this period that the pioneering work of individuals was so important in driving public health improvements. Often scorned by the public and sometimes derided by the medical profession, these far-sighted individuals had at the heart of their work their desire to improve the health of the public.

HOW EFFECTIVE WERE LOCAL INITIATIVES IN IMPROVING THE HEALTH OF THE PUBLIC, c1780–1939?

Local government action and reaction, c1780–1848

Unprecedented population growth in the 19th century (see pages 11–13) brought about a slow change to local and central government involvement in public health. Initially, local government intervention was the more prominent, with a whole series of Acts and regulations being applied locally, not nationally.

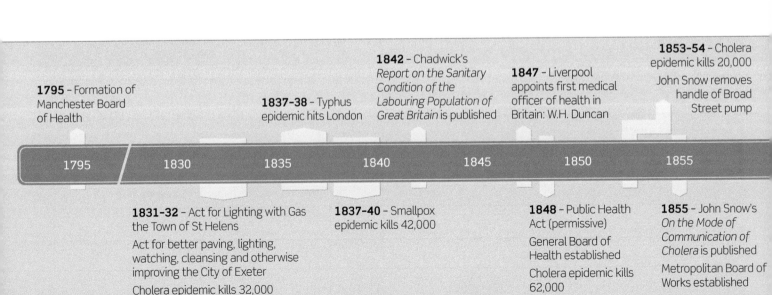

1795 – Formation of Manchester Board of Health

1831-32 – Act for Lighting with Gas the Town of St Helens

Act for better paving, lighting, watching, cleansing and otherwise improving the City of Exeter

Cholera epidemic kills 32,000

1837-38 – Typhus epidemic hits London

1837-40 – Smallpox epidemic kills 42,000

1842 – Chadwick's *Report on the Sanitary Condition of the Labouring Population of Great Britain* is published

1847 – Liverpool appoints first medical officer of health in Britain: W.H. Duncan

1848 – Public Health Act (permissive)

General Board of Health established

Cholera epidemic kills 62,000

1853-54 – Cholera epidemic kills 20,000

John Snow removes handle of Broad Street pump

1855 – John Snow's *On the Mode of Communication of Cholera* is published

Metropolitan Board of Works established

1795 | 1830 | 1835 | 1840 | 1845 | 1850 | 1855

This did not, however, mean that local authorities simply ignored the issue. Pioneering work was done in certain towns and cities by individual medical people and administrators. Thomas Perceval and John Ferriar of Manchester, for example, were behind the formation of the Manchester Board of Health in 1795, and in Scotland, Robert Graham, Robert Cowan and James Cleland published reports on public health in the early 19th century that prompted authorities to act. But this was piecemeal, and initiatives were only applied locally. Given a different local administration with different personnel and different priorities, public health schemes would collapse.

Equally piecemeal were the many **private Acts of Parliament** obtained by local authorities that related to public health. London, for example, was administered by 300 different bodies with an interest in public health, and these operated under some 250 Acts of Parliament. Just one London parish, St Pancras, had 16 paving boards, responsible for paving the streets of the parish, acting under 29 Acts of Parliament. It was an administrative nightmare that was repeated, to a lesser extent, throughout Britain. In 1831–32, for example, the county of Lancashire had an Act passed for 'Lighting with Gas the Town of St Helens'; and the City of Exeter asked for an 'Act for better paving, lighting, watching, cleansing and otherwise improving the City of Exeter'. These, along with many other private Acts of Parliament, allowed improvement commissioners to be elected by the ratepayers to deal with the specific problems detailed by the Acts. Many towns ended up with different sets of improvement commissioners dealing with, say, lighting, paving, street cleaning and other town improvements.

By the 1830s, many people were beginning to criticise the corrupt nature of town improvement committees and, sometimes, the town corporations themselves. In some towns, elections were rarely held and the various groupings of officials became self-perpetuating **oligarchies**. Many operated to serve the interests of selected groups of citizens. **Vested interests** – from night-soil men to clergy and owners of water companies – were either paid off or, which was far more likely, represented on the improvement committees themselves. It was becoming clear that the different ways of addressing public health issues were grossly inadequate.

Some towns, for example, Leeds and Manchester, took advantage of their new status under the Municipal Corporations Act 1835 (see Chapter 1, page 29) and assumed control of paving, sewerage, street cleaning and draining. Even so, they still needed a private Act of Parliament to enable them to do so, and this was by no means a cheap undertaking. In 1846, for example, the City of Liverpool obtained a Sanitary Act that made the corporation a health authority and empowered it to appoint a medical officer of health. The town council was given powers to carry out sewerage, drainage and water supply improvements – and it appointed W.H. Duncan as the first medical officer of health in Britain.

(see Chapter 1, page 29)

KEY TERMS

Private Act of Parliament
This gave specific powers or benefits to individuals or bodies rather than to the general public.

Oligarchy
Government by a small group of people; a self-perpetuating oligarchy would be a group of people who kept themselves in office, year-on-year.

Vested interest
This phrase is used to suggest that people are more likely to support a measure if they, their families or social group will benefit from the measure. People with power, whether that power rests in land, money, trade or industry, will look very carefully at measures that might damage that power.

1866–67 – Cholera epidemic kills 14,000

1875 – Public Health Act

1907 – Education (Administrative Provisions) Act

1919 – Housing Act

1860   1865   1870   1875   1880   1885   1900   1905   1910   1915   1920

1858 – Local Government Act The 'Great Stink'

1870 – Acceptance by medical profession that cholera is a water-borne disease

1888 – Local Government Act

1912 – TB becomes a notifiable disease

1922 – Ministry of Health orders the pasteurisation of milk

EXTRACT
1 From A. Briggs *Victorian Cities,* published in 1963.

The rise to power of the 'Economists' should be seen against a background of rising prices in the early 1850s. While the Leeds Town Council was building the Town Hall, the Birmingham Town Council was refusing to appoint a Medical Officer of Health and a stipendiary magistrate, cutting the costs of the jail, rejecting a public baths project, quarrelling with the Recorder and arguing noisily in public about the choice of a Town Clerk. In 1852 costly sewage schemes had been approved, and the Public Works Committee set about its task with vigour. Within a year, however, the city's finances showed that a borough improvement rate of two shillings in the pound – the limit set in 1851 – was inadequate to finance this and other schemes. The costs of reform had been badly underestimated. The financial position continued to deteriorate, and the excess of annual expenditure over income, on the Improvement Account, which stood at £36,392 at the end of 1853, rose to £71,192 at the end of 1855. The 'Economists' believed that a borough improvement rate of two shillings in the pound and borrowing powers of up to £150,000 were quite adequate for a city the size of Birmingham, and they succeeded in 1855 in having the borough rate, which was levied separately from the borough improvement rate, reduced from one shilling and three pence to ten pence in the pound. They dubbed their opponents the 'Extravagant' party, and used every opportunity to discredit them personally.

ACTIVITY
KNOWLEDGE CHECK

Local government involvement

1 Why did local authorities need private Acts of Parliament in order to carry out improvements?

2 a) In what ways could oligarchies and vested interests obstruct public health improvements?

 b) Why would they want to?

3 Read Extract 1. There were a number of problems associated with local council control of public health reform. Which problem is Briggs highlighting in this extract?

Implementing the Public Health Act 1848

It is immediately obvious that there were so many ways in which the Act could be avoided or undermined (see Chapter 1, page 30) that its implementation, and therefore effectiveness, was almost bound to be patchy. It got off to a bad start, too, in that the immediate implementation of the Act was overshadowed by the second cholera outbreak to hit Britain. The General Board of Health was almost totally caught up in coping with this, and only when the epidemic had died down could it focus its whole attention on more general public health issues.

There were some clear successes.

- By the beginning of 1850, 192 towns had asked for the new public health regulations to be applied and the Act had been applied to 32 of them.

- By 1853, this had risen to 284 petitions and there were 182 towns where the Act had been applied.

There were, too, town councils that took the Act even further, and, through private Acts of Parliament, obtained even more sweeping powers, as Source 1 shows.

SOURCE
1 Extracts from the Rochdale Improvement Act 1853.

X. That the Commissioners for executing this Act shall be called 'The Rochdale Improvement Commissioners' with Power to purchase, take, hold, and dispose of Lands and other property for the Purposes but subject to the Restrictions of this Act, and to put this Act in all respects into execution.

XIII. That the Qualifications for a Commissioner shall be his being of full Age and the Owner or Occupier of any Tenement within the Town which was rated in the... last Rate on a net yearly Value of Twenty Pounds or upwards.

XCVII. That the Commissioners, from Time to Time, as they think proper, may cleanse and otherwise improve the River Roche within the Town, and for such Purpose may remove or alter the Town Mill Weir on that River, and erect such other proper and sufficient Works as may be requisite.

XCIX. That the Commissioners may order any Land vested in them to be laid into any Street for the widening and rendering more commodious the same, or to be otherwise disposed of for making or improving any Street as they think proper.

CI. That, except with the Consent of the Commissioners, any new Street within the Town shall not be made of less Width than, if a Carriage Road, Thirty Feet, or, if not a Carriage Road, Ten Feet.

CXIX. That the Commissioners from Time to Time may make, alter, and remove, in such Places within the Town as they think fit, any public Privies or Water Closets, and may maintain and cleanse the same, and make such Regulations for the Use thereof.

CXXII. That if any Person discharge the Smoke of any Furnace or Fireplace or any Steam from any Building (otherwise than from the top of the same) into any Street within the Town, every person so offending shall for every such Offence forfeit any Sum not exceeding Forty Shillings.

However, the enthusiasm of towns like Rochdale has to be put into context and set against the strength of vested interests and the reluctance of many local authorities to pay for something they considered unnecessary, as the following examples show.

- In Lancashire, only 400,000 of its 2.5 million people were living under some sort of public health board.

- Of the 187 major towns (those with a mayor and corporation) in England and Wales, only 29 had the powers of draining and cleansing in the hands of one board; 30 had absolutely no powers over public health because such powers were in the hands of independent commissioners; 62 had no public health authority whatsoever.

- Local boards of health, where they were set up, were frequently simply the existing town corporation under a different guise. Consequently, they were governed by the same vested interests and moved in the same slow and cautious way. Sometimes this was because they were constrained by pre-1848 private Improvement Acts; more often, hesitancy was due to a reluctance to spend money and a general ignorance of sanitary engineering and of the need for it. Frequently, for example, lavatories flushed into sewers that emptied into the nearest watercourse from which drinking water was taken.

EXTEND YOUR KNOWLEDGE

Rochdale

Rochdale was, and still is, a market town on the River Roch in the south Pennines.

Coal mining and the production of woollen cloth were Rochdale's main industries until the middle of the 19th century, when the industrialised spinning and weaving of cotton became pre-eminent. The textile industry made Rochdale prosperous. By the end of the 19th century, there were flourishing woollen mills, silk manufacturers, bleachers and dyers, but the cotton industry was dominant. The Rochdale Canal was one of the major broad canals in Britain, important for the transport of cotton, wool and coal. The Rochdale Equitable Pioneers Society, the first co-operative society, was founded there in 1844 and the first co-operative shop opened in Toad Lane.

Rochdale's increasing prosperity throughout the 19th century was reflected in its governance. In 1825, the town council appointed commissioners for the social and economic improvement of Rochdale, and under the terms of the Reform Act Rochdale 1832 became a parliamentary borough. Despite intense local opposition, the Poor Law Amendment Act 1834 was forced on Rochdale, and the town became the lead town in the Rochdale Poor Law Union. In 1856, Rochdale became a municipal borough, obtaining the powers of improvement commissioners in 1858. Under the Local Government Act 1888, Rochdale became a county borough.

The Public Health Act 1848 did not have the same impact as the Poor Law Amendment Act 1834 (see Chapter 4). The reasons for this were many: the public and government were not convinced that order needed to be brought into the bewildering multiplicity of private Acts relating to public health; there was no existing structure that could be reformed; medical knowledge was not giving clear messages; vested interests in, for example, water companies, remained strong; local improvement commissioners, where they existed, feared the loss of their powers, and, to cap it all, sanitary engineering was expensive.

However, in many ways the Public Health Act 1848 was a watershed. It marked the beginning of the state's intervention in public health matters, and the beginning of the end of the need for private Acts of Parliament to deliver, albeit piecemeal, public health for the people for whom councils were responsible. In the years to 1939, increased understanding about the causes, transmission and prevention of disease, the pioneering work of individuals and the increasing willingness of local authorities to support public health initiatives meant that during the whole period the health of the public improved markedly. This is nowhere shown more clearly than in matters concerning housing.

SOURCE

2 From the *Quarterly Review* published in 1850. The *Quarterly Review* was a literary and political periodical founded in 1809. It tended to be conservative in its views.

And first – to strike at once into the heart of the debate – let us meet the charge of 'Centralisation', or the alleged tendency of the new Sanitary system to supersede Local Self-government by the arbitrary rule of a Metropolitan Board. To reduce this question to its proper terms, we must begin by laying down a well-marked preliminary distinction – that, namely, which exists between Local self-government, as it affects the *mass* of residents in any district, and as it concerns the *functionaries,* often corrupt and ignorant, by whom they are rated and ruled. Obviously, wherever district rates are squandered by jobbing or incompetent Local Boards, the corrective intervention of a Central power, so far from diminishing, may tend largely to increase, the *real* self-governing power of the place, as measured by the control of the population over the expenditure of their own funds.

Centralisation is, in fact, legitimate, provided that its action be based on ascertained public requirement, national or provincial. It is only when these limitations are disregarded, when the exception becomes the rule, and when, in opposition to the public wish, the imperial power exercises by its nominees a direct and permanent sway over local affairs, that Centralisation becomes excessive and obnoxious.

These distinctions have been clearly kept in view by the framers of that admirable sanitary code, the Public Health Act of 1848; an act which embodies the main principles laid down by Sir Robert Peel's Commission of Inquiry into the means of improving the Health of Towns; – and which will remain, we believe, an imperishable monument of that great statesman's far-reaching sagacity. This masterly enactment, while it places the *general* sanitary interests of the country under the care of a metropolitan Board (the pretext of the anti-centralisation cry), also recognises the principle of Local Self-government, by the simultaneous institution of District boards, elected by the ratepayers, to whom they are consequently responsible, and liable to central interference only in one of two cases: first, on an appeal or petition, emanating from district itself, and signed by not less than one-tenth of the ratepayers; secondly, on a duly certified district mortality exceeding the high annual of 23 in 1000. Even, indeed, when the regulating power of the Central Authority is thus called forth, either by the express prayer of a suffering district, or by official delays and restrictions, designed to afford time for local deliberation, and popular concurrence.

ACTIVITY
KNOWLEDGE CHECK

The Public Health Act 1848

1 The Public Health Act 1848 was welcomed by some local councils and ignored by others. Why was this?

2 Read Source 1. Use it to set up a debate between town councillors who supported the Act when it was proposed, and those who opposed it. Use the information in this section to support the argument of both sides.

3 Read Source 2. It addresses the relationship between local and central government. Summarise this relationship. Then use this summary to:

a) explain what problems could arise from too much centralisation

b) explain what problems could arise from too much local control.

Keeping the people healthy: housing

The pressures of a growing population upon the existing housing stock during the first half of the 19th century have been described and explained on pages 13–14. The health of the poorer and most vulnerable people in Britain was dependent to a large extent upon the provision of good-quality housing. The provision of a clean water supply, the construction of a sewerage system, an understanding of the ways in which disease was transmitted were nothing if the poor lived in overcrowded, squalid conditions. However, housing had to be cheap if the poor were to afford it, and herein lies the problem. No speculative builder was going to build good-quality housing that was also cheap. No landlord was going to charge lower rents than he could obtain on the open market for properties he owned.

Was the way forward to be one of compulsion or of state-built housing to the required standard that would be cheap enough to house the poorest in the community? There was no clearly defined government housing policy until the last two decades of the 19th century. Some towns and cities had inserted clauses in their own private Improvement Acts that empowered them to have some control over new building, sewerage connections and cellar dwellings. These were, for example:

- Leeds and Liverpool in 1842
- Manchester in 1844/45
- Nottingham and St Helens in 1845
- Burnley and Newcastle in 1846.

The Metropolitan Building Act 1844 gave the London authorities similar powers. It required all newly constructed buildings that were within 30 feet of a common sewer to be connected to it.

However, to give controls to an authority was not the same as that authority actually acting upon them. Without a building inspectorate, hundreds of new buildings did not conform to the regulations that were supposed to govern them.

It was the Local Government Act 1858 (see Chapter 1, page 32) that set out model by-laws, and ten years later some 568 towns were using them. However, although building regulations were generally available in the 1860s, their impact was less than it could have been. Vested interests fought them through the local courts; localities developed their own variants; and there was always the problem of enforcement. The Public Health Act 1875 (see Chapter 1, page 33) set out very clearly what the powers of local authorities were with regard to building regulations, and it was because of the firmness and clarity of this Act that standard local government by-laws were laid down in 1877. These sought to regulate such things as the width of streets, the height of buildings and systems of drainage.

However, all these measures were primarily concerned with new buildings. It was going to take years before these building regulations had any sort of cumulative effect on public health. Faced with cholera epidemics and endemic 'dirty' diseases, the authorities had to fall back on various expedients.

- The Common Lodging Houses Acts 1851 and 1853 laid down that all lodging houses were to be registered and inspected by the police. However, the Acts were badly drafted and rarely enforced.
- A Nuisances Removal Act 1855 empowered local authorities to combat overcrowding, as a nuisance, with fines and prosecution.
- The Sanitary Act 1866 (see Chapter 1, page 32) placed limitations on the use of cellars for occupation.
- The Artisans' and Labourers' Dwellings Act 1868 (sometimes called Torren's Act) gave local councils the power to force a landlord to repair an insanitary house. If he did not, the council could buy it and pull it down.
- The Artisans' and Labourers' Dwellings Improvement Act 1875 (sometimes called Cross's Act) gave local councils the power to clear whole districts, not just individual houses.

These last two Acts were permissive. Some councils adopted them with alacrity. Birmingham, for example, began a huge slum clearance programme under the direction of its progressive mayor Joseph Chamberlain. He persuaded the town council to buy four acres of slum houses and tumbledown workshops in the city centre. In their place, the council built new law courts and a shopping centre. However, the people who had lived there had to make do as best they could. This highlights the main problem with the Artisans' and Labourers' Dwelling Acts: that they made no provision for the compulsory housing of those made homeless by slum clearance. So the dispossessed simply moved on, to create a slum somewhere else. It was not until 1890 (for London) and 1909 (for the rest of the country) that councils were obliged to rehouse at least half of the people evicted in their slum clearance programmes.

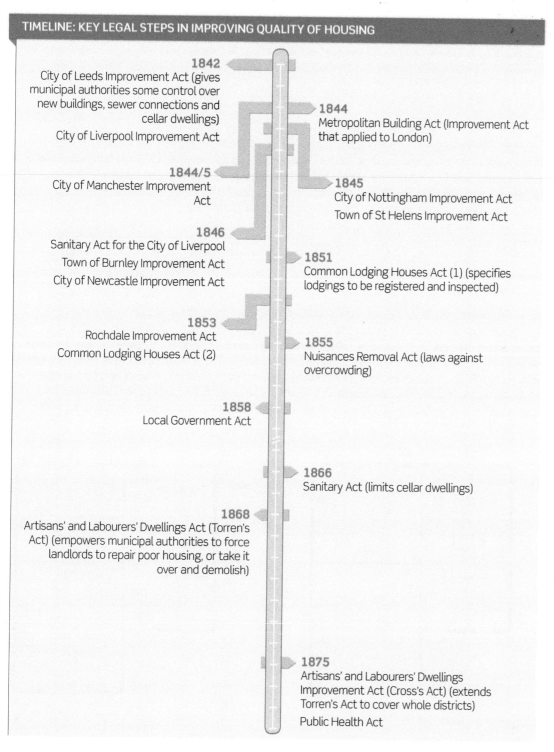

TIMELINE: KEY LEGAL STEPS IN IMPROVING QUALITY OF HOUSING

1842
City of Leeds Improvement Act (gives municipal authorities some control over new buildings, sewer connections and cellar dwellings)
City of Liverpool Improvement Act

1844
Metropolitan Building Act (Improvement Act that applied to London)

1844/5
City of Manchester Improvement Act

1845
City of Nottingham Improvement Act
Town of St Helens Improvement Act

1846
Sanitary Act for the City of Liverpool
Town of Burnley Improvement Act
City of Newcastle Improvement Act

1851
Common Lodging Houses Act (1) (specifies lodgings to be registered and inspected)

1853
Rochdale Improvement Act
Common Lodging Houses Act (2)

1855
Nuisances Removal Act (laws against overcrowding)

1858
Local Government Act

1866
Sanitary Act (limits cellar dwellings)

1868
Artisans' and Labourers' Dwellings Act (Torren's Act) (empowers municipal authorities to force landlords to repair poor housing, or take it over and demolish)

1875
Artisans' and Labourers' Dwellings Improvement Act (Cross's Act) (extends Torren's Act to cover whole districts)
Public Health Act

EXTEND YOUR KNOWLEDGE

Joseph Chamberlain (1836–1914)

Born in London, Chamberlain was educated at University College School and went to work in Nettlefold's screw factory in Birmingham. He retired when he was 38 years old, having made a fortune. He entered politics and in 1868 was elected a Birmingham town councillor, and in 1873-6 the city's mayor. He became MP for Birmingham in 1876; four years later he was in the Cabinet as President of the Board of Trade. A radical social reformer, he embarked on a massive slum clearance programme in Birmingham, built housing for the poor, set up free public libraries and art galleries, and took gas, water and sewerage systems into the control of the city council. He had little regard for the aristocracy, believing they should pay for their privileges. Queen Victoria was not amused. Chamberlain broke with the Liberal Party in 1886 because he distrusted Gladstone and opposed his Home Rule policies. In 1895, he became Colonial Secretary in Salisbury's Conservative–Unionist government, where he supported expansion in Africa. He resigned in 1903 so that he could promote his own policy of tariff reform, which was based on giving preferential treatment to imports from the colonies and protection for colonial industries. In 1906, he left public life because of a stroke and died on the eve of the First World War.

Under normal conditions, house building lagged behind population growth, but, during the First World War (1914–18) house building stopped altogether and house repairs were minimal. Returning soldiers found that Prime Minister Lloyd George's promise to clear slums and make a land 'fit for heroes' rang hollow. After 1918, a dramatic rise in the cost of building materials slowed any rebuilding programmes and made it virtually impossible to build houses that lower-paid workers could afford. Central government stepped in, and in 1919 parliament passed a Housing Act whereby government subsidies were given to local councils and private builders to enable them to build affordable housing for people on low incomes. Called council houses, estates of these houses with gardens, piped water and inside lavatories sprang up and were let to people on low incomes. Waiting lists were common.

Eleven years later, the government offered councils a special slum clearance subsidy to encourage councils to pull down slums and rehouse their inhabitants at rents they could afford. Clearly this wasn't wholly successful, because in 1933, councils were asked to prepare five-year programmes for the abolition of slums. Despite these initiatives, almost two-thirds of all houses built in the interwar years were sold to owner-occupiers. The housing problem had become one of providing sufficient houses to rent for those on a low income. However, by 1939, most houses in towns and cities had piped water and were connected to a sewerage system, but only about 50 percent had a hot water tap and a fixed bath.

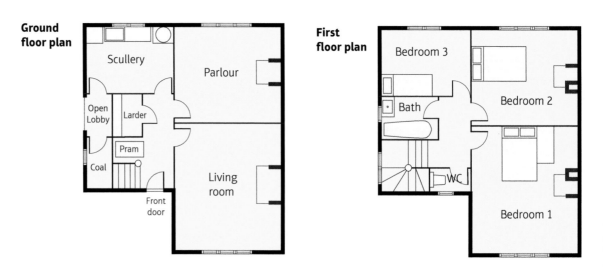

Figure 2.1 Plan for a standard council house, 1920.

ACTIVITY
KNOWLEDGE CHECK

Housing: local government initiatives

1 Assess the significance of the Local Government Act 1858 and the Public Health Act 1875 in improving Britain's housing stock.

2 What were the main drawbacks of the Artisans' Dwelling Acts of 1868 and 1875?

3 Look at Figure 2.1. How far would houses like this meet the public health concerns that were evident in the 19th century?

Individual initiatives in providing housing for the poor

Elsewhere, people of substance had a different attitude and were not dependent on Acts of Parliament before they could act.

- George Peabody (1795–1869), a London-based American banker, founded the Peabody Donation Fund (later the Peabody Trust) with the object of providing model dwellings for the London poor. The first block of 57 dwellings (flats) opened in Spitalfields in 1864 and contained water closets (one for every two flats), baths and laundry facilities. Larger estates were built in Bermondsey, Chelsea, Islington, Poplar, Shadwell and Westminster. By 1882, the Trust was housing more than 14,600 people in 3,500 dwellings, which had risen to over 8,000 dwellings housing over 33,000 people by 1939.

- Titus Salt (1803–76), a wealthy Bradford mill owner, in the 1850s moved his factory and its workers out of a filthy, polluted environment to the purpose-built village of Saltaire. He first built a new mill, and then houses, a school, park, almshouses and a hospital for his workers. Salt laid down strict rules for his workers: for example, he forbade his workers to join unions, refused to allow a public house to be built in Saltaire and did not allow washing to be hung out to dry on Sundays.

- Octavia Hill (1838–1912) bought up run-down artisans' cottages and renovated them by ensuring they were repaired, cleaned, decorated, connected to sewers and provided with clean water. She then let them at low rents to poor people and by the mid-1870s she had more than 3,000 tenants. Working with a team of women rent collectors, she was able to check on her tenants' habits. A strong believer in self-help (see Chapter 5), she was against municipal housing, believing that the poor should be encouraged to be self-sufficient and not become reliant on charity.

- Ebenezer Howard (1850–1928) wrote *To-Morrow: A Peaceful Path to Real Reform* in 1898, in which he developed the theory that people should live in harmony with nature in towns where there was plenty of space, light and fresh air, with an obvious emphasis on good public health. This started the garden city movement that supported the building of Letchworth, the first garden city, in 1903 and the second garden city, Welwyn, in 1920. Both these cities are in Hertfordshire.

- William Lever (1851–1925) found a new site for his soap-making business and alongside had a model village built for his workers. Between 1899 and 1914, some 800 houses were built at Port Sunlight on the Wirral, Merseyside, together with allotments, a cottage hospital, schools, a concert hall, an open-air swimming pool and a church. Lever introduced welfare schemes and provided entertainment in a society where there were strict rules of behaviour.

This level of benevolent paternalism was resented by some, derided by others, but accepted with alacrity by those who willingly swapped some individual freedoms for fresh air, clean water and decent housing.

EXTRACT

 From Richard Rodger *Housing in Urban Britain,* published in 1989.

While private gains to land and capital outweighed social costs, there was little reason to address the slum problem. In fact, suburbanisation temporarily sidestepped the environmental consequences and postponed intervention without disturbing either the mechanism of low wages or the structure and distribution of wealth and power. But, pricked by Christian consciences, panicked by fear of disease, and punctured by developing public transport, the insularity of suburbia could not indefinitely neglect deficient housing standards. How best to contain the contamination was approached with considerable reluctance. Successively the sequence of sanitary provisions, permissive legislation and bye-law regulation, 'model dwellings', municipal clearances and site redevelopment, and taxation proposals each sought to limit the concessions required from property interests and were geared to re-establishing working-class independence. Even council housing, town planning and inexpensive suburban transport, by ostensibly extending choice to those in housing need, sought to restore individual liberty and self-reliance.

This reluctant reformism was in fact overtaken in the last quarter of the nineteenth century by wider social and economic forces associated with rising real wages and reduced family sizes, and it was these influences more than the combined impact of housing reform efforts which contributed to the upward drift in standards of accommodation and comfort for a majority of the population. More fundamentally, perceptions of housing had altered with the realisation that it had a considerable impact on both the quality and quiescence of labour, as well as on military capabilities and national economic efficiency.

ACTIVITY
KNOWLEDGE CHECK

Housing: individual initiatives

1 On a scale of 1–5, where 1 = minimal impact and 5 = maximum impact, rate the contributions of George Peabody, Titus Salt, Octavia Hill, Ebenezer Howard and William Lever to improving the health of the public.

2 Consider the lowest-rated person, or select one if more than one, and explain why you gave that rating. Then consider the highest-rated person, or select one if more than one, and explain why you gave that rating.

3 How far do you agree with the view, expressed in Extract 2 lines 10–11, that improvements in working-class housing were made in order to restore individual liberty and self-reliance?

KEY TERMS

Smallpox
A highly contagious, and sometimes fatal, disease caused by the variola virus. It enters the body through the lungs, infects the internal organs and appears on the skin as a rash. The rash is preceded by a fever, headache and backache, and vomiting. The rash develops into blisters that eventually dry up and the scabs of which fall off, leaving a mark on the skin. Blisters can, in extreme cases, cover an individual's whole body. In severe cases, sufferers die of secondary infections that cause complications, including internal bleeding. Edward Jenner (see page 49) nicknamed the disease 'the speckled monster'.

Human beings are the only carriers of smallpox and so vaccination is very effective. It has been so effective, in fact, that today there have been no recorded cases of smallpox anywhere in the world for many years.

Vaccination
Against smallpox, this involved the introduction of cowpox, a different but similar virus to that of smallpox, into a healthy person, which triggers an immune response without giving the individual smallpox.

Keeping the people healthy: vaccinations

Smallpox had been a controllable disease since Edward Jenner's discovery of a vaccine in 1798 (see page 49) and a National Vaccine Establishment was set up in 1808, using a government grant, to promote **vaccination**. However, until the mid-1830s vaccination was, because of its cost and the activities of the anti-vaccination movement, used by the well-to-do and comfortably off only intermittently. Furthermore, in the days before Pasteur's discovery of the germ theory of disease (see page 17) and without antiseptics and an understanding of the need to sterilise needles, things could, and sometimes did, go badly wrong.

However, the dangers of having an unprotected population were highlighted by the smallpox epidemic of 1837–40 in which around 42,000 people died and thousands more were disfigured for life.

What was to be done? A vaccine was readily available but people were reluctant to use it. The government began a gentle move to compulsion.

- The permissive Vaccination Act 1840 meant anybody could be vaccinated free of charge by the Poor Law medical officers. These men were being used because at the time the Poor Law represented the only national administrative network, and the Poor Law medical officer the only widely available vaccinator.

- The compulsory Vaccination Act 1853 made it obligatory for parents to have their children vaccinated for smallpox within three months of birth. If parents failed to comply, they were fined £1 and the money went towards the poor rate. This made vaccination more common, but it was administered in a haphazard way.

In 1870–73, a second smallpox epidemic, in which 44,000 people died, resulted in a draconian Act.

- The compulsory Vaccination Act 1871 made it obligatory for local health boards to appoint vaccination officers and imposed fines of 25 shillings on parents who refused to have their children vaccinated, with imprisonment for those who did not pay the fine.

In theory, all should have been well. But this emphasis on compulsion resulted in a groundswell of opposition and a strong anti-vaccination movement. Their arguments ranged from fear of central government interference in local government affairs, through to the rights of the individual to choose to take a chance with death, to religious objections against the injection of impurities in the blood. The lead in the anti-vaccination movement was taken by the inhabitants of the city of Leicester, where deaths from smallpox fell without the need to resort to vaccination. Infected people were compulsorily quarantined, as were all those who had contact with them. This was accompanied by a vigorous programme of disinfecting the houses of the quarantined people, and, where necessary, burning their bedding and clothing. The Leicester Anti-Vaccination League was formed in 1869 and, together with the London Society for the Abolition of Compulsory Vaccination, carried out a determined campaign against the compulsion of central government. Town after town formed their own anti-vaccination committees, and a great demonstration held in Leicester in 1885 was joined by representatives from over 50 towns. The 'Leicester Method' of combating smallpox grew in popularity with the town councils of Bolton, Huddersfield and Leicester obtaining private Acts of Parliament making quarantining of smallpox victims compulsory.

The fears of those opposing vaccination were somewhat ameliorated in 1898 by the insertion of a 'conscience clause' in the Smallpox Act, and by the end of the year some 203,143 exemption certificates had been issued. Parents in Lancashire accounted for over one-third of the applications, with Leicester parents requesting 28,524 certificates. Even though it was often difficult to get life insurance, rent a room or get a job without a vaccination certificate, there were thousands of unvaccinated babies by 1900. In 1875, only 3.8 percent of all registered births in England and Wales were of unvaccinated babies, but by 1898 this had risen to 26.6 percent. Despite the lack of take-up in vaccinations, deaths from smallpox continued to fall.

The furore caused by vaccinations demonstrated that government initiatives, and even scientific discoveries, were not enough. What was needed, in addition, was the co-operation of local government officials and in particular the involvement of local medical officers of health and the commitment of local doctors. Without their co-operation and hard work, the health of the people would be at risk.

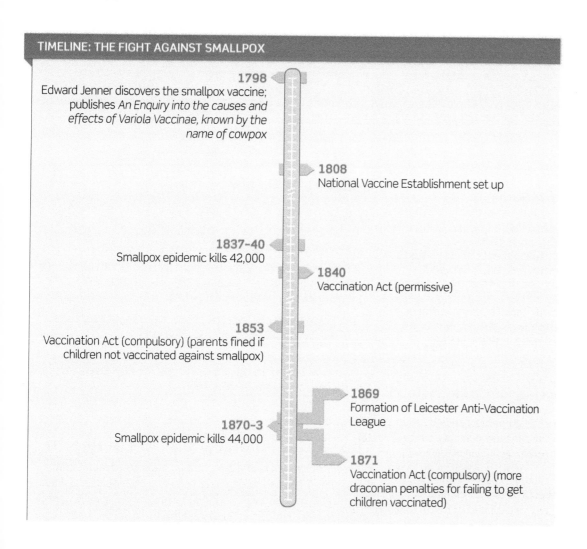

TIMELINE: THE FIGHT AGAINST SMALLPOX

1798
Edward Jenner discovers the smallpox vaccine; publishes *An Enquiry into the causes and effects of Variola Vaccinae, known by the name of cowpox*

1808
National Vaccine Establishment set up

1837–40
Smallpox epidemic kills 42,000

1840
Vaccination Act (permissive)

1853
Vaccination Act (compulsory) (parents fined if children not vaccinated against smallpox)

1869
Formation of Leicester Anti-Vaccination League

1870–3
Smallpox epidemic kills 44,000

1871
Vaccination Act (compulsory) (more draconian penalties for failing to get children vaccinated)

SOURCE
3
A pro-vaccination cartoon, drawn by Isaac Cruikshank in 1808.

SOURCE
4
From *The Times* newspaper, 24 March 1885.

The widespread opposition to the enforcement of the compulsory clauses of the Vaccination Acts which exists in Leicester culminated yesterday in a great demonstration, which was carried out very successfully. The position which the inhabitants of the town have assumed with regard to this question is due to a variety of causes. At the present moment there are over 5,000 persons being summoned for refusing to comply with the law. The total number of summonses issued in the year 1884 only reached seven or a little over one summons in every two months, while at the present moment forty-five summonses are being heard and disposed of every week. The last decade has witnessed an extraordinary decrease in vaccination, but nevertheless the town has enjoyed almost an entire immunity from smallpox, there never having been more than two or three cases in the town at any one time. Under such a system the Corporation have expressed their opinion that vaccination is unnecessary, as they claim to deal with the disease in a more direct and efficacious manner. This, and a widespread belief that death and disease have resulted from the operation of vaccination, may be said to be the foundation upon which the existing opposition to the Act remains.

ACTIVITY
KNOWLEDGE CHECK

Vaccination

1 Look at Source 3. How is the cartoonist setting out the argument in favour of vaccination?

2 Despite the smallpox epidemics of 1840 and 1873, why was the government unable to persuade the general public to become vaccinated?

3 Why was the city of Leicester so successful in reducing cases of smallpox without resorting to vaccination?

4 Organise a debate in which one side argues for compulsory vaccination and the other argues in favour of the regulations imposed by the city of Leicester.

The work of medical officers of health

However much legislation government introduced, ultimately the health of the nation depended on work at a local level. Here, the elected town councils and their willingness to spend money on public health improvements (and this included the salary of a medical officer of health) was key. Most town councillors were elected on the promise of keeping the rates low, and here there was an inevitable tension between maintaining low rates and raising money to spend on sanitary measures. The constitution of many councils, too, tended to skew any decision towards maintaining the status quo. Shopkeepers, manufacturers, farmers and gentlemen made up most of the membership of those responsible for public health in towns and cities, and these tight oligarchies were generally difficult to persuade to spend money on unseen developments, like drains, as opposed to the more obvious elements of civic pride, like town halls.

SOURCE 5

From James Hole *Homes of the Working Classes,* published in 1866. James Hole was active in the development of mechanics institutes and wrote a large number of books and articles that focused on improving the lives of working people. Mechanics institutes were founded to provide adult education in technical subjects for working men.

They, and those who elect them, are the lower middle class, the owners, generally speaking, of the very property which requires improvement. To ask them to close the cellar dwellings is to ask them to forfeit a portion of their incomes. Every pound they vote for drainage, or other sanitary improvement, is something taken out of their own pocket. To the ratepayers themselves, a little claptrap about centralisation, and still more an appeal to their pockets, is sufficient to cause the rejection of the most useful measures. When contemplating an ugly, ill-built town, where every little freeholder asserts his independent right as a Briton to do what he likes with his own; to inflict his own selfishness, ignorance and obstinacy upon his neighbours, and on posterity for generations to come; and where local self-government means merely mis-government – we are apt to wish for a little wholesome despotism to curb such vagaries.

The gradual change in attitudes has been explored in Chapter 1. What must be remembered is that change happened at different rates in different places and at different times. What does seem clear, however, is that the effectiveness of public health at a local level rested in the hands of the medical officer of health. Central government might devise codes of practice and local authorities form boards of health or sanitary committees, but the effectiveness of such matters as the notification of diseases, the application of sanitary by-laws and ensuring houses were fit for human habitation was dependent on the appointment of a qualified medical officer as the medical officer of health.

Although Leicester appointed two medical officers of health in 1846, it was the appointment, in 1847, of Dr William Henry Duncan as Liverpool's medical officer of health that provided an ideal model for other towns and cities to follow. A physician at the Liverpool Infirmary, a lecturer in medical jurisprudence at the medical school of the Royal Institution and in regular correspondence with Edwin Chadwick, Duncan was a man of considerable standing in the medical profession. That such a man could interest himself in public health was a signal to other local authorities of its importance. This, coupled with the early work of John Simon as medical officer of health for the City of London, should have provided ample evidence of the importance of such appointments to the community. However, local authorities were slow to follow the examples of Leicester, Liverpool and

London. Leeds did not appoint a medical officer of health until 1866, Manchester in 1868 and Wolverhampton did not have a full-time medical officer of health until 1921. Indeed, at the time of the Public Health Act 1875 (see Chapter 1, page 33), which made the appointment of a medical officer of health obligatory for all local sanitary authorities, there were approximately 50 medical officers of health holding down full-time appointments in England and Wales. Medical officers of health had, too, to become professionally qualified. The Local Government Act 1888 laid down that all medical officers of health in districts with a population of over 50,000 had to be qualified doctors holding a diploma in sanitary science, state medicine or public health. The low pay on offer compelled most medical officers of health to take on additional work as well. They also had uncertain tenure: they could be removed at the whim of the local authorities who employed them, and this could be done either because they were too rigorous in pursuing public health matters, or too lax.

However, by the end of the 19th century, public health had become an accepted part of local government and local elections began to include public health issues in the manifestos of various parties and candidates. It was clear that a commitment had been made by all local authorities to public health, and that it was their responsibility to create an environment that would engender a healthy population, and that the local medical officers of health were the key to this.

Keeping the people healthy: TB and sanatoria

Tuberculosis (TB) was by far the biggest 19th-century killer, perhaps accounting for one-third of all deaths from disease. It is not possible to be more specific than 'perhaps', because, on diagnosis for death certificates, it was sometimes confused with other diseases such as lung cancer and chronic bronchitis and was not separately notifiable until 1912. Nevertheless, it seems that between 1851 and 1910, deaths from TB almost halved. Even so, in the years to 1919, TB killed more people each year than smallpox, scarlet fever, measles, whooping cough and typhus put together.

KEY TERM

Tuberculosis (TB)
Also known as consumption, phthisis or the white plague, TB is an infectious disease caused by bacteria that attacks the lungs of an infected person. It spreads through the air when an infected person coughs or sneezes and can be transmitted in infected cows' milk. A person with TB usually coughs up blood-spotted sputum and suffers with fevers, night sweats and weight loss. It affects people of all ages.

Because it was a respiratory disease, TB spread most rapidly in overcrowded, poorly ventilated conditions, and was particularly prevalent amongst the urban working class because of their poor living conditions. Indeed, the prevalence of TB in a community can be seen as indicative of the quality of working-class housing, and arguably any improvement in housing standards would impact on the prevalence of the disease. This, however, was long term. The removal of a slum and the provision of good-quality housing with ventilation, space, piped water and sewerage took time. It was the actions of local officers of health that had a more immediate impact, as the following examples show.

- In Oldham, the local medical officer of health ordered the leafleting of all houses, stressing that TB was highly infectious and could be transmitted in the spit of an infected person. It forbade spitting in public places and railway carriages, advised the burning of all handkerchiefs used by sufferers and stated that the local authority would disinfect all houses lived in by TB sufferers.

- In Brighton, the local medical officer of health issued similar leaflets, urging people only to spit in bowls provided for that purpose that should be emptied before the contents became dry.

Actions such as these on a local basis brought home to people how simple, easily achievable steps on their part could significantly help to stop the spread of TB. A similarly important preventative measure was undertaken by central government in 1922, when the Ministry of Health ordered the **pasteurisation** of milk, thus preventing the spread of TB from cattle to humans. Even so, this had to be put into action and monitored at a local level. In 1934, an Act was passed empowering local authorities to make free, or subsidised, pasteurised milk available to schoolchildren and by 1937 school milk was being provided for 3.2 million children either free or at ½d for one-third of a pint.

KEY TERM

Pasteurisation
The process of heating milk to a specific temperature in order to kill sufficient bacteria so that the milk will not transmit tuberculosis from cows with bovine tuberculosis.

Although the tubercle bacillus had been isolated in 1882, the appropriate antibiotic and chemotherapeutic cures had to wait until after the Second World War. In the years to 1939, the most effective 'cure' was fresh air, sunlight, good food and rest, and considerable effort went into the provision of sanatoria where the focus was on these treatments. In 1911, there were 84 sanatoria in the country, providing 8,000 beds; by 1930, this had risen to 500 sanatoria providing 25,000 beds. Even so, surgery for glands, bones and joints affected by TB was common and, for example in 1910, accounted for one-sixth of all surgical operations.

ACTIVITY
KNOWLEDGE CHECK

Tuberculosis

1 In what ways did improvements in housing help to prevent the spread of TB?

2 What part did medical officers of health play in reducing the spread of TB?

Keeping the people healthy: the children

Children did, of course, benefit from all the changes made to sanitation, clean water supplies, housing and the control of 'dirty' diseases. In the 19th century, various Factory Acts legislated for the hours and conditions under which children worked. However, it was the early years of the 20th century, and as part of the raft of reforms instituted by the Liberal governments (see Chapter 6, pages 143–51) that the focus was for the first time on the domestic welfare of children.

Many local authorities were, at the turn of the century, beginning to bring in schemes that helped the children of the poor when their parents were unwilling, or unable, to do so. They opened clean milk depots, appointed health visitors to give advice to poor parents and they started schemes for feeding poor schoolchildren. The Liberal governments (1905–15) built on these local initiatives.

The Education (Provision of Meals) Act 1906
Public concern for feeding needy children has always been there, but in a more organised form stems from voluntary efforts in the 1860s (see Chapter 5). This came to a head with the publication in 1904 of the Report of the Interdepartmental Committee on Physical Deterioration. This highlighted the poor physical condition of army recruits for the second Boer War (1899–1902) and urged the medical inspection and the feeding of children within the state system of education. Public concern focused on the fear that a generation of children was being raised who were not sufficiently physically fit to sustain an Imperial army and, by extension, the Empire.

This Act allowed local authorities to use public money to provide free school meals for the children of needy parents. In some ways, the government had been rushed into this by the introduction of a private member's bill by the Labour MP William Wilson. The Liberal government, partly through fear of being seen as less radical than the Labour Party, took it on and in doing so established the important principles that the state could, in some circumstances, take over the role of parent where the needs of children were concerned. This had always been done, post-1834, when a family was split up on entering a workhouse and parental rights were taken over by the state. However, this assumption of parental rights was associated with the taint of pauperism. This Act made it clear that parents of children taking advantage of free school meals were not regarded, by the state, as paupers. This heralded a philosophical and practical break from the giving of state help only through the Poor Law system.

The Education (Administrative Provisions) Act 1907
This Act set up a school medical service, run by local authorities. This was no great Liberal government initiative, but more of a sleight of hand by Sir Robert Morant, the permanent secretary at the Board of Education. He managed to slip clauses relating to school medical inspection into a technical and complicated piece of legislation. Few MPs realised the significance of what they were debating. Morant, however, was fully aware of what medical inspections of schoolchildren would reveal, certainly before the impact of free school meals could be seen. He was anxious to

have medical treatment linked to medical inspection, and in this he succeeded. A medical department was established within the Board of Education and this was to supervise the provision of the new school medical service. Once the bill was passed, Morant issued directives and circulars to local authorities, regulating the service and authorising them to provide treatment as well as inspection. Whether or not these regulations were implemented effectively was the responsibility of the local authorities. Local authorities began establishing school clinics and, from 1912, grants were available from central government for local authorities to provide treatment, too.

The Board of Education attached great importance to the co-ordination of school medical work with other branches of public health, and urged all local education authorities to appoint the local medical officer of health as their school medical officer. Some local authorities ignored this, and appointed their own separate school medical officers, arguing that to subordinate the school medical service to general public health was to minimise its importance. However, by the end of the 1930s, most local authorities had appointed their local medical officer of health as their school medical officer.

It is evident that, in the early years of the 20th century, the school medical service had expanded considerably. By 1935, there were 2,300 doctors and 5,300 school nurses involved in the service, and 1,650 school clinics providing medical treatment.

EXTEND YOUR KNOWLEDGE

Margaret McMillan (1860–1931)

In 1892, the newly formed Independent Labour Party invited Margaret McMillan to Bradford, West Yorkshire, in order to establish the Party as a force in the city. Standing as a representative of the ILP for the Bradford School Board, she was elected, the only woman member, in 1894. Once on the Board, Margaret fought long and hard for the health and welfare of the children of the poor, believing that it was impossible for dirty, hungry children to learn. The first baths were installed in the Wapping Road School and this was followed by the building of baths in others. Working with Bradford's school medical officer, Dr James Kerr, Margaret persuaded the School Board to institute medical inspections, set up a school clinic and establish a system whereby hungry children were given free school meals.

This Bradford initiative was one of many instituted by Margaret and her sister Rachel. It is indicative of the work that was undertaken in the localities in advance of central government legislation.

The Children and Young Persons' Act 1908

This Act was brought in after serious lobbying by the National Society for the Prevention of Cruelty to Children. As with the Public Health Act 1875 (see page 33), its importance lies partly in consolidating several older Acts and then it carried their provision further.

- Children were made 'protected persons', which made it possible to prosecute their parents for neglect or cruelty.
- Poor Law authorities were made responsible for visiting and supervising children who had suffered cruelty or neglect.
- Nursing and private children's homes were to be registered and inspected.

- Publicans were forbidden to let children under 14 years old into public houses.
- Shopkeepers were forbidden to sell cigarettes to children under 16 years old.
- Juvenile courts and remand homes were set up to separate children from adult offenders.

This Act represented a radically new relationship between the state, parents and children. It is perhaps too early to talk about children's rights, but children were certainly seen, from the beginning of the 20th century, as individuals for whose welfare the state had responsibility. No longer should children suffer for the shortcomings of their parents insofar as their health and welfare were concerned.

ACTIVITY
KNOWLEDGE CHECK
Looking after the children

1 In your view, which helped children the most – the Education (Provision of Meals) Act 1906, or the Education (Administrative Procedures) Act 1907? Explain your answer.

2 The Children's and Young Persons' Act 1908 is often referred to as the 'Children's Charter'. Would you agree?

3 In your judgement, how far do these three Acts of Parliament represent a significant change in the relationship between the state and the public?

A Level Exam-Style Question Section C

How accurate is it to say that, in the years 1780–1939, the key actions that improved the health of the public came from local government? (20 marks)

Tip

Consider the role of local government as a factor, and identify and analyse their key actions in improving the health of the public. Then move on to a consideration of alternative factors that could be seen to impact on change, such as the work of individuals and legislation passed by parliament that applied nationally. There will be overlaps; for example a report on the state of a town written by an individual may be acted upon by local government, so you need to be aware of this when you come to weigh up factors.

HOW SIGNIFICANT WAS THE WORK OF INDIVIDUALS IN IMPROVING PUBLIC HEALTH, c1780–1939?
Edward Jenner (1749–1823): vaccination against smallpox

Smallpox was a disease feared almost as much as cholera. In Jenner's time, smallpox killed approximately ten percent of the population, rising to 20 percent in towns where poor living conditions and overcrowding enabled the infection to spread easily. In children, it accounted for one-third of all deaths.

Inoculation
Another term for vaccination. Against smallpox, this involved the introduction of the smallpox virus into a healthy person by arm to arm or scab to arm. The individual concerned should develop a mild form of smallpox and become immune to any future contact with the disease.

Early inoculation

Inoculation as a means of combating smallpox had been known since the early 18th century. It was a technique brought back to England from Turkey by Lady Mary Wortley Montagu, the wife of the British ambassador there. Basically, it consisted of taking some pus from a smallpox sufferer's pustule, scratching a healthy person and putting some of the pus into the scratch. Obviously this was somewhat hit or miss in its success. Sometimes the inoculated person would develop a mild form of smallpox and be protected from the disease, as was intended; sometimes the inoculated person would develop a severe and disfiguring version of the disease, and sometimes they would die. However, so great was the fear of smallpox that many people, including the Princess of Wales, risked having their families protected in this way. Jenner himself, as a child, had been inoculated against smallpox in this way. Jenner had been starved, purged and bled in order to prepare his body for the process, known as variolation. He was infected with smallpox and locked in a stable with other boys until the disease had run its course. It was a particularly distressing experience, and one Jenner never forgot.

Jenner, the family doctor

In 1773, Edward Jenner was working as a local doctor in his home town of Berkeley, Gloucestershire. He maintained his interest in experimentation and observation, learned when he studied as a surgeon in London, and in 1788 was made a Fellow of the Royal Society. He became interested in local stories about the efficacy of cowpox in preventing smallpox when local people refused inoculation, claiming immunity because of a previous cowpox infection. Indeed, it did seem, anecdotally, that dairymaids who caught cowpox were less likely than those in other occupations to become infected. Deciding to revisit the experimental work he had undertaken when he was a student, Jenner aimed to prove that someone who had been infected with cowpox could not catch smallpox.

SOURCE

From Edward Jenner *An Enquiry into the causes and effects of Variola Vaccinae, known by the name of cowpox,* published in 1798. Jenner gave details of 23 cases before reaching his conclusion.

CASE 16

Sarah Nelmes, a dairymaid near this place, was infected with the cowpox from her master's cows in May 1796. A large sore and several symptoms were produced.

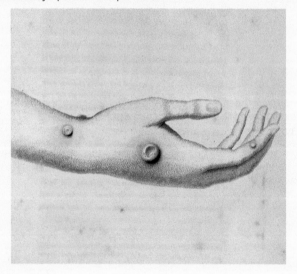

CASE 17

James Phipps. I selected a healthy boy, about eight years old. The matter was taken from the sore on the hand of Sarah Nelmes and it was inserted on 14th May 1796 into the arm of the boy by two cuts each about half an inch long. On the seventh day he complained of uneasiness, on the ninth he became a little chilly, lost his appetite and had a slight headache and spent the night with some degree of restlessness, but on the day following he was perfectly well.

In order to ascertain whether the boy was secure from the contagion of smallpox, he was inoculated with smallpox matter, but no disease followed. Several months later he was again inoculated with smallpox matter, but again no disease followed...

I conclude that the cowpox protects the human constitution from the infection of the smallpox.

Jenner, the experimental scientist

In 1796, a dairymaid, Sarah Nelmes, consulted Jenner because she had believed she had caught cowpox from Blossom, one of the cows she milked regularly and who had developed blisters on her udders. This was Jenner's opportunity. He took some pus from one of Sarah's blisters and rubbed it into the scratches he had made on one of the arms of James Phipps, the eight-year-old son of his gardener. The boy developed a mild fever but was quickly well again. Jenner had established that cowpox could be passed from human to human. He then had to test James to see whether the cowpox had given the boy immunity from smallpox. Undeterred, Jenner variolated the boy with smallpox. The boy suffered no ill effects. Jenner repeated the experiment with 23 different patients, none of whom caught smallpox. Jenner had proved, to his own satisfaction, that cowpox gave immunity against smallpox.

Acceptance of Jenner's work?

Jenner submitted his findings to the Royal Society, which refused to publish them; he was, after all, a country doctor, few learned men in the medical profession had ever heard about cowpox, let alone worked with it and, most importantly, Jenner could not explain how and why his experimentation worked. It could all just be a lucky coincidence. Furthermore, many of them were making a nice income from variolation – inoculating people with smallpox.

In 1798, Jenner published his results at his own expense in *An Enquiry into the causes and effects of Variola Vaccinae, known by the name of cowpox*. He called his technique 'vaccination' from the Latin *vacca*, meaning cow. Over 100 leading London doctors signed a letter supporting his research and declaring their intention to vaccinate. Parliament voted him £30,000 to establish a vaccination clinic in London, yet still vaccination did not sweep the country (see page 43). Jenner spent most of the rest of his professional life in supplying doctors around the world with cowpox material and, in order to do this safely and without contamination, he developed a technique that dried the cowpox matter into threads or onto glass. He participated, too, in conferences and learned discussions about the nature of immunity.

ACTIVITY
KNOWLEDGE CHECK

Edward Jenner

1 In your view, what was the main significance of Jenner's work: that he had discovered a 'cure' for smallpox, or that he had developed a technique that could be used to combat other killer diseases?

2 Read Source 6. Is Jenner's conclusion supported by the evidence he has produced to back it up?

3 Why was Jenner's discovery not immediately taken up by the medical profession and the general public?

Edwin Chadwick (1800–90): innovative administrator

Underlying philosophy

Edwin Chadwick is associated both with Poor Law reform (see Chapter 4) and with public health reform. Irascible, hard-working and arrogant, Chadwick can be credited with using his various positions to persuade and even bully the government to invest in public health reform. Chadwick's attitude to reform was coloured by his early experiences. Despite his legal training, limited finances drove Chadwick to writing essays for publication in journals such as the *Westminster Review*. Interestingly, these essays were rarely, if ever, on law but were more usually on topics relating to the ways in which scientific principles could be applied to various areas of government. This drew him to the attention of Jeremy Bentham, with whom Chadwick worked as his literary secretary. It was Bentham's belief in the doctrine of Utility (see page 82) that drove Chadwick throughout his professional life.

Making the connection between poor public health and disease

It was while working with the Poor Law Commission that Chadwick became convinced of the significance of the connection between disease caused by poor public health and pauperism. The typhus epidemic that hit London in the years 1837–38 resulted in a dramatic increase in the numbers applying for poor relief. As a result of the epidemic, East London Poor Law guardians spent money from the poor rates on removing filth from the streets and on prosecuting negligent landlords. It was Chadwick's defence of this expenditure in the face of it having been disallowed by the government auditors that led to the eventual commissioning of the *Report on the Sanitary Condition of the Labouring Population of Great Britain* (see Chapter 1, page 21).

Setting up the enquiry

It was important to Chadwick that the people he selected to work on the initial investigation that was focused on the poor of London were likely to come up with the solutions he favoured. Any reforms they recommended had to be based on the need for sanitary engineering, the disposal of refuse and the provision of clean water. The three doctors Chadwick chose were all well known to him and all had previous experience in sanitary investigations: Neil Arnott had worked as a ship's surgeon for the East India Company, where he had a particular interest in improving seamen's health and had made considerable progress in identifying connections between 'exotic' diseases such as cholera and sanitation; James Kay had worked among, and reported on, the poor in Manchester (see Chapter 1, page 20); and Southwood Smith had worked for over ten years at the London Fever Hospital and as a physician to the Eastern Dispensary and the Jews' Hospital in Whitechapel.

Drawing conclusions

Underlying the initial reports on London, collected and collated by Chadwick and the three doctors, was the argument that, no matter how expensive sanitary improvements would be, the cost of pauperism that would result from inaction would be even higher. They made the important points that in areas inhabited by thousands of people, healthy conditions could not be achieved under existing circumstances and that the personal habits of people were of less significance in producing disease than overcrowding, poor ventilation, an inadequate water supply and a lack of proper refuse control. These points were later corroborated by the much larger investigation that resulted in the *Report on the Sanitary Condition of the Labouring Population of Great Britain*, published in 1842.

SOURCE

7

From Edwin Chadwick's *Report on the Sanitary Condition of the Labouring Population of Great Britain*, published in 1842.

The chimneys of the furnaces which darken the atmospheres and pour out volumes of smoke and soot upon the inhabitants of populous towns, afford most frequent examples of the inefficiency of the local administration, and the contempt of the law for the protection of the public against nuisances which are specially provided for. As smoke in Manchester and other towns becomes more dense, the vegetation declines...

Whenever the adult population of a physically depressed district, such as Manchester, is brought out on any public occasion, the preponderance of youth in the crowd and the small proportion of aged, or even middle-aged, amongst them is apt to strike those who have seen assemblies of the working population of more favourably situated districts.

In the Metropolis [London] the experience is similar. The mobs from such districts as Bethnal Green are proportionately conspicuous for a deficiency in bodily strength.

The facts indicated will suffice to show the importance of moral and physical considerations, namely, that a noxious physical environment depresses the health and bodily condition of the population, and hinders education and moral culture. In cutting short the duration of adult life amongst the working classes, it checks the growth of productive skill, social experience and steady moral habits in the community. Instead of a population that preserves instruction and is steadily progressive, it creates a population that is young, inexperienced, ignorant, credulous, irritable, passionate and dangerous, having a perpetual tendency to moral as well as physical deterioration.

	Average age of the deceased		
Place	Professional	Trade	Labourers
Truro	40	33	28
Derby	49	38	21
Manchester	38	20	17
Rutland	52	41	38
Bolton	34	23	18
Bethnal Green (London)	45	26	16
Leeds	44	27	19
Liverpool	35	22	15
Whitechapel (London)	45	27	22
Strand (London)	43	33	24
Kensington (London)	44	29	26
Kendal	45	39	34

The Tory government of 1842 effectively rejected Chadwick's report by using a well-known and well-tried delaying tactic – setting up a Royal Commission. This Royal Commission on the Health of Towns received regular, detailed briefings from Chadwick, backed up by anecdotal and statistical evidence. Unsurprisingly, the commission's report, published in 1844, upheld all of Chadwick's findings.

Working with the General Board of Health

The Public Health Act 1848, passed by parliament largely as a result of the report from the Royal Commission and Chadwick's previous 1842 report, set up a General Board of Health, to which all local and regional boards reported. Chadwick was appointed as one of the General Board of Health's sanitary commissioners and, once appointed, was intent on seeing his ideas about sanitation implemented. These included the supply of clean water to all dwellings, water closets in every house and the building of a sewerage system that would carry raw sewage to outlying farms where it could be used on the fields as a fertiliser. One of his innovations was to recommend, forcefully, the installation of glazed, egg-shaped earthenware pipes to carry sewage and this, coupled with the abolition of shallow drinking wells, considerably reduced the contamination of drinking water by sewage. However, the General Board of Health was not well liked. Its imperious tone and directives were resented in the localities, and doubtless much of this was due to Chadwick's impatience with those who worked at a slower pace. He agreed to resign in 1854. Indeed, the House of Commons had only agreed to renew the Board's mandate provided Chadwick was no longer a commissioner.

Chadwick's involvement in public health reform did not end with his work on the General Board of Health. Awarded a pension of £1,000 a year, he continued to give voluntary advice on all issues concerning sanitation and health. In January 1884, he was appointed the first president of the Association of Sanitary Inspectors, and received a knighthood the following year.

ACTIVITY
KNOWLEDGE CHECK

Edwin Chadwick

1 How would the recommendations contained in Chadwick's report (Source 7) improve the health of the public?

2 What conclusions can be drawn from the table in Chadwick's Report (Source 7)?

3 Use your own knowledge to explain what obstacles might prevent the implementation of Chadwick's recommendations.

4 Edwin Chadwick was neither an empirical scientist nor an engineer. How significant, then, was his contribution to effective public health?

John Snow (1813–58) and the Broad Street pump

Cholera was unknown in Britain before 1831. Endemic in India, it was believed to have spread from there to China and then along the trade routes to Europe. It hit Britain in four massive epidemics: 1831–32, resulting in 32,000 deaths; 1848–49, resulting in 62,000 deaths; 1853–54, resulting in 20,000 deaths; and 1866–67, resulting in 14,000 deaths.

Fighting the 1832 cholera epidemic

In 1831, Dr John Snow had fought single-handed a cholera outbreak at Killingworth colliery, Newcastle. In the years that followed, reflecting on that experience, he became increasingly convinced that cholera was a water-borne disease, but few people were inclined to agree with him. This was partly because his own retiring nature didn't allow him to push himself forward, and partly because of the hold that miasmic theory had on the minds of doctors, surgeons, administrators and the general public.

Making connections with the Broad Street pump

The third cholera epidemic was to change this. The 1853 outbreak found Snow working as a general practitioner in Frith Street in Soho, London, and again struggling to contain and control the terrifying disease. His suspicions fell upon a pump in Broad Street, the water from which enjoyed a high reputation locally for taste and purity. However, once Snow had persuaded the authorities to lock the pump handle and its users were forced to go elsewhere, the number of deaths in the Soho area fell dramatically.

The problem was to make the connection between the fall in the Soho death rate and closing down the Broad Street pump, and make it so that the scientific and medical community would accept it. Dr John Snow did this by first making a meticulous study of the area around the Broad Street pump during the 1853–54 cholera epidemic. Using careful observation, house-to-house interviews and meticulous research he constructed a detailed picture of the progress of the cholera epidemic there.

SOURCE

8 From John Snow *On the Mode of Communication of Cholera*, published in 1855.

The most terrible outbreak of cholera which ever occurred in this kingdom is probably that which took place in Broad Street and the adjoining streets a few weeks ago. Within two hundred and fifty yards of the spot where Cambridge Street joins Broad Street, there were upwards of five hundred fatal attacks of cholera in ten days.

As soon as I became acquainted with the situation, I suspected some contamination of the water of the much frequented street pump in Broad Street, near the end of Cambridge Street.

On proceeding to the spot, I found that nearly all the deaths had taken place within a short distance of the pump. There were only ten deaths in the houses situated decidedly nearer to another street pump. In five of these cases, the families of the deceased persons informed me that they always sent to the pump in Broad Street, as they preferred the water to that of the pump that was nearer. In three other cases the deceased were children who went to school near the pump in Broad Street. Two of them were known to drink the water, and the parents of the third think it probable that it did so, too.

With regard to the deaths occurring in the locality belonging to the pump, there were sixty-one instances in which I was informed that the deceased persons used to drink the pump water from Broad Street. This water was used for mixing with spirits in all the public houses around. It was used in the same way at dining rooms and coffee-shops. The keeper of a coffee shop in the neighbourhood, which was frequented by mechanics, and where the pump water was supplied at dinnertime, informed me she was already aware that nine of her customers were dead.

There is a brewery in Broad Street, near to the pump, and on perceiving that no brewer's men were registered as having died of cholera, I called on Mr Huggins, the proprietor. He informed me that there were about seventy workmen employed in the brewery and none of them had suffered from cholera – at least not in a severe form – only two having been indisposed, and that not seriously, at the time the disease raged. The men are allowed a certain quantity of malt liquor, and Mr Huggins believes they do not drink water at all; and he is quite certain that workmen never obtained water from the pump in the street.

I had an interview with the Board of Guardians of St James' parish on the evening of Thursday 7th September and represented the above circumstances to them. In consequence of what I said, the handle of the pump was removed on the following day.

Snow supported his theory with a vast amount of anecdotal evidence.

- Seven workmen, who lived outside the area but who were working in Broad Street and drinking from the pump, all died.

- Five hundred and thirty-five people lived in the local workhouse close to the Broad Street pump, but they got their water from another source. Only five inmates died from cholera.

- A widow, who used to live in the area and had a large bottle of Broad Street pump water delivered to her Hampstead home, died of cholera and none of her neighbours caught the disease.

- Two hundred people worked in a factory on Broad Street and got their water from the Broad Street pump. Eighteen factory workers died.

Even so, the medical establishment was not impressed, and for some years the idea that cholera was water-borne was referred to as 'Dr Snow's theory'.

SOURCE 9

A copy of John Snow's map of 1854, plotting cholera deaths in the Broad Street area of Soho, London. The black rectangles represent deaths from cholera; the bigger the cluster of rectangles, the greater the number of deaths.

MAP 1.

SOURCE 10

From the *Report of the Committee for Scientific Enquiry into the Recent Cholera Epidemic*, published in 1855.

If the Broad Street pump did actually become a source of disease to persons dwelling at a distance, we believe that this may have depended simply on the fact of its impure waters having participated in the atmospheric infection of the district. On the evidence, it seems impossible to doubt that the geographical distribution of cholera in London belongs less to the water than to the air.

**SOURCE
11**
A cartoon published in the magazine *Fun* in August 1866.

F U N.—August 18, 1866.

DEATH'S DISPENSARY.

OPEN TO THE POOR, GRATIS, BY PERMISSION OF THE PARISH.

Corroborating Snow's findings

A much larger study than that of John Snow was made by John Simon, the medical officer of health for the City of London. John Simon's study covered some 500,000 south Londoners and was published in 1856. He showed that customers of the Lambeth Water Company had a death rate in the 1854 cholera epidemic of 37 per 1,000 compared with 130 per 1,000 among those who took their water from the Southwark Water Company. What was the difference? Lambeth took its water from Ditton, up-river from London, while Southwark took its water close to an outflowing sewer in Battersea.

Even so, it was another 14 years before the medical establishment accepted that cholera was a water-borne disease. It was not until 1870 that John Snow's breakthrough in showing that cholera was water-borne received universal acclaim. John Simon (see page 32), by then chief medical officer of health to the Privy Council, finally abandoned his attachment to the miasmic theory of disease.

A Level Exam-Style Question Section C

To what extent was the work of John Snow in discovering how cholera was transmitted the key turning point in public health reform in the years 1780–1939? (20 marks)

Tip
Think about what changed and what stayed the same as a result of Snow's discovery, and then consider at least two other possible turning points within the time period in order to judge whether Snow's was 'key'. These might be, for example, the work of Edward Jenner, Joseph Bazalgette or one of the Public Health Acts. Make sure that what you write covers the whole period of 1780–1939.

ACTIVITY
KNOWLEDGE CHECK

John Snow

1 a) What methods of investigation did Dr John Snow use to try to discover the reasons why the cholera epidemic was so much worse in the area around the Broad Street pump? Use Sources 8 and 9 to inform your answer.

   b) Do you find the evidence Snow has produced convincingly supports his conclusions?

2 Why were the authors of Source 10 not convinced by Snow's conclusions?

3 The cartoon (Source 11) was published in 1866. Use your own knowledge to explain whether or not you find the date of publication surprising.

4 a) Despite the investigations of Dr Snow and Dr Simon, why did it take so long for the medical establishment to accept that cholera was a water-borne disease?

   b) To what extent would this delay have harmed the health of the public?

Joseph Bazalgette (1819–91): combining ideas and technology

It is one thing to have ideas and theories, even proven theories, and quite another to be able to act upon them. So there would be little point in believing, or even knowing, that cholera was a water-borne disease, if there was not the technology, the civil engineering skills and the will to put theories into action.

London's local government

London's local government was chaotic, with various different specialist authorities and improvement commissions having authority over different streets or even parts of streets. All of these bodies had to agree in order to provide services (such as drains, water and sewerage) that crossed their boundaries. This clearly made any public health initiatives virtually impossible to implement. In 1837, an attempt was made to set up a London-wide elected authority to provide and administer services, but it was defeated by the vested interests of the wealthy districts of Marylebone and Westminster. In 1854, there was another attempt to rationalise the administration of London. The Royal Commission on the City of London proposed dividing London into seven boroughs, with each borough represented on a Metropolitan Board of Works. The proposal relating to the boroughs was defeated, but the Metropolitan Board of Works was set up in 1855.

Bazalgette: chief engineer

The Metropolitan Board of Works took over the responsibilities of the Metropolitan Buildings Office and the Metropolitan Commission of Sewers. Both these bodies were short-lived. Indeed, the only marked 'success' of the Metropolitan Commission of Sewers had been to order all cesspits to be closed and that house drains should connect to sewers and empty into the River Thames, thus markedly adding to the death rate in the 1848–49 cholera epidemic. The new Metropolitan Board of Works was not an elected body, but consisted of 45 nominees from the principal local authorities in London. One of its earliest, and possibly best, actions was to appoint Joseph Bazalgette as its chief engineer.

By the time Bazalgette was appointed chief engineer in 1856, the River Thames as it flowed through London was little more than an open sewer. No fish swam in its water and there was no wildlife along its banks. The problem was that the rapid growth of London had not been accompanied by the development of an infrastructure that could deal with the huge amount of sewage produced every day. Instead, the sewage contributed to the severity of the cholera epidemics and to other 'dirty' diseases such as diphtheria and typhoid.

Bazalgette drew up a comprehensive plan whereby London's sewage was channelled through miles of street sewers into a series of larger intercepting sewers. These large sewers took the waste far to the east of London where it could be pumped into the tidal part of the River Thames where it would be swept far out to sea. The plans were good, but the members of the Metropolitan Board of Works and its political boss became locked in fruitless arguments, mostly about money, until the summer of 1858.

The 'Great Stink'

The summer of 1858 was unusually hot. The River Thames was overflowing with raw sewage, and the warm weather encouraged bacteria to thrive. The resulting smell was so powerful that business in the House of Commons was suspended while members decided whether or not to move up-river to Hampton Court, and plans were made to evacuate the law courts either to Oxford or to St Albans. In the event, MPs decided to stay put and debate the state of the river. Nicknamed the 'Great Stink' by the press, the episode led to a vociferous campaign for change, led by *The Times* newspaper. In July 1858, the Metropolis Local Management Amendment Act was passed, giving the Metropolitan Board of Works permission to improve the drainage of London and, as far as was possible, prevent sewage from passing into the River Thames. Joseph Bazalgette could begin work.

SOURCE 12 Joseph Bazalgette inspecting a sewer being dug at Abbey Mills pumping station, east London, in 1862.

Sanitising London

Bazalgette's project was a massive one, involving over 2,000 km of interconnecting brick-lined sewers linked to four massive pumping stations, two on each side of the Thames. This involved redesigning the Thames embankment so that it housed the huge, final sewers connecting the smaller ones with the pumping stations. These pumping stations were to carry the untreated sewage to treatment plants rather than dumping it in the lower Thames or the sea. Bazalgette designed large, brick-lined egg-shaped sewer tunnels rather than the narrower pipes favoured by Chadwick, and this was a sensible decision because they rarely got blocked. When planning the size of the sewers, Bazalgette started with the densest areas of population, calculated the amount of sewage each person would generate and then doubled it. In building the sewers, 318 million bricks and 670,000 cubic metres of concrete were used. The whole sewerage system was opened by Edward, Prince of Wales in 1865, thus giving it the royal seal of approval.

ACTIVITY
KNOWLEDGE CHECK

Joseph Bazalgette

1 How far would you agree that Bazalgette's improvements to London's sewerage system only came about because of the 'Great Stink'?

2 How would Bazalgette's sewerage system have satisfied the following?

   a) Those who believed in the miasma theory of disease.

   b) Those who thought that John Snow was correct.

3 What questions would you want to ask of Source 12 before it could be used as evidence of a serious intention to improve the health of London's public?

SOURCE 13

Marcus Varro, writing in the 1st century BC.

When building a house or farm especial care should be taken to place it at the foot of a wooded hill where it is exposed to health-giving winds. Care should be taken when there are swamps in the neighbourhood because certain tiny creatures which cannot be seen by the eyes breed there. These float through the air and enter the body through the mouth and nose and cause serious diseases.

SOURCE 14

Sextus Julius Frontinus, writing in the 1st century AD.

As a result of the increase in the number of works, reservoirs, fountains, and water basins, the air is purer, and the causes of the unwholesome atmosphere, which gave the air of the city such a bad name, are now removed. With such an array of indispensable structures carrying so many waters, compare, if you will, the idle pyramids or the useless, though famous, works of the Greeks.

SOURCE 15

A Roman aqueduct, the Pont du Gard near Nîmes, southern France, built c19 BC.

SOURCE 16

Roman lavatories.

THINKING HISTORICALLY   Cause and consequence (6c)

Connections

Sources 13–16 are some typical aspects of the Roman Empire regarding its approach to public health.

Work in groups or individually and answer the following:

1 Read Source 13. How might this be seen as similar to John Snow's belief about the way in which cholera was transmitted between people?

2 Read Source 14.

   a) What did Edwin Chadwick believe about the need for clean water?

   b) How is this similar to Sextus Julius Frontinus' ideas about water supplies?

3 Look at Sources 15 and 16. What did the 19th century copy from the Roman Empire?

4 Make a list of other similarities between public health at the time of the Romans and in the 19th century. How likely is it that 19th-century public health reformers built on their understanding of Roman practices?

5 Why it is important for historians to see these links across time and be able to explain how causal factors can influence situations much later in time?

Marie Stopes (1880–1958): smaller, healthier families

The major contribution Marie Stopes made to public health and the health of the public was to provide information and direct practical advice about limiting family size.

The attitude of the authorities

In the years 1906–8, parliament concerned itself with the welfare of children, and passed legislation regarding the provision of meals and medical treatment for the children of the poor (see pages 47–49). What parliament could not do was to pass legislation enabling people to have ready access to information about birth control methods in order to limit their family size. Opposition from both the Anglican and Catholic Churches, and the fear of offending the electorate by discussion about such a sensitive issue, made governments unwilling to legislate in this field. Maternity and child welfare clinics were not allowed to give advice on birth control, even when a mother's life would be at risk from further pregnancies. Indeed, in 1922 a nurse, Elizabeth Daniels, was dismissed from her post as a health visitor in the London district of Edmonton because she gave birth control advice. This attitude of the authorities was held despite clear evidence that to a very large extent it was the number of children in a working-class family that kept it, and its health, poor. Families of 12 to 14 children were not uncommon, with women giving birth year on year. With limited incomes and more and more mouths to feed, providing adequate food, clothing and warmth was a struggle. Overcrowded in poor housing, the health of this large section of the public was at risk.

The need for information

Middle- and upper-class families tended to have fewer children than working-class families, and this was most probably due to their being able to afford access to private clinics where advice on contraception, whether natural or artificial, could be obtained. This was at a time when anyone openly disseminating advice, particularly written advice, on birth control could be prosecuted under various obscene publication laws. For poorer families, the traditional methods of birth control – abstention, the use of *coitus interruptus* (the withdrawal method) and induced abortion – were the principal methods of birth control. *Coitus interruptus* meant that women had to trust their husbands and this could be combined with various pessaries that women could use with or without their husband's knowledge; extended breast feeding, erroneously believed to inhibit conception, and attempts to establish a safe period in a woman's cycle when conception could not occur, could also give women some sort of control. For many women, finding themselves pregnant against their will, abortion was the last resort, even though it remained illegal until 1967 unless carried out for medical reasons.

There was clearly a demand for information. Cheap women's magazines carried advice about contraceptives in sections headed discreetly 'Women's Ailments' and abortive agents were advertised as medicines to restore health. All kinds of contraceptive appliances, too, could be bought from visiting speakers who gave 'women only' lectures. All this, however, was very risky and open to all kinds of quacks and fraudsters.

Married Love

It was the work of Marie Stopes that cut across all of this and provided straightforward, detailed and practical advice. In 1913, and involved in divorcing her first husband for what was claimed to be an unconsummated marriage, Marie Stopes began writing a book about the ways in which she thought marriage should work. Strongly opposed to abortion, Stopes believed that the size of a family should be limited by the use of effective contraception, and it was the chapter on contraception as well as explicit descriptions as to what married women should expect from sexual relationships, that led to publishers refusing to handle her manuscript, believing it to be too controversial. Finally, the philanthropist Humphrey Verdon Roe (who was to become Stopes' second husband) had the book *Married Love* published at his own expense. The book was an immediate success, selling over 2,000 copies in the first fortnight of publication, and over 400,000 copies by 1924. Marie Stopes became a household name. However, *Married Love* was aimed at middle-class women, as was her *Wise Parenthood: A Book for Married People*, which focused almost exclusively on contraception. Stopes then condensed *Wise Parenthood* into a 16-page booklet, aimed at the working-class poor and distributed free of charge.

The first birth control clinic

Despite her somewhat flowery language and difficult prose, Stopes clearly met a massive public demand for birth control advice, and attracted correspondence from hundreds of women and some men of all classes asking for further advice and help with their sexual problems. Pressed to do more than disseminate printed advice, Stopes and her husband Roe opened a Mother's Clinic in Holloway, north London, in March 1921. This free clinic was run by midwives supported by visiting doctors, and not only gave face-to-face contraceptive advice, but also taught mothers how to use different methods of contraception. In 1925, the clinic moved to a more central position close to Tottenham Court Road, where it flourished. Stopes gradually built up a network of clinics across Britain, and by 1939 there were clinics in Leeds and Aberdeen (1924), Belfast (1936) and Cardiff (1937).

Meeting opposition

Not everyone took a positive view of Marie Stopes' work. In 1922, a Dr Halliday Sutherland, secretary of the League of National Life, which was an anti-contraception (mainly Catholic) organisation, wrote *Birth Control: A Statement of Christian Doctrine Against the Neo Malthusians*. In this, Sutherland was highly critical of Marie Stopes and her work, and he made defamatory attacks that could be considered libellous. Stopes challenged him to a public debate and when he failed to respond, she sued him for libel. At the end of the trial, the jury found in favour of Stopes, but the judge disagreed. The Court of Appeal reversed the judge's decision, finding in favour of Stopes. However, the ultimate British court of appeal, the House of Lords, reversed that decision, finding in favour of Sutherland. This legal furore hit Stopes financially, but the trial had brought the issue of birth control to the attention of the public – and the number of clients visiting her clinics doubled.

The medical profession, too, was divided in its attitude to Stopes' work in the field of birth control. Indeed, in 1917 Humphrey Roe offered to endow a birth control clinic in St Mary's Hospital, Manchester. His offer was declined even though he proposed that all patients should be married and that no abortions were to be carried out. Dr C. Killick, medical officer of health for Leicester, was a strong supporter of birth control; other doctors did not go beyond accepting the 'safe period' in a woman's cycle as being the only acceptable method, whereas Dr George Jones, of the West End Hospital for Women (London) maintained that birth control was even more important in the case of unmarried women and should be offered to them.

The Catholic Church was implacably opposed to Marie Stopes and to her work in promoting birth control. Anglican clergy were, too, less than impressed. In 1920, Stopes addressed the **Lambeth Conference** as a result of claiming to have received a message direct from God that led her to write *A New Gospel to All Peoples*. Stopes' message to the bishops was that sexual intercourse was not only for the procreation of children, but was for the giving and receiving of pleasure by husband and wife. Her message was received in silence.

Marie Stopes and her work clearly did help many individual married couples to limit the size of their families, either directly by visiting her clinics, or indirectly by her opening up of the whole subject of birth control to public debate. In doing so, she had an impact on the general health and welfare of the public.

KEY TERM

Lambeth Conference
A meeting of Anglican bishops, held every ten years since 1867, at Lambeth Palace, London and presided over by the Archbishop of Canterbury.

ACTIVITY
KNOWLEDGE CHECK

Marie Stopes

1 The connection between large families, poor living conditions and public health problems was a clear one. Why, then, was Marie Stopes' work so controversial?

2 How important was the contribution of Marie Stopes to the health of the public?

Marie Stopes and eugenics

Marie Stopes was an enthusiastic supporter of the science of eugenics – the belief that the quality of a race can be improved by controlling the fertility of certain groups and classes. In 1921, Stopes became a Fellow of the Eugenics Society, and in the same year founded the Society for Constructive Birth Control and Racial Progress. In her book *Radiant Motherhood,* she maintained that those unfit for parenthood should be sterilised, and in other forums she argued that people with mental and physical disabilities should not be allowed to breed. It is possible, therefore, to see her mission to extend knowledge and understanding of birth control as more to do with her eugenic concerns than a desire to improve the lot of the poor.

Conclusion

There was a clear improvement in public health between the years 1780 and 1939. This was due to a unique combination of three factors: the inventiveness and determination of individuals; the drive of local authorities to improve the lot of the people for whom they had responsibility; and the move of central government from laissez-faire to active involvement in the lives of the citizens. The balance between these three factors was not constant throughout the period, but changed according to local and national issues. What was important was that all three elements existed in combination throughout the period and, working together, produced effective public health reforms.

 THINKING HISTORICALLY   Cause and consequence (7c)

The value of historical explanations

Historical explanations derive from the historian who is investigating the past. Differences in explanations are usually about what the historians think is significant. Historians bring their own attitudes and perspectives to historical questions and see history in the light of these. It is therefore perfectly acceptable to have very different explanations of the same historical phenomenon. The way we judge historical accounts is by looking at how well argued they are and how well evidence has been deployed to support the argument.

Approach A	Approach B	Approach C
Public health reform happens because of decisions taken by politicians. It is imposed from the top by parliament. Local councils and individuals then obey the laws that parliament has passed.	Public health reform happens because of decisions taken at a local level by town councils. The councils raise money either by borrowing it or by raising the local rates, and use it for local improvements to public health.	Public health reform happens because of the ideas, discoveries and inventions of individual people. These are then taken up by local councils and/or the government, who impose them either in their localities or nationally.

Work in groups of between three and five. (You will need an even number of groups in the class.)

1   In your groups, devise a brief explanation of what drove public health reform, of between 200 and 300 words, that matches one of the approaches above. Present your explanation to another group, who will decide on two things:

   a)   Which of the approaches is each explanation trying to demonstrate?

   b)   Considering the structure and the quality of the argument and use of evidence, which is the best of the three explanations?

2   If you choose a 'best' explanation, should you discount the other two? Explain your answer.

ACTIVITY
SUMMARY

The health of the public

1 'Local government initiatives were more important than the work of individuals in improving the health of the public.' Explain how far you agree with this statement.

2 To what extent was improvement in housing the key to all other improvements in public health?

3 Consider the work of Edward Jenner, Edwin Chadwick, John Snow, Joseph Bazalgette and Marie Stopes.

   a) Working in groups, agree an order of priority as to the importance of the contribution each made to public health reform.

   b) Compare your order of priority with those of other groups, and write an account that defends your prioritisation and challenges that of the other groups.

4 Create a table or flow chart to show the drivers of change in improvements in drainage, sewerage and water supply. Explain which was the most successful and why.

 WIDER READING

Briggs, A. *Victorian Cities*, Odhams Press (1963)

Fraser, D. *The Evolution of the British Welfare State*, Macmillan (1973)

Pugh, M. *State and Society 1870–1997*, Arnold (1994)

Rodger, R. *Housing in Urban Britain, 1780–1914*, Macmillan (1989)

Stevenson, J. *British Society 1914–45*, Penguin Books (1984)

Wohl, A.S. *Endangered Lives*, Dent (1983)

3.3 Paupers and pauperism, 1780–1834

KEY QUESTIONS

- How effectively did parish outdoor relief deal with the able-bodied paupers?
- What impact did the provision of parish indoor relief have upon pauperism?
- Why did the pressure for change intensify in the years 1780–1834?

INTRODUCTION

The Elizabethan Poor Law of 1601 supplied the philosophical and practical basis for providing assistance to those who were unable to support themselves. Called the 'old Poor Law' in order to distinguish it from the 'new Poor Law' resulting from the Poor Law Amendment Act 1834 (see Chapter 4), it was not one law, but a collection of laws that parliament had passed between the end of the 16th century and the end of the 18th century. Overlaying central legislation was a host of local rules and regulations agreed by a range of different parishes throughout the country. This ragbag of laws, rules and regulations was driven by the assumption that the Elizabethan Poor Law provided the philosophical and practical basis for providing assistance to the needy.

Critical to the administration of the old Poor Law was the parish. It was parish officials who set the **Poor Rate**, and who determined whether the poor were eligible for relief, how much relief should be given and whether this should be provided as indoor or outdoor relief (see page 9). Here, the concept of settlement was central. Was a parish to be responsible for all those born there but living elsewhere and facing destitution? Or for those living within its boundaries, but born elsewhere, and in desperate need of help?

By the beginning of the 19th century, many people were coming to believe that the Poor Law was failing to cope with the growing and very different demands upon it caused by a mobile and increasingly industrialised population. This belief was overshadowed, and possibly exaggerated, by the pressures placed on the Poor Law by the **Napoleonic Wars**. Indeed, many of the attacks on the Poor Law were made against systems of relief that were introduced and applied as emergency measures during this time of war. However, the belief that reform was necessary was bolstered by the views of economists and political theorists who urged different 'solutions' to the problem of the poor, and driven by a government fearing revolution. Reform was welcomed, too, by those weary of paying an ever-increasing Poor Rate.

KEY TERMS

Poor Rate
A tax levied at parish level and used to provide relief for the parish poor.

Napoleonic Wars
A series of wars fought by different combinations of European powers against revolutionary France and the armies led by Napoleon. The wars ended on 18 June 1815 with the Battle of Waterloo, when the forces of Prussia under Blücher and Britain under Wellington defeated those of Napoleon.

1601 – Poor Law
Parishes become the administrative unit for raising money for poor relief and for distributing such relief

1697 – Settlement Act
Strangers could be denied entry to a parish unless they could produce a Settlement Certificate stating their parish of origin would take them back if they needed relief

1789 – Publication of *An Introduction to the Principles of Morals and Legislation* by Jeremy Bentham lays the foundations of Utilitarianism

1798 – Publication of *An Essay on the Principle of Population* by Thomas Malthus suggests abolition of the poor laws

| 1600 | 1650 | 1700 | 1780 | 1785 | 1790 | 1795 | 1800 |

1662 – Settlement Act
Individuals could be returned to the parish of their birth in order to receive relief

1782 – Gilbert's Act
Parishes could combine to build a workhouse and so share the cost of poor relief

1795 – Speenhamland system, and variations, in use in some southern and eastern counties of England
Roundsman system and Labour Rate also used

HOW EFFECTIVELY DID PARISH OUTDOOR RELIEF DEAL WITH ABLE-BODIED PAUPERS?

Reliance on the parish

The basis of the administration of the Elizabethan Poor Law lay in the parish as a unit of government with unpaid, non-professional administrators. It was not until the mid-to-late 18th century that rapidly growing towns began to employ paid officials. Each parish was to administer relief to its own poor and collect taxes in order to provide appropriate relief. The setting to work of the poor was in the hands of churchwardens and overseers of the poor, who were appointed annually by the local justices of the peace (JPs). In practice, this work was usually undertaken in rotation by local farmers and respectable householders – those liable to pay the poor rates.

By embedding the administration of the Poor Law in the 1,500 or so parishes in England and Wales, the Elizabethan legislators had ensured that local needs would be met appropriately. However, they had also laid the foundations for an immense diversity in practice, and therefore in fairness and in effectiveness, that was to be found throughout the country by the early years of the 19th century.

It can be argued that, because the dispensing of relief was based on an administrative unit as small as a parish, greater humanity and sensitivity could be shown to the poor and needy, because those seeking relief and those dispensing it would be known to one another. Local people would be better able to distinguish between those who genuinely needed help, and those who did not. On the other hand, the opportunities for tyrannical behaviour on the part of local **overseers of the poor**, and for the settling of old scores and the perpetuating of grievances, were manifold. It was not surprising, too, that local class relationships and the habit of deference to one's 'betters' tended to prevail. Furthermore, any local crisis such as a poor harvest could place an almost intolerable burden on locally raised finances. To bring about some consistency in the treatment of the poor and paupers, attempts were made, in theory and in practice, to categorise the poor.

Categorising the poor

Many late 18th- and 19th-century social writers and reformers regarded poverty as both inevitable and necessary. For most writers and legislators, a distinction was drawn between poverty, which was seen as the lot of most people, and pauperism (see page 8). Poverty was believed to be necessary because it was only through fear of poverty that people would work. Working people could be poor and still support themselves and their families. What was wrong, however, was '**indigence**': the inability of individuals to support themselves. It was this desire to force the poor to stand on their own feet and participate in a healthy economy that drove much of the thinking behind legislation for and about the poor.

KEY TERMS

Overseer of the poor
Each year every parish appointed one or two overseers of the poor, who were approved by the local magistrates. These overseers were usually churchwardens or landowners. Overseers were responsible for administering poor relief in their parish. They levied a Poor Rate and supervised its distribution.

Indigence
A term, frequently used in the 19th century, meaning a person's inability to support themselves, so that they became indigent.

1815 – Ending of wars with France
Parliament passes the Corn Laws; price of bread kept high, leading to widespread protests

1819 – The Six Acts passed, confirming the government's policy of repression in the face of protest
Sturges-Bourne Acts enable distinction to be made between 'deserving' and 'undeserving' poor

1828 – Publication of report of the Select Committee on the Employment or Relief of Able-Bodied Persons

1832 – The government sets up the Royal Commission of Enquiry into the Operation of the Poor Laws

1815   1820   1825   1830   1835

1817 – Habeas corpus suspended
Report of the Select Committee on the poor laws
Publication of *On the Principles of Political Economy and Taxation* by David Ricardo

1824 – Publication of report of the Select Committee on labourers' wages

1830-31 – Swing riots, mainly in south and east of England

It is important to realise that the poor laws had nothing to do with trying to bring about the end of poverty. They had everything to do with preventing the 'indigent' from starving while at the same time forcing the poor to work rather than become indigent and dependent upon the authorities for support.

In the 19th century, social commentators and legislators were greatly concerned with establishing and quantifying the links between poverty and what they saw as morality. The 'deserving poor' were those who were poor through no fault of their own and were therefore deemed worthy of help and support. These were, for example, the old, the sick and children. The 'undeserving poor' were those whose poverty was the result of some sort of perceived moral failure such as drunkenness or prostitution. While they would be kept from starvation, any help directed towards this group would have to contain within it elements of both punishment and improvement. One of the main reasons, then, for trying to categorise the poor in the 19th century was to determine those who were deserving of help and those who were not.

The great fear, of course, was that if too much help was provided for the undeserving poor they would see no reason to look for work. Worse, the deserving poor might see the attractions of an idle life with adequate support and be tempted into immoral, jobless living. The army of the undeserving poor would grow and fewer and fewer poor people would be leading responsible and independent lives.

Some kind of balance was required. A system was needed that would adequately support the genuinely needy, while at the same time deterring the feckless and the work-shy from using it as a permanent solution to their needs.

The importance of settlement

In order for any system that was based on parishes as administrative units to work, it was essential that each parish knew for whom it was responsible. It seemed simple and straightforward to make each parish responsible for its 'own' poor. But this in itself created problems with a population that was growing increasingly mobile. Was a parish to be responsible for all the individuals who had been born within its boundaries, no matter how far they had travelled since? Or was a parish to be responsible for those who were currently living and/or working there, no matter how brief their sojourn, or where they had been born? What happened to married couples needing relief but who were born in different parishes and, maybe, had children born in several different parishes, too? From where would a family such as this claim relief?

The Elizabethan Poor Law, which still held good albeit with minor amendments in the late 18th and early 19th centuries, stated that a person claiming relief had to be returned to the place of their birth in order to receive it; or, if the place of birth was not known, to a place where he or she had lived for a year or more, or to the last parish through which the person had passed without getting into trouble with the law.

The Settlement Act 1662 tried to clarify matters. After this date, legal settlement was by birth, marriage, apprenticeship or inheritance. So, for any one individual claiming relief, the responsible parish could be the one in which that person was born, married, served an apprenticeship or inherited property. Strangers staying in a parish could be removed, if they were not working, within 40 days and if the overseers considered they were likely to end up claiming poor relief. In practice, most strangers were left alone until they tried to claim relief. Then, removals were common. Settlement legislation was further tightened up in 1697, when strangers could be barred from entering a parish and finding work there unless they could produce a settlement certificate issued by their home parish which stated that they would be taken back and given relief there should they become needy. The Removal Act 1795 modified the Settlement Act 1662. It prevented strangers from being removed unless they applied for relief. Over the years, the Settlement legislation was a genuine attempt to provide every man, woman and child with a clearly defined legal settlement and equally clearly defined criteria for removal.

Once these criteria were clearly understood, overseers and paupers became skilled at using the system to their advantage, as Sources 1 and 2 show. It was common for magistrates to enquire closely into a pauper's background and circumstances before agreeing to a parish's application for the removal of a pauper family. Indeed, so frequent were applications for removal that pre-printed forms were used, with the parish clerk only having to fill in the gaps with the names and situation of the paupers they wanted to remove.

SOURCE

1

Part of an order for the removal of William Pyman and his family from Watton, Norfolk, to Clerkenwell, Middlesex, in 1819. It was made by Norfolk magistrates and sent to the churchwardens and overseers of the poor in Watton and in Clerkenwell. The order was suspended for three months due to Mrs Pyman's pregnancy. When it was eventually carried out, the overseers of Clerkenwell were ordered to pay the costs incurred by its suspension.

Upon the complaint of the Churchwardens and overseers of the poor of the parish of Watton in the county of Norfolk, made unto us being two of His Majesty's Justices of the Peace acting in and for the county of Norfolk, that William Pyman, Carpenter, Elizabeth his wife, Henry aged 10 years, Charles aged 4 years, Francis aged 2 years and William aged 1 year, being their children have come to inhabit the said parish of Watton not having gained a legal settlement there, nor produced any Certificate owning them to be settled elsewhere; and that the said William Pyman, his wife Elizabeth and Henry, Charles, Francis and William their children are now actually chargeable to the said parish of Watton.

We, the said Justices, upon due proof being made thereof, as well upon the examination of the said William Pyman upon oath, do judge that the legal settlement of them, the said William Pyman, Elizabeth his wife, and Henry, Charles, Francis and William their children is in the parish of Clerkenwell in the said county of Middlesex.

We do therefore require you, the churchwardens and Overseers of the Poor of the said Parish of Watton, or your deputy, to convey the said William Pyman, Elizabeth his wife, and Henry, Charles, Francis and William their children from and out of your said parish of Watton to the said Parish of Clerkenwell and then to deliver them to the Churchwardens and Overseers of the Poor there, or to some or one of them, together with this our Order.

And we do also hereby require you, the said Churchwardens and Overseers of the Poor of Clerkenwell, to receive and provide for them as settled inhabitants of your Parish. Given under our hands and seals the nineteenth day of June in the year of Our Lord one thousand eight hundred and nineteen.

The **Settlement Laws**, as well as being designed to control a migrant population, were at the same time intended to ensure that the burden of providing for the poor did not overwhelm some parishes. However, they were not applied consistently over time or from place to place. They gave rise to an immense amount of squabbling, prevaricating and litigation between overseers of different parishes. Overseers were always mindful of the burden of the Poor Rate levied on their own parish property owners, who had elected them to their position in the first place, and were anxious to keep their own Poor Rate as low as possible. The struggles of overseers to prevent paupers from becoming a charge on their particular parish took up a considerable amount of time and were not always necessarily in the best interests of the paupers themselves. Local **vestry minutes** frequently recorded the fortunes of pauper families and the manoeuvrings of overseers as paupers were shunted back and forth across parish boundaries. Hated and evaded by the poor and manipulated by administrators, the Settlement Laws were, in the end, unable to prevent a mobile population creating the growing cities of the late 18th and early 19th centuries. This was because so many thousands of people were on the move that local overseers of the poor and the magistrates simply couldn't keep up with issuing, and carrying out, settlement orders.

SOURCE

2

A letter sent by Robert Fitch to the overseers of Royston, Hertfordshire, early in the 19th century, while he and his family were living in Kent. The exact year in which the letter was written is not known, but the letter is dated 21 February. The 'examination' to which he refers is his Certificate of Settlement.

Sir

I have sent you my examination in a letter. But you have sent me no word about it as to whether you mean to relieve me or not. But if you don't believe me, I shall send my wife and five children home to your parish anyway. I have enquired into the law and you can't take only the two of my children into the House [workhouse] which are above seven years old for you can't take the others away from her until they are seven years old. So if you don't think it proper to relieve me I shall sell my things to pay my debts. Then I shall go to sea or for a soldier. So then you will have to keep them all. It seems to me that you mean to drive me to it for I can't maintain them with my pay. And if you will get me a house to live in and find me work at my trade I will come home. And then I must have things to put in, for I am sure that I shan't have any money to buy goods with. So I will be glad if you will send me an answer about it.

From
Yours truly, Robt Fitch
(Brasted, Kent)

A Level Exam-Style Question Section A

Study Source 1 before you answer this question.

Assess the value of the source for revealing the attitude to paupers of those administering the old Poor Law, and the importance of settlement.

Explain your answer, using the source, the information given about it and your own knowledge about the historical context. (20 marks)

Tip
Consider the ways in which the magistrates and overseers are acting towards the Pyman family, and the importance of settlement as it related to the poor rates.

KEY TERMS

Settlement Law
This is a general term referring to the Act of Settlement 1662 and subsequent amendments.

Vestry minutes
A vestry is a room in an Anglican Church where meetings are held. Vestry minutes would therefore be a written account of those meetings.

ACTIVITY
KNOWLEDGE CHECK

The role of the parish

1 a) What were the advantages of using the parish as an administrative unit for poor relief?

    b) What were the disadvantages of using the parish as an administrative unit for poor relief?

    c) In your judgement, did the advantages outweigh the disadvantages?

2 How far does Source 2 challenge the view of settlement given in Source 1?

3 To what extent would you agree with the view that the Settlement Laws were unworkable?

Outdoor relief

Parishes generally provided outdoor relief for their able-bodied paupers in their own homes, largely because it was easy to administer and could be applied flexibly. Families might, for example, have sudden and urgent calls upon their funds at a time when the principal breadwinner was ill; **cyclical unemployment** might cause only short-term distress and long-term provision of relief in a residential poorhouse or a workhouse would not be appropriate.

Inevitably, different parishes worked out different systems of outdoor relief. These were geared to a pre-industrial economy and were, more or less, effective. However, from about 1750 industrialisation and a growing, mobile population began to test to the limits the ingenuity of magistrates and vestries in devising effective ways of meeting the needs of the able-bodied poor. In the last years of the 18th century, a series of bad harvests coupled with the stresses and strains of the Napoleonic Wars brought the Poor Law almost to breaking point. Lagging wages and increasing food prices meant that, even when the main breadwinners were in full-time work, thousands of families struggled on the edge of starvation. Central government could not, or would not, provide any answers and it was the parishes themselves that had to find solutions to the crisis. Indeed, the national solutions proposed by MP Samuel Whitbread in 1795 and Prime Minister William Pitt a year later, were barely debated in the Commons, largely because their proposals involved the raising of wages to lift families out of poverty and the creation of a national poor law budget. This was a step too far for a Commons dominated by employer, wage-paying landowners. They, and their fellow landowners outside the legislature, favoured the flexibility of an allowance system, whereby low wages would be topped up by the parish.

What different solutions did the parishes develop?

Parishes adopted, developed and amended over time several different ways of providing relief to the poor outside workhouses and poorhouses. All attempted to supplement the wages paid by employers; all were open to abuse by employers and paupers.

- The Speenhamland system was one of the most widely used allowance systems, and was introduced in 1795 by magistrates at Speenhamland in Berkshire. It was a way of providing relief by subsidising low wages and, as such, it was not new. What was new about it was that it established a formal relationship between the price of bread and the number of dependants in a family. Parishes did not always give relief in cash. Newton Valance (Hampshire), for example, made up the wages of the parish able-bodied paupers by giving them flour. Some parishes took each child into consideration, while others did not increase the relief given until there were more than a certain number of children in a family.

The Speenhamland system and its variations were widely adopted in the south and east of Britain at the beginning of the 19th century, where they were generally used only in the slack times during the agricultural year which generally occurred after harvest. The problems of seasonal unemployment had always been there, but in the late 18th and early 19th centuries these problems were exacerbated by the loss of **cottage industries** and the lack of availability of allotments on which villagers could grow their own vegetables, combined with the loss of common land due to **enclosures**. Allowance systems were rarely, if ever, used in rural areas in the north where livestock farming usually provided full employment throughout the year. However, the system was never given legal backing, although some politicians tried, and it was often abandoned or modified out of all recognition as overseers struggled to cope with changing economic conditions, particularly after 1815.

KEY TERM

Cyclical unemployment
Unemployment that would only be short term and was related to trade cycles.

KEY TERMS

Cottage industry
Paid work that could be done at home, like spinning and weaving before the Industrial Revolution.

Enclosure
Many large landowners enclosed open fields by putting fences and hedges around them. This enabled the landowners to breed cows and sheep for specific characteristics. Thousands of agricultural labourers were thrown out of work and, if the landowners enclosed the common land, they had nowhere to graze what few animals they had.

SOURCE

From F.M. Eden *The State of the Poor,* published in 1797. Here, Eden sets out the table agreed by the magistrates at Speenhamland, Berkshire, for the outdoor relief of the poor. A gallon loaf is one weighing 4 kg. The relief was paid weekly.

A meeting of the magistrates for the county [Berkshire] was held about Easter 1795, when the following plans were submitted to their consideration: 1st, that the magistrates should fix the lowest price to be given for labour, as they were empowered to do...; and secondly, that they should act with uniformity, in the relief of the impotent and infirm poor, by a Table of universal practice... The first plan was rejected... but the second was adopted, and the Table [below] was published as the rule for the information of magistrates and overseers.

Income should be		For a Man	For a Single Woman	For a Man and his Wife	With One Child	With Two Children
When the gallon loaf is	1s 0d	3s 0d	2s 0d	4s 6d	6s 0d	7s 6d
When the gallon loaf is	1s 1d	3s 3d	2s 1d	4s 10d	6s 5d	8s 0d
When the gallon loaf is	1s 2d	3s 6d	2s 2d	5s 2d	6s 10d	8s 6d
When the gallon loaf is	1s 3d	3s 9d	2s 3d	5s 6d	7s 3d	9s 0d
When the gallon loaf is	1s 4d	4s 0d	2s 4d	5s 10d	7s 8d	9s 6d
When the gallon loaf is	1s 5d	4s 0d	2s 5d	5s 11d	7s 10d	9s 9d
When the gallon loaf is	1s 6d	4s 3d	2s 6d	6s 3d	8s 3d	10s 3d
When the gallon loaf is	1s 7d	4s 3d	2s 7d	6s 4d	7s 5d	10s 6d
When the gallon loaf is	1s 8d	4s 6d	2s 8d	6s 8d	8s 10d	11s 0d
When the gallon loaf is	1s 9d	4s 6d	2s 9d	6s 9d	9s 0d	11s 3d
When the gallon loaf is	1s 10d	4s 9d	2s 10d	7s 1d	9s 5d	11s 9d

SOURCE

The Allowance system used by the parish of Winfarthing, Norfolk, in the 1820s.

Number in family	In the summer	In the winter
3	1s 9d	2s 4d
4	2s 4d	2s 8d
5	2s 11d	3s 4d
6	3s 6d	4s 0d
7	4s 1d	4s 8d
8	4s 8d	5s 4d
9	5s 3d	6s 0d
10	5s 10d	6s 8d

- The Roundsman system was a way of making sure that, in parishes where there were too many paupers for the work available, at least some work was found for each able-bodied pauper. Here, able-bodied pauper labourers were sent in rotation to local farmers who would provide them with work that either genuinely needed doing, or that had been invented for the purpose. The Roundsman's wages were paid partly by the farmer and partly by the parish. Locals often called this a 'billet' or 'ticket' system. This was because the overseer would sign a 'ticket' for the pauper to take to a potential employer, authorising the pauper to work under the parish relief system. When the work was completed, the pauper would return the 'ticket' to the overseer, signed by the employer to show that the work had been done and a wage paid. The overseer would then make up the difference from the poor rates. In some parishes this would be based on the price of bread and the size of a pauper's family; in other parishes, a flat rate would be paid. Unsurprisingly, over time the proportion of a Roundsman's wage paid by the parish increased as farmers took advantage of a system that did not require them to pay a set proportion of the wages of the paupers they employed.

- The Labour Rate was a different way of providing relief that avoided the pitfalls of the Roundsman system. This involved an agreement between parishioners to establish a labour rate in addition to the usual Poor Rate. The total parish labour bill was worked out according to what was assumed to be the going market rate. Ratepayers who employed pauper labourers, and paid them at the rate set by the parish, were exempt from paying poor rates into the general fund. Those who did not pay the going rate had to pay the difference between the wages they were paying and the going rate into the Poor Rate 'pot'. The Labour Rate prevented the most obvious abuse of the Roundsman system, whereby wages became nominal and for most of each pauper's wages to be paid by the parish, with an obvious impact on the poor rates. The popularity of the Labour Rate system is not clear, but it does seem that, by 1832, about one parish in five was operating some sort of Labour Rate.

SOURCE 5

The composition of the pauper population 1802–03 in eight counties using the Speenhamland system. Compiled by Eric Evans in *Victorian Social Life: British Social History 1815–1914* (2002), using data from J.D. Marshall *The Old Poor Law 1795–1834* (1968).

County	Total number of paupers	Total number of elderly paupers	Total number of paupers receiving outdoor relief	Total number of pauper children (aged 0–15) living inside a workhouse or poor house
Sussex	37,000	3,330	7,400	19,000
Wiltshire	42,100	5,052	12,500	16,900
Berkshire	22,600	2,938	5,300	7,500
Buckinghamshire	19,600	2,548	6,500	6,500
Dorset	15,900	3,180	5,800	4,600
Huntingdonshire	4,700	611	1,600	1,500
Suffolk	36,100	4,332	8,100	8,100
Bedfordshire	7,300	1,168	2,500	2,000
England/Wales	**1,041,000**	**166,560**	**236,200**	**315,100**

SOURCE 6

From William Cobbett *Rural Rides*, published in 1830. Here, he is commenting on what he saw as he rode towards Warminster, Wiltshire, on 31 August 1826. Cobbett was a farmer and a radical journalist and pamphleteer.

I set out from Heytesbury this morning about six o'clock. Last night, before I went to bed, I found that there were some men and boys in the house who had come all the way from Bradford [Bradford on Avon, in West Wiltshire] about twelve miles in order to get nuts. These people were men and boys that had been employed in the cloth factories at Bradford and about Bradford. I had some talk with these people, and I am quite convinced, not that cloth making is at an end, but that it will never be again what it has been. Before last Christmas these manufacturers had full work, at one shilling and three pence a yard at broadcloth weaving. They now have a quarter of the work at one shilling a yard! Nothing can show more clearly than this, and in a stronger light, the great change which has taken place in the payment for labour. These poor people were extremely ragged. I saved my supper and I fasted instead of breakfasting. That was three shillings I had saved and I added five to them in order to give these chaps a breakfast for once in their lives.

From Heytesbury to Warminster is a part of the country singularly bright and beautiful. The labourers here look as if they are half-starved. For my own part, I really am ashamed to ride a fat horse, to have a full belly, and to have a clean shirt upon my back, while I look at these wretched countrymen of mine; while I actually see them reeling with weakness; when I see their poor faces present me with nothing but skin and bone, while they are toiling to get the wheat and the meat ready to be carried away by the tax-eaters.

We are reversing the maxim of the scripture: our laws almost say, that those that work shall not eat, and that those who do not work shall have the food. I repeat, that the baseness of the English landowners surpasses that of any other men that ever lived in the world. The cowards know well that the labourers that give value to their land are skin and bone. They are not such brutes as not to know that this starvation is produced by taxation. They know well how unjust it is to treat their labourers in this way.

A Level Exam-Style Question Section A

Study Source 6 before you answer this question.

Assess the value of the source for revealing the extent of poverty and the effectiveness of relief in the years before 1834.

Explain your answer, using the source, the information given about it and your own knowledge about the historical context. (20 marks)

Tip
Consider the position of the author to give an unbiased view of rural poverty as well as the likelihood of those he describes being typical.

ACTIVITY
KNOWLEDGE CHECK

Able-bodied paupers and outdoor relief

1 Why did people believe it was essential to categorise the poor?

2 Why did able-bodied paupers present such a problem to the authorities?

3 Consider the three main systems of outdoor relief.

   a) How would it be possible for each system to be abused by the overseers?

   b) How would it be possible for each system to be abused by the paupers?

   c) Set up a debate in which 'overseers' defend their own system.

4 Study Source 5.

   a) Which age group formed the largest group of paupers?

   b) Which counties seem to be problem counties in terms of the composition of their pauper population?

   c) All the counties in the table use some form of the Speenhamland system to supplement wages based on the price of bread or flour. How, then, can you account for such differences in the composition of their pauper populations?

5 How far does Source 6 prove that the poor laws were not working?

WHAT IMPACT DID THE PROVISION OF PARISH INDOOR RELIEF HAVE UPON PAUPERISM?

Poorhouses, workhouses and houses of correction

The Elizabethan Poor Law abandoned the more obvious sorts of earlier repression in favour of 'assistance' and 'correction'. The **impotent poor** – the sick, old, infirm and mentally ill – were to be looked after in poorhouses or almshouses (receiving what was known as indoor relief). The able-bodied poor who wanted relief were to be set to work in a 'workhouse' while they continued to live at home. Those who refused work and continued a life of begging and general vagrancy were to be punished in a 'house of correction'. Pauper children were to be apprenticed to a trade so that they could support themselves when they grew up. It all seemed so simple and straightforward. But was it?

The initial division of institutions for the giving of relief into 'poorhouses' for the impotent poor, 'workhouses' for the able-bodied poor and 'houses of correction' for the idle never really worked in practice. It simply was not cost effective for each parish to provide for paupers in this way. However, in the latter half of the 18th century, some parishes tried out a variety of experimental approaches aimed at making poor relief more cost effective. Those considering reform of the poor laws ranged from people driven by humanitarian motives to ameliorate the lot of the poor, and those, equally driven, who sought to reduce the burden on the ratepayers. What united them was the realisation that the days of a single parish as a unit of administration were numbered insofar as indoor relief was concerned. Urban parishes, for example in Exeter, Hereford, Gloucester and Plymouth, had already combined for the purpose of workhouse building. This was followed by, for example, landowners in the rural parishes of East Anglia and Shropshire driving parish amalgamation for workhouse provision. This resulted, by 1780, in about half the parishes in Suffolk being in some form of combination or incorporation with neighbouring parishes in order to build workhouses for their paupers. Indeed, by that year there were some 2,000 workhouses throughout England and Wales providing around 90,000 places for paupers. Even so, outdoor relief, whereby paupers remained in their own homes, remained the most common way of giving them help.

One significant feature of this amalgamation of parishes was the transfer of authority away from parish overseers to elected and appointed guardians of the poor. With larger units to administer, there was obvious concern that administration should be in the hands of those perceived to have the requisite judgement and experience. Overseers tended to be local farmers and tradesmen; guardians were drawn from the ranks of magistrates, gentry and upper ranks of tenant farmers.

KEY TERM

Impotent poor
People, such as the sick, the disabled, the old and children, who could not look after themselves even when times were good, and who were deemed worthy of relief.

Gilbert's Act 1782

Towards the end of the 18th century, there were various reasons why the attention of parliament was drawn to a more formal reform of the poor laws.

- The ending of the American War of Independence in 1782 resulted in demobilised soldiers and sailors flooding the labour market where not all could find employment.

- Enclosure of the great open fields, while creating some immediate employment opportunities regarding, for example, fencing and ditching, resulted in generalised long-term rural unemployment.

- The early stages of industrialisation attracted people to the growing towns, searching for work. This led to some depopulation of the countryside and an increase in the pressure on urban parishes to provide adequate relief.

There were very real fears that there would be a considerable increase in people seeking relief and that parishes, whether combined or not, would find it difficult to cope. Thomas Gilbert, MP for Lichfield, presented a bill to the House of Commons that rapidly passed through all its stages to become law. Basically, it sought to overhaul the local administrative system of relief.

- Parishes could combine in Poor Law unions for the purpose of building and maintaining a workhouse if two-thirds of the major landowners and ratepayers voted in favour. Voting was weighted according to the rateable value of the voters' property.

- In these Gilbert Unions, overseers were to be replaced by paid guardians, appointed by local magistrates chosen from a list supplied by ratepayers.

- Able-bodied workers were to be excluded from Gilbert Union workhouses, which were to be solely for the aged, the sick and children.

- The parish guardian was to find work for the able-bodied worker; only if this could not be found could outdoor relief be provided.

This was a permissive Act (see page 30), despite Gilbert's attempts in 1786 to make it a **mandatory Act**.
He did, however, manage to get two further pieces of legislation through parliament.

- Overseers were required to submit annual returns of Poor Law expenditure, thus providing hard evidence of the cost of poor relief that was to be used by later reformers.

- Ministers and churchwardens were required to provide information about local charities that mirrored, or supplemented, the support given by the Poor Law.

KEY TERM

Mandatory Act
An Act of Parliament that has to apply to everyone.

SOURCE

7 The parish workhouse of St James', London, a hand-coloured aquatint produced in 1809 by T. Rowlandson and A.C. Pugin.

The state was moving in on the provision of poor relief. However, parishes were slow, initially, to adopt Gilbert's Act, and were under no compulsion so to do. By 1834, when a new Poor Law was introduced, 924 parishes had combined into 67 Gilbert Unions. It was becoming clear that, by the end of the 18th century, there were two sets of largely rural Poor Law unions in existence. One was created by local initiatives to amalgamate parishes and the other created under the stricter terms of Gilbert's Act. All of these were in rural areas of the Midlands, south-east and east of England.

The Sturges-Bourne Acts, 1818 and 1819

Sometimes known as the Select Vestries Acts, these were a direct outcome of the House of Commons' Select Committee on the poor laws that was chaired by William Sturges-Bourne in 1817. Like Gilbert's Act, these Acts were permissive and only applied to those parishes whose vestries voted to adopt the new provisions. The intention behind both Acts was to tie the landowners, gentry and well-to-do more firmly into the administration of the poor laws. The first Act did this by laying down how voting was to be managed when electing men to the parish **select vestries** that were responsible for the local administration of the poor laws. Those occupying land worth less than £50 in rateable value had one vote; for every further £25 a man had another vote up to a maximum of six. Thus, major landowners would have six times the power and influence of smallholders.

SOURCE

8 The workhouse in Eversholt, Bedfordshire. The print is entitled 'A house near the church, the property of the Poor.' It was drawn in 1815 by Thomas Fisher, but was clearly built much earlier.

The following year, a second Act added a resident clergyman to the members of the vestry. This Act instructed vestries to take account of an applicant's character and circumstances, distinguishing between the 'deserving' and the 'undeserving' poor when considering who should receive relief. Destitution was not of itself sufficient to obtain relief. However, if a select vestry refused to grant relief, this decision could be overturned only if two JPs agreed that it was wrong.

By 1825, a total of 46 select vestries had been formed, and many experienced a remarkable drop in the cost of relief. For example, two parishes in Berkshire, where the Speenhamland system of outdoor relief was used: Bray and White Waltham, saw a reduction of 33 percent during the first year of the operation of their select vestries. Nationally, however, the reduction after the first year of administering relief via a select vestry was in the order of nine percent. Reductions of this size must have been at the expense of the destitute: not all those who were refused relief were scroungers and thousands must have been genuinely destitute and remained destitute.

KEY TERM

Select vestry
A vestry (a group of parishioners who meet in the vestry of a church) where members were selected according to specific criteria – usually the amount of property or land they owned. These were different from open vestries, where every ratepayer was entitled to be a member and to decide how poor relief was to be distributed.

A Level Exam-Style Question Section B

To what extent did Gilbert's Act (1782) and the Sturges-Bourne Acts (1818 and 1819) change the ways in which paupers were treated? (20 marks)

Tip
Consider what changed and what stayed the same in the ways in which all classes of paupers were treated by these Acts, and then reach a judgement as to the extent of change.

SOURCE

From an article written by Isaac Wiseman and published in the *Norwich Mercury* on 7 March 1829. He is describing the Norwich workhouse.

In 1826, and for some years previously, the workhouse was, in every part of it, a scene of filth, wretchedness and indecency, which baffles all description, without regulations of any kind. Imagine, too, paupers who for weeks, months and years together, breakfasted, dined and supped, without any order or regularity; who had neither knife, fork or plate; they were to be seen in groups with their hot puddings and meat in their hands, literally gnawing it. Imagine 600 persons indiscriminately lodged, crowded into rooms seldom or never ventilated, the beds and bedding swarming with vermin; single and married, old and young, all mixed without regard to decency.

Less eligibility and the workhouse test

These two concepts are more usually connected with the operation of the new Poor Law after the passing of the Poor Law Amendment Act in 1834 (see Chapter 4). In reality, they were in operation, albeit in a limited area, in the years prior to 1834 and were an important innovation stemming from local initiatives.

In 1823, Nottinghamshire had established a large Gilbert Union of some 49 parishes, largely due to the enthusiasm and hard work of the Rev J.T. Beecher, vicar of Southwell and chairman of the Quarter Sessions of the Newark Division, who had been actively involved since the 1790s in trying to put the Poor Law in his locality on a sounder footing. In 1819, Beecher appointed George Nicholls, a retired sea captain, to the post of overseer of the poor in the parish of Southwell. Working with the Rev Robert Lowe in the neighbouring parish of Bingham, the two men were determined to eradicate outdoor relief. Lowe is credited with introducing the policy of '**less eligibility**', believing that order within the Poor Law system could only be restored and then maintained if potential paupers were forced to provide for themselves because they feared the workhouse; it followed that conditions inside the workhouse had to be less eligible – less desirable – than conditions outside. This was one part of the **workhouse test**, which was itself a self-selecting test of destitution. Only the genuinely needy (and, some would say, desperate) would accept relief on these terms. Children, the sick, disabled and the elderly were exempt from the policy of less eligibility and the workhouse test because they were deemed worthy of relief. However, because these people, and children in particular, were usually part of a family, relief frequently resulted in families being split up or remaining in destitution.

EXTRACT

From J.D. Marshall *The Old Poor Law 1795–1834*, published in 1968.

The first characteristic of the Old Poor Law was that of great reliance on the parish as a unit of government, and, accordingly, on unpaid, non-professional administrators. The small size of the administrative unit meant that its finances were feeble, and that any unusual burden, as in 1815–21, might appear disastrous to those working at parish or county levels.

The second characteristic, connected closely to the first one, was a profound adherence to the tenets, if not always to the practice, of the Poor Law of 1597–1601, and especially of the famous 'Act of Elizabeth' of 1601. This Act was under strong attack in the 1820s - a consideration which is, in itself, startling testimony to its influence - and it laid down that each parish was to be responsible for its own poor. At the same time the impotent poor were to be maintained and work was to be provided for the able-bodied.

This brings us to a third characteristic of the Old Poor Law, the tendency to rationalise, repeatedly, what had already been done in practice for a number of years, in localities or generally. Even the immensely important Act of Settlement [Settlement Act] of 1662 was based on an already recognised principle or principles, while deterrent workhouses, roundsmen systems, unions of parishes, and allowances in aid of wages were all known or utilised in given places before, often long before, they became central places of particular enactments or policies.

A fourth characteristic, moreover, is the absence of any very consistent body of practice (ie pursued for any length of time), between 1601 and 1834. On the one hand, one can say that the Old Poor Law was inconsistent; on the other, that it was profoundly adaptable!

An undoubted fifth characteristic of the Old Poor Law was geographical variation. It may eventually be shown, however, that these local differences in policy or attitude were not by any means fortuitous; just as the great if somewhat blurred differences between the southern or Speenhamland counties and the northern counties of England corresponded, in the broadest possible terms, to an economic division, so the variation in Poor Law administration as between one part of a county and another has been known to correspond to differences in trade, industry or agriculture.

Indoor relief and links to outdoor relief

1 What were the main differences between Gilbert's Act (1782) and the Sturges-Bourne Acts (1818 and 1819) insofar as the paupers were concerned?

2 How useful would Sources 8 and 9 be for a historian investigating the impact of the old Poor Law on local communities?

3 How far does the article written by Isaac Wiseman (Source 9) challenge the view of workhouses presented in Source 7?

4 J.D. Marshall (Extract 1) lists five characteristics of the old poor laws. Draw a flow chart, mind map or spider diagram to show how they are all linked.

WHY DID THE PRESSURE FOR CHANGE INTENSIFY IN THE YEARS 1780-1834?

The Elizabethan Poor Law of 1601 remained the basis of Poor Law administration for over 200 years. Changes were made in response to local conditions; some simply became enshrined in custom and practice whilst others found their way onto the statute books – but always as permissive, not mandatory legislation. So what happened to focus the attention of the rate-paying public and legislators on what they saw as the problem of poor relief to the extent that mandatory change on a national level was seen as essential?

What were the financial pressures for change?

There were always poor and vulnerable people in any society, and Britain was no different in this from any other country. It was the poor and the vulnerable who were forced to seek relief and it was anticipated by the authorities that this **underclass** would remain fairly constant in numbers and demands over time. However, political and economic changes in the early years of the 19th century led to an increase in pauperism and put a huge and unexpected strain on the relief services.

The impact of the wars with France

The ending of the wars with France (1783–1815) led to greater demands for poor relief. Indeed, pressure on the Poor Law to provide sufficient relief, and at a level required by its own regulations, brought it almost to a state of collapse.

- The harvests of 1813 and 1814 were good in England and on the continent. Cheap foreign corn could again be imported from Europe, which forced English farmers to keep their prices low. This created problems for many as they had wartime taxes to pay and some, too, had interest to pay on loans to cover the cost of enclosure. Many went bankrupt, which meant unemployment for their labourers. With little work to be had, many were forced to ask for relief. Farmers who survived were forced to reduce the wages they paid to their workers. Those whom they employed were therefore pushed closer to pauperism.

- In 1815, the Tory government tried to improve the situation. Persuaded by parliament to do so, it introduced Corn Laws to protect British farmers. The new Corn Laws would not allow the import of foreign corn until the price of British corn reached 80 shillings a quarter. In this way, the government hoped to hold the price of corn steady and so keep the price of bread steady, too. Since the landowners' profits would not fluctuate wildly, wages would also remain stable. That was the theory. In practice, many people resented the Corn Laws, which they believed kept the price of bread artificially high. There were riots and outbreaks of violence up and down the country as the poor found they could not afford to buy sufficient bread – their staple diet. Systems pegging relief to the price of bread struggled to provide sufficient relief.

- Post-war distress meant that more people than ever before claimed relief and, to the horror of some observers, began to regard relief as a right. The crisis years were 1817–19, when the problems experienced by returning soldiers, the continuing dislocation of trade, appalling weather and poor harvests resulted in expenditure on poor relief reaching a hitherto unimaginable £8 million per year, somewhere between 12 and 13 shillings per head of population.

- The situation was exacerbated by continuing radical protests, which forced the government to suspend **habeas corpus** in 1817, and introduce the **Six Acts** two years later, confirmation of its policy of repression and the curtailing of individual liberties in the face of protest. A repressive government was unlikely to legislate for any easement in the provision of relief.

In the midst of all this, the 1817 report of the Select Committee on the poor laws comprehensively condemned the evils of the Poor Law as being themselves the creators of poverty. While abolition might have seemed to some commentators to be the only way forward, no sensible government could go down that road at a time when distress was at its height and society seemed to many to be so unstable. Instead, their recommendations led directly to the Sturges-Bourne Acts (see page 73).

(see page 73)

KEY TERMS

Habeas corpus
Literally meaning 'you have the body', the Act of 1679 was intended to prevent people from being imprisoned in secret. Its suspension meant that people could be imprisoned without trial for an indefinite period.

Six Acts 1819
These Acts prohibited meetings of more than 50 people, increased stamp duties on newspapers, made the publication of blasphemous and seditious material a transportable offence, forbade military training by civilians, limited the right of an accused person to delay a trial in order to prepare the defence, and gave magistrates powers to search private houses for arms.

EXTEND YOUR KNOWLEDGE

The Corn Laws (1815–46)
The Corn Laws, introduced in 1815, imposed restrictions and tariffs on imported grain in an attempt to protect the profits of British farmers. The Laws forbade the importation of foreign grain until the price of home-grown grain reached 80 shillings a quarter and even then the foreign produce was subject to high import duties. In the 1820s, the figure of 80 shillings was replaced by a sliding scale that went down as the price of British wheat rose. Intended to stabilise the price of bread, the Corn Laws did, in fact, keep the price of food artificially high. The Laws had political as well as social and economic outcomes. Supported by landowners, who had an overwhelming majority in the unreformed parliament and a significant one in the reformed parliament after 1832, they were opposed by the rising industrial interests who saw them as limiting the spending power of the domestic market. They were universally hated by the poor who regarded them, with some justification, as keeping the cost of bread, their staple food, artificially high. A strong and vociferous Anti-Corn Law League, founded by Richard Cobden, campaigned for the repeal of the Corn Laws, more so that manufacturers could lower their costs than that the poor could afford bread. The Corn Laws were eventually repealed in 1846, largely prompted by the distress caused by the Irish famine. In championing repeal, Prime Minister Robert Peel split the Conservative Party, of which he was leader, and forced his resignation.

The impact of agricultural unrest: the 'Swing' riots
Urban protest was matched by rural discontent that came to a head in 1830.

In over 20 counties, mainly in southern and eastern England, the rural poor burned hayricks and barns, smashed threshing machines and intimidated their employers. What did the rioters want? Initially, their demands were for higher wages and the removal of the steam-powered threshing machines that deprived them of autumn and winter employment. As the rioting spread, there were repeated arson attacks against the property of overseers of the poor and their assistants; poorhouses and workhouses were burned down and demands were made for increased relief as the farmers' use of the hated threshing machines was forcing them into pauperism.

- In the village of Brede, Sussex, close to the towns of Rye and Hastings, a group of labourers launched a local movement against the overseers of the poor, demanding higher allowances and the removal of Mr Abel, an assistant overseer who had made himself objectionable by his constant use of the parish cart to remove paupers. The frightened gentry agreed to both demands, and a posse of labourers removed Mr Abel from the parish in the self-same parish cart. Rye had already been the centre of radical agitation and the scene of violent popular riots earlier in 1830 against the election of an unpopular Tory MP. William Cobbett had lectured at various places in the county and it was popularly believed that he deliberately incited the paupers to arson.

- Headley and Selbourne, two villages in Hampshire, witnessed a combined operation against threshing machines, tithes and overseers of the poor. Labourers extracted written assurances from the two vicars that tithes would be reduced, then they moved on and broke a threshing machine and pulled down workhouses in both parishes, having given notice of their intention so that no pauper was harmed.

- In Wiltshire, the major landowner John Bennett MP had drawn up a particularly harsh allowance scale for poor relief in 1817 and, 13 years later, became the target of violent demonstrations. Leading a troop of yeomanry against the rioters, Bennett was wrong-footed by local farmers who invited the labourers to a vestry meeting where their grievances were discussed and resolved.

Petitions and threats signed 'Captain Swing' gave the impression of an organised revolt under a single leader. In fact, there was no such leader and no organised revolt. The Swing riots, while revealing pent-up grievances against changes in farming practice and harsh poor-relief policies, do not demonstrate revolutionary intent or even radicalism on the part of the rioters. However, it was enough for the authorities to think that the revolt was organised, and to believe they had to face up to a very real threat of revolution. The home secretary, Lord Melbourne, ordered that the rioters should be dealt with harshly. A revolution had just happened in France and he couldn't risk one breaking out in Britain. Afraid that local magistrates would be sympathetic and too lenient, a special commission of three judges was appointed to try the rioters. Although no deaths had happened as a result of the Swing riots, 19 rioters were themselves sentenced to death, over 400 were sentenced to transportation to Australia, 644 sentenced to imprisonment, seven were fined, one was whipped and 800 were either acquitted or **bound over to keep the peace**.

One positive outcome of the Swing riots was that they created a political climate, especially in parliament, where reform of the poor laws was becoming more than a possibility: it was an urgent necessity.

EXTRACT

From W.H. Hudson *A Shepherd's Life,* published in 1910. Hudson grew up on farms in South America. He began writing about 19th-century rural England when he came to live in England in 1869, married and settled down to the life of a writer on rural matters.

I can understand how it came about that these poor labourers, poor spiritless slaves as they had been made by long years of extremist poverty and systematic oppression, rose at last against their hard masters and smashed the agricultural machines, and burnt ricks and broke into houses to destroy and plunder their contents. It was a desperate, a mad adventure but oppression had made them mad; the introduction of the threshing machines was but the last straw. It was not merely the fact that the wages of a strong man were only seven shillings a week at most, a sum barely sufficient to keep him from starvation and rags, but it was customary, especially on the small farms, to get rid of the men after harvest and leave them to exist the best way they could during the bitter winter months. Thus every village, as a rule, had its dozen or twenty or more men thrown out each year. The misery of these out-of-work labourers was extreme. They would go to the woods and gather logs of dead wood, which they would try to sell in the villages; but there were few who could afford to buy them; and at night they would skulk about the fields to rob a swede or two to satisfy the cravings of hunger.

The impact of the increasing cost of providing poor relief

It was becoming clear that the cost of poor relief was rising at an alarming rate, and that the old Poor Law was creaking under the strain.

Date	Average expenditure (in £000)	Per head of population
1783-85	2,004	5s 2d
1803	4,268	9s 2d
1813	6,656	12s 5d
1814-18	6,437	11s 7d
1819-23	6,788	11s 2d
1824-28	6,039	9s 2d
1829-33	6,758	9s 8d

Figure 3.1 Expenditure on poor relief in England and Wales.

Traditionally, parishes looked after their own poor and raised the money to do so by a tax on property, and income from this was obviously limited. In stable conditions, this way of providing relief for a parish's paupers worked reasonably well. However, society in the early years of the 19th century was far from stable, with thousands crossing the line that divided poor from pauper and enlarging the existing underclass. The situation was worsened by the mobility of the population, with hundreds of people crowding into parishes in industrialising areas and claiming poor relief that the parishes could hardly afford to pay. To the issue of increasing poor rates, and the perception amongst the rate-paying classes that the poor were increasingly idle, was added the fear of their revolutionary potential. However, whether a parish was urban, rural or somewhere in-between, the overall cost to the nation of poor relief was rising.

ACTIVITY
KNOWLEDGE CHECK

Pressures for change

1 How did the government hope the introduction of the Corn Laws in 1815 would help the poor?

2 Why did the years 1817-19 put enormous pressure on the various systems of poor relief?

3 Explain whether the Swing riots of the 1830s were 'a desperate, a mad adventure' (Extract 2) or a serious protest against the poor laws.

4 How could the data in Figure 3.1 be used to argue for and against the need to reform the poor laws?

Regional differences

Different parishes, as has been shown, operated poor relief before 1834 in many different ways. As well as differences between parishes, there were clear regional differences in the numbers and sorts of people claiming relief.

SOURCE

10 A comparison of the composition of the pauper population in agricultural and industrial areas, 1802–03. Compiled from *Abstract of Returns relative to the Expense and Maintenance of the Poor, 1802-3*. This was published by the government and was compiled from information sent in from the parishes.

Region	Total in receipt of relief (and as a percentage of total population)	Non-able-bodied receiving relief	Able-bodied receiving relief	Able-bodied as percentage of total population relieved	Permanent workhouse/ poorhouse residents as percentage of total population relieved
Industrial/ commercial					
Lancashire	46,200 (6.7)	6,928	39,272	85.0	5.9
London area	63,173 (7.5)	8,407	54,766	86.7	24.0
Yorkshire, West Riding	54,365 (9.3)	9,867	44,498	81.9	4.7
Agricultural counties					
Berkshire	22,588 (20.0)	2,872	19,716	87.3	5.2
Sussex	37,076 (22.6)	3,231	33,845	91.3	10.3
Wiltshire	42,128 (22.1)	5,219	36,909	87.6	3.8
Total: England and Wales	**1,040,716 (11.4)**	**166,829**	**873,887**	**84.0**	**8.0**

The Nottinghamshire experiment

Nottinghamshire, the fifth-most industrialised county in Britain, was relatively prosperous. It had a thriving framework knitting industry, and industrial expansion provided alternative work when there was a downturn in rural employment. In 1820–23, the per capita relief expenditure was less than 11 shillings, well below the national average. There was an allowance system in operation, but clearly this did not impact too heavily on the poor rate. It is therefore somewhat surprising that by the 1820s, Nottinghamshire was regarded by contemporaries as radical in its experimentation with poor law reform. This was due to the individuals concerned.

- The Reverend J.T. Becher of Southwell, Chairman of Quarter Sessions for the Newark Division, had been the driving force behind the amalgamation in 1823 of 49 parishes into a large Gilbert Act Union and the building of two new workhouses at Upton and Southwell. These were deterrent workhouses, with an emphasis on strict segregation and classification of inmates. Even so, Becher insisted on kindness being shown to the aged and infirm, and workhouse schools were established for the children that were also open to children from 'outside' if there were more than four children in a family.

- The Reverend Robert Lowe of Bingham, a magistrate, agreed with Becher about the need for deterrence, but went further, insisting as early as 1818 that outdoor relief should be abolished and that the way to do that was by making the workhouse a place of fear. He worked hard to bring greater rigour to the workhouses with which he was involved.

- George Nicholls, a retired sea captain, moved to Southwell in 1819. Appointed an overseer of the poor by Becher, he agreed with Lowe about the need for deterrence, and reached the conclusion that allowance systems were themselves responsible for the continuation of poverty. His writings on the poor law, and in particular his *Eight Letters on the Management of the Poor* (1822), in which he claimed to have ended outdoor relief through the creation of a well-regulated workhouse, created a high profile for himself as a reformer. He gave evidence to the 1824 Select Committee enquiring into the poor laws, and was appointed one of the three Poor Law Commissioners in 1834. (See page 90.)

Success in Gloucestershire

In 1830, J.H. Lloyd Baker, a Gloucestershire JP, started reforming poor law administration in Uley, a community of some 2,641 inhabitants and with little regular employment from the failing woollen industry. An allowance system was in full swing, with an annual relief bill of £3,185. Under guidance from Lowe, Baker introduced rigorous reforms and within two years the number of paupers fell from 977 to 125. The secret of Baker's success was to abolish outdoor relief and to make the workhouse so dreadful that only the desperate would seek admission.

Similar policies were introduced in Cornwall and Derbyshire.

Challenge in Cookham, Berkshire

The Reverend Thomas Whately of Cookham in Berkshire, adopted a somewhat different approach. When the able-bodied applied for relief, he offered them work at a lower rate than that which was generally paid in the parish. He claimed that 63 long-term recipients immediately left the parish.

Parishes in cities like London, Bristol and Norwich adopted similar policies.

These are all examples of parishes and even whole counties adopting aggressive policies in an attempt to lower the cost of poor rates and to reduce pauperism. It was by no means a universal approach. There were still areas where local magistrates and overseers of the poor retained their paternalistic approach to the poor in their care, doing their best to provide relief without demoralising the recipients.

ACTIVITY
KNOWLEDGE CHECK

Regional differences

1 Study Source 10.

   a) What were the main differences in the pauper population of agricultural and industrial areas?

   b) How would you account for these differences?

2 In what ways was the Nottinghamshire experiment successful?

3 How far were the new approaches developed in Nottinghamshire, Gloucestershire and Berkshire successful in solving the problem of pauperism?

4 Why do you think there were so many regional differences in the relief of poverty?

What were the ideological arguments for change?

Philosophers, commentators, political theorists and economists all had views, particularly about the poor laws, that they made known. Ideas and theories, like these outlined below, which influence the ways in which contemporaries think and act, are called 'prevailing ideologies'.

Thomas Malthus (1766–1834)

Malthus was an economist specialising in demography – the study of population. He argued that population had an inbuilt propensity to rise and outstrip all available food supplies. The Poor Law made the situation worse because it encouraged the poor to have more and more children so that they could claim more and more relief. He favoured the abolition of the Poor Law altogether. The poor would then have to keep their families small because there would be no financial advantage to them in having a lot of children; wages would rise because the Poor Rate would no longer be levied and employers could afford to pay their employees more; everyone would prosper.

SOURCE 11 From Thomas Malthus *An Essay on the Principle of Population,* published in 1798.

I feel no doubt whatever that the parish laws of England have contributed to raise the price of provisions and to lower the real price of labour. They have therefore contributed to impoverish that class of people whose only possession is their labour. The labouring poor always seem to live from hand to mouth. Their present wants employ their whole attention, and they seldom think of the future. Even when they have an opportunity of saving they seldom exercise it, but all that is beyond their present necessities goes to the alehouse. The poor laws of England may therefore be said to diminish both the power and the will to save among the common people, and thus to weaken one of the strongest incentives to sobriety and industry, and consequently to happiness.

The poor-laws of England were undoubtedly instituted for the most benevolent purpose, but there is great reason to think that they have not succeeded in their intention. They certainly mitigate some cases of very severe distress which might otherwise occur, yet the state of the poor who are supported by parishes, considered in all its circumstances, is very far from being free from misery. But one of the principle objections to them is that for this assistance which some of the poor receive, in itself almost a doubtful blessing, the common people of England is subjected to a set of grating, inconvenient and tyrannical laws, totally inconsistent with the genuine spirit of the constitution. The whole business of settlements, even in its present form, is utterly contradictory to all ideas of freedom. The parish persecution of men whose families are likely to become chargeable, and of poor women who are near lying-in, is a most disgraceful and disgusting tyranny.

The tyranny of Justices, Churchwardens and Overseers is a common complaint among the poor, but the fault does not lie so much in these persons but in the nature of all such institutions.

The evil is perhaps gone too far to be remedied, but I doubt that if the poor-laws had never existed, though there might have been a few more instances of very severe distress, yet that the aggregate mass of happiness among the common people would have been much greater than it is at present.

David Ricardo (1772-1823)

Ricardo was a political economist who reached the same conclusions as Malthus about the poor laws, but by a slightly different route. In his work *On the Principles of Political Economy and Taxation*, published in 1817, he put forward the idea of an iron law of wages, believing that there was a wages fund from which money for wages and poor relief was paid. It therefore followed that, the more that was paid out in poor relief, the less there was available for wages. Because less money was available for wages, more and more people were being drawn into pauperism, thus draining the wage fund still more. The only way to break out of this cycle was to abolish the poor laws altogether.

Not all theorists favoured abolition!

Thomas Paine (1737-1809)

Paine was a writer and republican who criticised the Poor Law because it was so inadequate. He proposed a property tax on the very rich to be used for a variety of support systems for the poor, among these being family allowances and old age pensions. He, like others, had a problem with the able-bodied poor and implied that they had to go into workhouses before they could receive relief.

SOURCE

 12 From Thomas Paine *The Rights of Man,* published in 1791.

In the first place the poor-rates are a direct tax which every house-keeper feels, and who knows also, to a farthing, the sum which he pays. In the present state of things, a labouring man, with a wife and two or three children, does not pay less than between seven and eight pounds a year in taxes. He is not sensible of this, because it is disguised to him in the articles which he buys, and he thinks only of their dearness; but as the taxes take from him, at least a fourth part of his yearly earnings, he is consequently disabled from providing for a family, especially if himself, or any of them are afflicted with sickness.

The first step, therefore, of practical relief, would be to abolish the poor-rates entirely, and in lieu thereof, to make a remission of the taxes of the poor of double the amount of the present poor-rates, viz. four millions annually out of the surplus taxes. By this measure, the poor will be benefitted two millions, and the house-keepers two millions.

I shall now enumerate the several particulars:

First	Abolition of two millions of poor-rates.
Secondly	Provision for two hundred and fifty-two thousand poor families.
Thirdly	Education for one million and thirty thousand children.
Fourthly	Comfortable provision for one hundred and forty thousand aged persons.
Fifthly	Donation of twenty shillings each for fifty thousand births.
Sixthly	Donation of twenty shillings each for twenty thousand marriages.
Seventhly	Allowance of twenty thousand pounds for the funeral expenses of persons travelling for work, and dying at a distance from their friends.
Eighthly	Employment, at all times, for the casual poor.

Cases are continually occurring in a metropolis, different to those which occur in the country, and for which a different, or rather, an additional mode of relief is necessary. The plan would be first, to erect two or more buildings, or take some already erected, capable of containing at least six thousand persons, and to have in each of these places as many kinds of employment as can be contrived, so that every person who shall come may find something which he or she can do. Second, to receive all who shall come without enquiring who or what they are. The only condition to be that for as much, or so many hours a week, each person shall receive so many meals of wholesome food and a warm lodging, at least as good as a barrack.

By the operation of this plan, the poor laws, those instruments of civil torture, will be superseded...

Robert Owen (1771–1858)

Owen was a radical factory owner who blamed the capitalist economic system for creating poverty and, in particular, abuse of the factory system. At his New Lanark site in Scotland, which consisted of a huge cotton-spinning mill and a mill workers' village, he tried to put his ideas into practice by building a new sort of community. No adult was allowed to work for more than ten-and-a-half hours a day and sick pay was provided when illness or accident prevented a person from working. Children had to be educated in the New Lanark school until they were ten years old, and only then could they work in his mills; corporal punishment of children and adults was forbidden. To the surprise of Owen's fellow mill owners, his mills ran at a profit. A large store at New Lanark sold goods to Owen's workers at cost price. This, again, was part of Owen's concept of a fair community. He suggested that, if workers were employed in co-operative communities, everyone would share in the profits of whatever organisation they worked for. In this way, the harder they worked the greater would be their income, and they would have no need for poor relief. Care would only need to be taken of the impotent poor.

The influence of utilitarianism

The thinking of men like Paine and Owen, Malthus and Ricardo was important in shaping the philosophical and theoretical debate centring on the ways in which the destitute underclass should be treated. However, it was the philosophy of **Utilitarianism**, developed by Jeremy Bentham, that was to have a profound and far-reaching influence on the thinking of those who developed and administered a new poor law.

Bentham's unconventional and daringly critical approach to contemporary issues inspired a group of men who were known as the Philosophical Radicals, and who had as their main purpose the complete overhaul of Britain's laws and institutions. The judiciary, education, prisons and, in particular, the poor laws were all subject to a forensic appraisal, and recommendations made according to the basic philosophy of Utilitarianism. Any society, Bentham argued, should be so organised as to enable the greatest amount of happiness to be delivered to the greatest number of its people. It followed that legislators, therefore, should be guided only by a desire to maximise happiness and minimise misery. How did this revolutionary thinking relate to the treatment of paupers? Bentham believed that:

- relief was a public responsibility that should be organised by central government

- there should be a government minister responsible for, for example, keeping statistics and inspecting workhouses

- all outdoor relief should be abolished, and relief only given to those prepared to enter a workhouse, where conditions would be no better than those enjoyed by the poorest labourer outside the workhouse

- there should be no discrimination between 'deserving' and 'undeserving' poor. There were only the destitute, without the means of support and so worthy of relief.

Bentham was no philanthropist; his views were based purely upon Utilitarianism. A starving underclass would be highly likely to turn to revolution, and a revolutionary situation was one where no one's life or property was secure. Hence, revolution had to be avoided in order to maximise happiness.

KEY TERM

Utilitarianism
A theory that society should be organised so as to secure the greatest happiness for the greatest number of people. Actions, Acts of Parliament and institutions should be judged according to whether or not they added to this sum total of happiness. Utilitarianism underpinned the reforms of the first half of the 19th century, in particular the Poor Law Amendment Act 1834 and sanitary reform. Jeremy Bentham was one of the thinkers who developed this theory and it had a profound impact on his secretary, Edwin Chadwick.

SOURCE

From Jeremy Bentham *An Introduction to the Principles of Morals and Legislation*, published in 1789.

Nature has placed mankind under the governance of two sovereign masters, pain and pleasure. It is for them alone to point out what we ought to do, and to determine what we shall do. They govern us in all we do, in all we say, in all we think: every effort we can make to throw off our subjection, will serve but to demonstrate and confirm it. In words a man may pretend to abjure their empire: but in reality he will remain subject to it all the while. The principle of utility recognises this subjection.

By the principle of utility is meant that principle which approves or disapproves of every action whatsoever, according to the tendency which it appears to have to augment or diminish the happiness of the party whose interest is in question: or, what is the same thing in other words, to promote or oppose that happiness. I say that of every action whatsoever, and therefore not only of every action of a private individual, but of every measure of government.

The interest of the community is one of the most general expressions that can occur in the phraseology of morals: no wonder that the meaning of it is often lost. When it has a meaning, it is this. The community is a fictitious body, composed of individual persons who are considered as constituting, as it were, its members. The interest of the community then is, what? – the sum of the interests of the several members who compose it.

It is vain to talk of the interest of the community, without understanding what is the interest of the individual. A thing is said to promote the interest of an individual when it tends to add to the sum total of his pleasures: or, what comes to the same thing, to diminish the sum total of his pains.

An action then may be said to be conformable to the principle of utility when the tendency it has to augment the happiness of the community is greater than any which it has to diminish it.

A measure of government (which is but a particular kind of action, performed by a particular person or persons) may be said to be conformable to or dictated by the principle of utility, when in like manner the tendency which it has to augment the happiness of the community is greater than any which it has to diminish it.

EXTEND YOUR KNOWLEDGE

Jeremy Bentham (1748–1832)

Born in London into a wealthy Tory family, Bentham attended Westminster School, Oxford University and trained as a lawyer. He never worked as a lawyer, but instead gained eminence as a philosopher and social reformer who developed the theory of Utilitarianism. Any society should, he argued, be so organised as to enable the greatest amount of happiness to be delivered to the greatest number of its people. He believed that this could be achieved if wages and prices found their true level in a free market and all state institutions, like the Poor Law, were centrally controlled to agreed standards. All responsibility for the poor, he argued, should be given to a profit-making private company. He wanted all outdoor relief to be abolished. The poor would only get help if they entered an 'industry house' where conditions inside would be bad so that only the genuinely destitute paupers would be helped.

Bentham advocated individual and economic freedom, equal rights for women, and the abolition of slavery and the death penalty. Bentham had considerable influence over John Stuart Mill and Edwin Chadwick. Mill developed Bentham's Principle of Utility and applied it to, for example, welfare issues, maintaining the aim of all welfare measures should be to maximise happiness. Chadwick became Bentham's secretary and, after Bentham's death, wrote extensively on public health and was a major force behind the implementation of the Poor Law Amendment Act.

A life-long atheist, Bentham ordered his body to be permanently preserved after his death and it was for some years on view at University College, London.

ACTIVITY
KNOWLEDGE CHECK

Ideologies

1 Summarise, in no more than 150 words, Bentham's Principle of Utility.

2 Which of the four ideological approaches to poor laws do you find the most convincing?

3 Work in groups of four. Each person takes one of the four ideologies given here and tries to persuade the other three that this is the best way of dealing with paupers.

A Level Exam-Style Question Section B

'The only reason the government decided to set up a Royal Commission of Enquiry into the Operation of the Poor Laws in 1832 was the rising cost of the poor rate.'

How far do you agree with this statement? (20 marks)

Tip

Consider the other factors that led to the decision not only to enquire into the working of the poor laws, but to set up the commission at that point in time.

THINKING HISTORICALLY Cause and consequence (7a & b)

Questions and answers

Questions that historians ask vary depending on what they think is important. It is the questions that interest us that define the history that is written. These questions change with time and place. Different historians will also come up with different answers to the same questions, depending on their perspectives and methods of interpretation, as well as the evidence they use.

Below are three historians who had different areas of interest.

John Stuart Mill	E.P. Thompson	Norman Gash
A British philosopher who lived in the 19th century. He was interested in social and political theories relating to freedom and state control.	An economic and political historian who lived in the 20th century. He was interested in the role of the lower classes and how they contributed to historical change.	A political historian who lived in the 20th century. He was very interested in English politics and prime ministers.

These are some key events, developments and issues relating to the old Poor Law.

Gilbert's Act 1782	The problem of the able-bodied pauper	The increasing cost of poor relief, 1780–1830
The ending of the Napoleonic Wars in 1815	The Swing riots of the 1830s	The concept of less-eligibility
The Speenhamland system of poor relief	The theory of Utilitarianism	The introduction of the Corn Laws in 1815

Work in groups of between three and six.

1 Which of these events would have been of most interest to each historian? Explain your answer.

2 a) Each take the role of one historian and devise a question that would interest them about each of the events.

  b) Discuss each event/development/issue in turn. Present the questions that have been devised for each historian, and offer some ideas about how they would have answered them.

  c) For each event, decide as a group which question is the most interesting and worthwhile of the three.

Answer the following questions in pairs:

3 Identify the different ways that each historian would approach writing an account of the old Poor Law.

4 In what ways would Thompson and Gash differ in their explanations of the significance of Gilbert's Act 1782? What would be the focus of their arguments?

Answer the following questions individually:

5 All three historians may produce very different accounts and explanations of the same piece of history. Of the three historians, whose account would you prefer to read first? Explain your answer.

6 a) Do the differences in these accounts mean that one is more valid than the others?

  b) Explain why different historical explanations are written by different historians.

  c) Explain why different explanations of the same event can be equally valid.

Why did the government take action in 1832?

There had been enquiries, investigations, comments, theories and reports on the Poor Law since the end of the 18th century. Why, then, did matters come to a head in the early 1830s? The general election of 1831 brought about a change of government, with the reforming Whigs having a clear majority in the House of Commons, although, in 1831, they were more intent on parliamentary reform than reform of the poor laws. However, this, combined with a general consensus among the propertied classes that something had to be done about the escalating costs of maintaining the poor, pushed the government into action. In this, the government's hands were forced by the Lord Chancellor, Lord Brougham. Responding to a parliamentary question in the Lords, Brougham (a committed **Benthamite**) made the surprising announcement that the government was to consolidate and simplify the existing poor laws in the next session or two of parliament. It's doubtful he had consulted with government colleagues, but they rose to the occasion. In February 1832, Lord Althorpe, the chancellor of the exchequer, told the House that a Royal Commission would be appointed to conduct an investigation into the operation of the poor laws. The ways in which the commission conducted its enquiries and the outcome of those enquiries had a profound and lasting impact on attitudes to, and treatment of, paupers throughout the rest of the century and beyond.

KEY TERM

Benthamite
A follower of Jeremy Bentham and who believed in his theory of Utilitarianism.

ACTIVITY
SUMMARY

The old poor laws

1 a) What were the strengths and weaknesses of the old Poor Law?

   b) In your judgement, did the weaknesses outweigh the strengths, and so justify reform?

2 The many pressures for change to the poor laws came to a head in the 1830s. Which do you think was the overriding one? Explain your answer.

WIDER READING

Brundage, A. *The English Poor Laws 1700-1930,* Palgrave Macmillan (2002)

Cobbett, W. *Rural Rides,* Penguin (2005; first published 1830)

Hobsbawm, E.J. and Rude, G. *Captain Swing,* Lawrence & Wishart (1969) / Verso Books (2014)

Marshall, J.D. *The Old Poor Law 1795-1834,* Macmillan (1968)

Rose, M.E. *English Poor Law 1780-1930,* David and Charles (1971)

Thompson, E.P. *The Making of the English Working Class,* Victor Gollancz (1963) / Penguin edition (2013)

3.4 Less eligibility: the Poor Law Amendment Act and its impact, 1832–47

KEY QUESTIONS

- In what ways did central government set about reforming the poor laws?
- What impact did the workhouse have on the lives of paupers?
- How effective was opposition to the implementation of the Poor Law Amendment Act?

INTRODUCTION

In February 1832, the Whig government, prompted by long- and short-term concerns (see Chapter 3), set up a Royal Commission of Enquiry into the Operation of the Poor Laws. The Royal Commission took two years to compile data and write its report, which recommended radical changes to the poor laws. That the main recommendations of the report became law in less than a year is a measure of the strong all-party acceptance of its recommendations. Indeed, the Poor Law Amendment bill passed through all its stages in Commons and Lords with never more than 50 votes being cast against it, and gained the royal assent in August 1834.

The Poor Law Amendment Act set up a central Poor Law Commission that was responsible for implementing and administering the Act throughout the country. In doing this, it was given almost a free hand: the Act itself did not lay down a programme of implementation. Here, the views of the commissioners and, more importantly, those of the commission's secretary, Edwin Chadwick, came to be of paramount importance. There was a determined attempt on their part to ensure that, in order to obtain relief, the poor had to enter a workhouse. So as to discourage pauperism, conditions in workhouses had to be worse than those of the independent labourer outside. Despite the best efforts of the commissioners, outdoor relief remained.

Implementation of the Poor Law Amendment Act was neither simple nor straightforward. The commissioners faced opposition from parishes in both the north and south of the country, some of which was well organised and serious. Nevertheless, by 1847 all paupers were subject to the Act they had come to loath and fear.

1834 – Parliament passes the Poor Law Amendment Act

Poor Law Commission established to implement and administer the Act

1835 – Commission begins work in southern England

Sampson Kempthorne appointed architect to the Poor Law Commission

1837 – Commission begins work in industrialised north of England

Protests, riots and the formation of the anti-Poor Law movement

| 1834 | 1835 | 1836 | 1837 | 1838 | 1839 |

After 1834 – Commission issues orders to individual Poor Law unions, prohibiting outdoor relief

1836 – Commission issues General Prohibitory Order forbidding outdoor relief

1838 – General Prohibitory Order set aside for unions in Lancashire and the West Riding of Yorkshire

IN WHAT WAYS DID CENTRAL GOVERNMENT SET ABOUT REFORMING THE POOR LAWS?

In the politically charged atmosphere surrounding the bitterly contested passage of the **Parliamentary Reform Act**, the Whig government set up the Royal Commission of Enquiry into the Poor Laws in February 1832. Many middle- and upper-class people, wary of the reforming Whigs who had been out of power until 1830, viewed the establishment of a Royal Commission as being suspiciously radical. It was against this background, as well as the pressures for change detailed in Chapter 3, that the commission started work.

How did the Commission of Enquiry set about its work?

The Royal Commission of Enquiry consisted, ultimately, of nine commissioners, the most influential of whom were Nassau Senior and Edwin Chadwick. Nassau Senior, Professor of Political Economy at Oxford University, deeply disapproved of the allowance system; Edwin Chadwick was a committed follower of Jeremy Bentham and the doctrine of Utilitarianism (see Chapter 3). It was not very likely that a survey of the old poor laws, and any recommendations for their amendment, would be impartial and unbiased. Additionally, 26 assistant commissioners were appointed who put in the leg-work, collecting and collating the evidence.

The data was collected in two ways. First, the commissioners devised three different questionnaires. Two were sent to parishes in rural areas and the third to parishes in towns. Around ten percent of the parishes replied: there was no compulsion to do so, but from this first trawl came an immense amount of information that was difficult to analyse. So difficult, in fact, that assistant commissioners were sent out to talk to the poor, attend vestry meetings and magistrates' sessions. The assistant commissioners were hard-working and in receipt of a daily allowance, not a salary. Each was given responsibility for a specific district in which to conduct their enquiries. Between them they visited around 3,000 parishes, covering about one-fifth of the Poor Law districts. All the information they collected was published by the commissioners in 13 volumes of appendices to their report.

Unsurprisingly, the assistant commissioners found what they were looking for. Indeed, the questions were skewed in order to elicit the answers that were required – or that at least were ambiguous and open to interpretation. A prime example was the use of the word 'allowance' in the questionnaires, which was interpreted in different ways by different informants. The final report made it appear that allowances to supplement wages (as in the Speenhamland system) were commonplace, ignoring the fact that these systems had largely died out in the 1820s. In reality, most parishes did not increase relief until the birth of a third or even a fourth child. Many of the interviews were similarly skewed, as witnesses were led along predetermined paths. This made it possible for a report to be constructed that was seemingly based on a mass of evidence, but which in fact obscured the complexity of existing poor relief. Any challenge to the conclusions drawn from the 'evidence' that filled nine volumes would be time consuming and very difficult.

Flawed as it was, this survey was the first of its kind and it would be unrealistic, even setting aside the bias of the commissioners, to expect a more systematic and sophisticated approach to have been taken. Furthermore, it must be remembered that the enquiry was not intended to be impartial.

KEY TERM

Parliamentary Reform Act 1832
An Act that extended the franchise so that one adult male in seven had the vote in general elections, and reorganised the constituencies to give greater representation to the industrialising Midlands and the North.

1841 – Poor Law Commission sets rules, regulations and disciplines to be observed in workhouses

1844 – General Outdoor Relief Prohibitory Order. This applied to all unions and forbade outdoor relief to the able-bodied poor

1840	1841	1842	1843	1844	1845

1842 – Labour Test Orders state that outdoor relief can only be given in return for some form of parish work and may not be given wholly in cash

Its function was to focus specifically on how the old Poor Law worked with a view to reforming it. The maintenance of the status quo was not an option. Interestingly and significantly, later investigations by historians, demographers and economists have reached the conclusion that relief under the old Poor Law was essentially a response to, and not the cause of, population growth, low wages and underemployment. The Royal Commission's report argued the exact opposite.

SOURCE

1 From the reports of assistant commissioners and published in the appendix to the *Report of the Royal Commission on the Poor Laws*, published in 1834. They were intended to provide evidence in support of the need for change to the 'old' poor laws.

From the evidence of Mr Richmond, one of the guardians of the poor in St Luke's parish, Middlesex.

When I came into office it was a recognised principle that purchase of commodities for relief of the poor should be confined to the tradesmen of the parish. This patronage was exercised by those who were themselves shopkeepers or connected with shopkeepers. For several years I have contended, unsuccessfully, for the universal application of the principle that contracts should be given to those who made the lowest tenders. On investigating the purchase of goods within the parish, I found that some of the charges were upwards of forty per cent above the market prices.

From the evidence of Thomas King, a victualler, whose poor rate was assessed at £6. Here he complains about the effect of the Labour Rate.

It has a very injurious effect on me, as it charges me for labour which I do not need, unless I stand still myself in order to have a man do the work which I can do myself.

From the report of Assistant Commissioner S. Walcott, North Wales.

As a body, I found the annual overseers wholly incompetent to discharge the duties of their office. This was either because of the demands of their private occupations, or from a lack of experience and skill, or both. Their object is to get through the year with as little unpopularity and trouble as possible. Their successors, therefore, complain of demands left unsettled, and rates uncollected, either from carelessness or a desire to gain popularity from having called for fewer assessments than usual.

What did the Royal Commission's report recommend?

Published in early 1834, the first part of the report attacked the old Poor Law, citing examples of corrupt practices and demoralised paupers. The second part contained the commissioners' conclusions and recommendations. Throughout, the reader is led inexorably to one conclusion: that the old Poor Law was itself the cause of poverty. At the core of the commissioners' analysis was their unshaken belief in the need to keep the distinction between poverty, which was part of the natural order of things, and indigence – the inability to earn enough to live on – which was not. The commissioners, too, had no problem with the impotent poor – those who could not work. They clearly had to be cared for in an appropriate way. Their problem, as generations before them had found, and generations after were to find, was with the able-bodied poor who either could not, or would not, earn sufficient income to keep themselves from grinding poverty.

The commissioners recommended radical changes, designed to save money and improve efficiency.

- Separate workhouses should be provided for the aged and infirm, children, able-bodied women and able-bodied men.

- Parishes should group into unions for the purpose of providing these workhouses.

- All relief outside workhouses should stop, and conditions inside workhouses should be such that no one would willingly enter them.

- A new, central authority should be established, with powers to make and enforce regulations concerning the workhouse system.

Aims of Poor Law policy

The aims of the policy were to:

- reduce the cost of providing relief for the poor

- ensure that only the genuinely destitute received relief

- provide a national system of poor relief.

What were the main terms of the 1834 Poor Law Amendment Act?

The bill reflected closely the recommendations of the report of the Poor Law Commission and the report itself, its supporters argued, was based on a mass of carefully collected evidence. What was more, the bill did exactly what MPs and the Lords wanted: it aimed to reduce the cost of providing for the poor by providing for them efficiently. Significantly, what opposition there was to the bill in the Commons came from MPs in the industrial west Midlands and north of England. There was little opposition as the bill went through its various stages to become an Act.

Why, indeed, should there be any opposition? The Tories, who might have stood out against it as an encroachment on traditional paternalism, were in a minority in the Commons and were overwhelmed by the arguments of the Whigs, seduced as they were by utilitarian arguments. Leading Whigs like Brougham, Althorp, Russell and Lansdowne were receptive to ideas of change. Indeed, several of them had helped create the climate of change. Brougham, for example, had contributed to the *Edinburgh Review*, a journal that throughout the 1820s published a stream of articles on social problems of the day. Thus, it was not surprising that old-stagers – radicals like William Cobbett who argued that the poor had a right to relief and that the object of the bill was to rob the poor and enrich the landowner – were barely listened to. Most of those who argued against the bill were not concerned with its underpinning philosophy. They were more worried by the centralisation involved, and the increased opportunities for patronage this would provide. But theirs were voices in the wilderness.

The purpose of the Act was to radically reform the system of poor relief in England and Wales, making it cost effective and efficient. To this end, it laid down that:

- a central authority should be set up to supervise the implementation and regulate the administration of the Poor Law

- parishes were to be grouped together to form Poor Law unions in order to provide relief efficiently

- each Poor Law union was to establish a workhouse in which inmates would live in conditions that were worse than those of the poorest independent labourer

- outdoor relief for the able-bodied poor was to be discouraged but, significantly, was not abolished.

However, the actual programme of reform was not laid down by parliament. Parliament simply set down the administrative arrangements through which the three commissioners were to implement and, indeed, interpret the Act.

ACTIVITY
KNOWLEDGE CHECK

The Royal Commission and the Poor Law Amendment Act

1 What were the strengths and what were the weaknesses of the report of the Royal Commission on the Poor Laws?

2 Read Source 1. How far would the Poor Law Amendment Act meet these concerns?

EXTEND YOUR KNOWLEDGE

The Poor Law Amendment Act and bastardy

The original Poor Law Amendment bill included a clause that made illegitimate children (referred to as bastards, and illegitimacy as bastardy) the sole responsibility of their mothers. This was a break with the past. The administrators of the old Poor Law pursued fathers of illegitimate children in an attempt to force them to contribute to their children's upkeep. Affiliation orders, whereby the relationship between father and child was legally determined, were made by a single magistrate. Why change a system that worked? The change was mainly due to the prevailing belief, expressed by men in the evidence collected by the male assistant commissioners and reinforced by evangelicals, that working-class women were immoral, lying predators, who nine times out of ten seduced the men who fathered their children. It was not the Commons but the Lords who protested at this change. The Bishop of Exeter launched an attack on the bastardy clauses, with the Bishop of London defending them fiercely. In the end a compromise was reached. Affiliation could continue, but it had to be determined by two magistrates at the quarter sessions (law courts held four times a year in every county). The expense of doing this made such affiliation actions impossible for the poor. If an affiliation order was successful, maintenance payments ceased when the child was seven years old, and fathers could not be prosecuted for non-payment.

How was the Poor Law Commission set up?

A central Poor Law Commission was established to administer the Poor Law Amendment Act throughout the country. The commission worked in Somerset House, London; there were three commissioners:

- Thomas Frankland Lewis, who had been a Tory MP actively involved in the Sturges-Bourne's select committee of 1817–18 (see Chapter 3, page 73)

- George Nicholls, a retired sea captain and bank of England official, who had been a radical overseer in Nottingham under the old Poor Law

- John Shaw-Lefevre, a lawyer who had been a Whig MP and under-secretary of state for war and the colonies.

The secretary to the commission was the utilitarian lawyer, Edwin Chadwick.

The commissioners were assisted by nine assistant commissioners (the number varied over time), whose job it was to make sure that decisions made centrally were implemented at local level in the parishes.

What power did the commission have?

The commission was independent of parliament, which was at once its great strength and its great weakness. Independence meant that the commission had no spokesman in parliament to defend it against the criticisms levelled against it by MPs. Outside parliament – in the press, books and journals, songs and broadsides – the commissioners were lampooned, and in the parishes, commissioners and assistant commissioners were almost universally hated.

The commission had a powerful constitutional position because it had been established by parliament, but it did not have the direct power that many people assumed it could wield. The commissioners could issue directives, draw up regulations and monitor their implementation, but in reality there was no mechanism for making recalcitrant parishes do what they were told. The commission did, however, have a considerable range of negative powers at its disposal. It could, for example, veto appointments it thought unsuitable; refuse to allow certain types of building; set **dietaries** for the workhouses; centralise accounting procedures; and generally make life very difficult for those parishes that opposed it.

What was the Poor Law Commission's work, 1834–47?

The Poor Law Commission policy, after 1834, had two priorities:

- the transfer of out-of-work and underemployed workers in rural areas to urban areas where employment was plentiful

- the protection of urban ratepayers from a sudden surge of demand from rural migrants prior to their obtaining regular employment.

It was possible to meet both priorities. A programme of workhouse construction met the first one: the setting up of a string of workhouses, offering relief to the able-bodied poor on the less eligibility principle (see Chapter 3, page 74), would, it was anticipated, drive potential paupers to find work in towns and cities. The Settlement Laws tackled the second priority: the poor rates would be kept low, and would not fall disproportionately on the towns if the Settlement Laws were stringently applied, returning the seekers of relief to their home parishes.

> **KEY TERM**
>
> Dietary
> Types and amounts of food that could be supplied by a workhouse for their resident paupers.

Priority 1: A programme of workhouse construction

SOURCE
2
A photograph of the workhouse in Oundle, Northamptonshire, taken in 1894. The workhouse was built in the years 1836–37, using £4,400 authorised by the Poor Law commissioners for its construction, and was built to house up to 150 paupers.

The programme of reducing able-bodied pauperism by building deterrent workhouses carried with it the assumption that outdoor relief for the able-bodied poor would stop, even though it was not expressly forbidden by the Poor Law Amendment Act 1834. In this key area, the commissioners were only able to act fairly slowly. Amalgamating unions and building or adapting workhouses took time, even when there was no organised opposition (see pages 101–06) against the implementation of the Act. The commission then acted to try to forbid outdoor relief for the able-bodied poor.

- Throughout the 1830s, the commission began issuing orders to specific unions in the rural south of England, prohibiting outdoor relief to the able-bodied poor.

- This was extended to the rural north of England in 1842.

- The 1844 General Outdoor Relief Prohibitory Order applied to all unions and forbade outdoor relief to the able-bodied poor.

However, the issuing of orders and directives was one thing. Their implementation and effectiveness, as the commissioners were to find, was quite another. Outdoor relief did continue, and continued to be the most common form of relief given to paupers, particularly in industrial northern towns. These towns were subject to enormous swings of cyclical unemployment beyond the control of mill and factory owners. There, outdoor relief was not only the most humane of alternatives, it was also the cheaper alternative to building huge workhouses that would remain half empty for most of a working year.

Priority 2: The Settlement Laws

Settlement legislation had been in operation since the 16th century (see page 66) and here, in the mid-19th century, the Settlement Laws were seen as necessary if the cost of maintaining paupers was to be fairly spread between urban and rural parishes, and if workhouses were indeed to be true deterrents. By 1840, around 40,000 paupers had been removed from the parishes in which they were living and claiming relief, back to their parishes of settlement, theirs by virtue of birth or marriage. This was a costly process, both in practical and administrative terms, whilst the cost in terms of human suffering was incalculable.

A Level Exam-Style Question Section B

How accurate is it to say that the recommendations of the Royal Commission's report on the poor laws fully met the concerns of those who wanted the old Poor Law reformed? (20 marks)

Tip
Focus on the word 'fully' when you match the recommendations of the report to the various pressures for reform.

The role of Edwin Chadwick

Working for two years as Jeremy Bentham's secretary, Edwin Chadwick became a fervent believer in the doctrine of Utilitarianism (see Chapter 3, page 82) and, because of the roles he played, this permeated the Royal Commission's report, the Poor Law Amendment Act and the work of the commission in implementing the Act.

A young barrister, Chadwick, was first appointed to the Royal Commission as an assistant commissioner, where his prodigious output as an investigator and report writer led to his rapid promotion to the post of commissioner. Indeed, his skill was so exceptional that he and Nassau Senior wrote the final report between them. Senior wrote the first part of the report, detailing the abuses that had been uncovered; Chadwick wrote the second part, setting out the remedial measures that had to be taken if the poor laws were to be put onto a sound footing. It is clear that here his object was to deter applications for relief by making both the relief itself, and the conditions under which it was given, repugnant. This was driven by the principle of less eligibility, which ensured that the condition of the pauper was worse than the poorest person not in receipt of relief. This could be achieved by making relief available only in a workhouse, whereby the workhouse test – their preparedness to enter such an institution in order to obtain relief – would be a genuine test of their destitution.

Drafting the parliamentary bill was the responsibility of the parliamentary solicitor John Meadows White, assisted by Nassau Senior and William Sturges-Bourne. But Chadwick's influence was not absent. His 'Notes for the Heads of a Bill', which he had written even before the report was finalised and which set out his recommendations for what should be included in the bill, was circulated to cabinet ministers as well as to his fellow commissioners. Two important recommendations made by these notes, and which did not appear in the report, were firstly that local control of poor relief should be vested in elected boards of guardians, and secondly that magistrates could become *ex officio* Poor Law guardians. Both these recommendations were implemented.

Chadwick, who had been the driving force behind both the report and the Act, fully expected to be appointed as one of the three Poor Law commissioners, charged with implementing the Act. Indeed, it has been argued that the recommendations of the report and the subsequent Act were less than specific because Chadwick had expected to be implementing them himself, along the utilitarian lines he wanted. Nassau Senior recommended his appointment but was overruled by the Cabinet who believed Chadwick was not of sufficient rank to make his appointment acceptable. He was, instead, made secretary to the commission. Bitterly disappointed and clashing frequently with the commissioners, Chadwick used his influence to the full for 14 years. He issued literally hundreds of notes, circulars, regulations and replies to queries from parishes in a determined attempt to impose his understanding of the doctrine of Utilitarianism on the operation of the new Poor Law.

EXTRACT

1 From E.C. Midwinter *Victorian Social Reform* (1968). Here he is writing about Edwin Chadwick.

His austere and severe pedantry gained him many enemies, not least in Parliament, amongst the working classes and on the press. John Walter, of *The Times* carried on a virulent campaign against him. Like many an incorruptible, he was unattractive; like many an enthusiast, he was impatient and abrasive.

In his grim way, the greatest happiness for him was synonymous with gross national product. Unimpeded, men would contribute to this as richly as possible, but impeded they were, particularly by disease, crime and pauperdom. The synthetic allowance system, by subvening wages, dislodged the free play of the labour market, and the individual, whether employer or employee, was unable to buy and sell in labour naturally. The allowance system stopped labour from finding its free and natural level by creating a system in which the pauper was better off than the labourer. Edwin Chadwick promulgated the belief in 'less eligibility'. Outdoor relief would be abolished and the workhouse test would be imposed on the potential pauper. Life in the workhouse would be so dreary and unpleasant that it would be 'less eligible' or attractive than the lowest form of work, and men would automatically be forced on to the labour market.

Chadwick and his henchmen were probably helped by one critical factor: namely the pressure of the problem on the commercial and industrial classes. Not only were they paying most heavily in rates, but it was their businesses that suffered from whatever was synthetic in the labour market.

Edwin Chadwick and the poor laws (1800–90)

1 Edwin Chadwick was a strong believer in the doctrine of Utilitarianism. Explain how this doctrine can be seen in the *Report of the Royal Commission on the Poor Laws*, which was largely the work of Chadwick.

2 Chadwick was secretary to the Poor Law Commission. To what extent did the Poor Law Commission's work in 1834–47 reflect his Utilitarianism?

3 Using Extract 1, set up a debate in which one side argues in favour of the beneficial impact Chadwick had on the changes to the poor laws, and the other side argues that his impact was harmful.

WHAT IMPACT DID THE WORKHOUSE HAVE ON THE LIVES OF PAUPERS?

The workhouse was intended to be the last refuge for the destitute. It was intended that the principle of less eligibility, together with the deterrent conditions offered by the workhouse test, would be self-regulating. However, conditions inside workhouses could not, insofar as cleanliness, food and clothing were concerned, be made deliberately worse than the poorest labourer living outside. The state could not be seen to institutionalise dirt, disease and starvation. What was to be done? The Poor Law Commission attempted, in the face of this problem, to make the workhouses repellent by insisting on a monotonous routine and strict discipline, by building workhouses that looked like prisons and by trying in every way to dehumanise the paupers by removing from them their own individual identities. In these ways, the commission argued, the principle of less eligibility would be upheld. However, regardless of the intentions of the Poor Law reformers, outdoor relief continued to be the most common form of relief given to those who sought help from the authorities.

Workhouse architecture: designed to deter?

The design and structure of workhouses were intended, in themselves, to act as a deterrent to would-be paupers. They were also supposed to instil discipline in the paupers they were designed to house. How were they to do this? Sampson Kempthorne, an architect with a London practice, was appointed architect to the Poor Law Commission in 1835. He produced designs for the approval of the Poor Law commissioners that were then issued to boards of guardians as indicative of the standards to which they should work when commissioning new workhouses or altering existing ones.

Kempthorne produced two basic designs.

- The Y-shaped workhouse, two or three storeys high, inside a hexagonal boundary wall is shown in Source 3. The boundary wall held workrooms; one wing of the Y, kitchen, dining hall and chapel; the other two wings, dormitories and day rooms. The master's rooms were in the middle of the Y, where he and his staff could watch the three exercise yards that were divided from each other by the wings of the Y. This design was intended to accommodate around 300 paupers.

- The cruciform-shaped workhouse, two storeys high, inside a square boundary wall is shown in Source 4. The wall held workrooms and the cruciform shape divided the space into four exercise yards. Each 'arm' of the cross held dormitories and dining rooms, a chapel and kitchens, schoolrooms and stores – sufficient accommodation for between 200 and 500 paupers.

Kempthorne's designs provided for the division and segregation of paupers. Segregation enabled the workhouse officers to provide appropriately for each class of pauper; it added to the deterrence factor by splitting up families, and prevented the moral 'contagion' that would occur if the different categories mixed freely. Paupers, as soon as they entered the workhouse, were beginning to lose their individuality and were beginning to be treated as impersonal units.

SOURCE 3

Sampson Kempthorne's design for a Y-shaped workhouse. One Poor Law union that adopted this design for its workhouses was the Winchester Union.

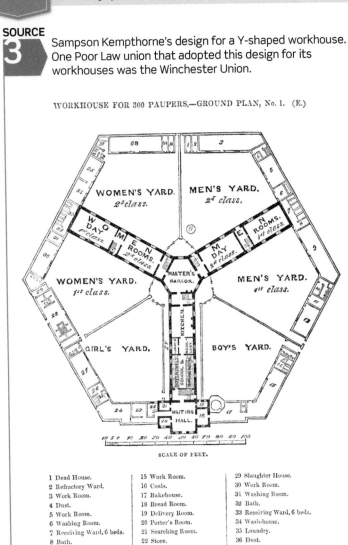

WORKHOUSE FOR 300 PAUPERS,—GROUND PLAN, No. 1. (E.)

1 Dead House.	15 Work Room.	29 Slaughter House.
2 Refractory Ward.	16 Coals.	30 Work Room.
3 Work Room.	17 Bakehouse.	31 Washing Room.
4 Dust.	18 Bread Room.	32 Bath.
5 Work Room.	19 Delivery Room.	33 Receiving Ward, 6 beds.
6 Washing Room.	20 Porter's Room.	34 Wash-house.
7 Receiving Ward, 6 beds.	21 Searching Room.	35 Laundry.
8 Bath.	22 Store.	36 Dust.
9 Work Room.	23 Potatoes.	37 Washing Room.
10 Dust.	24 Coals.	38 Work Room.
11 Washing Room.	25 Receiving Ward, 4 beds.	39 Refractory Ward.
12 Flour and Mill Room.	26 Washing Room.	40 Dead House.
13 Washing Room.	27 Work Room.	41 Well.
14 Receiving Ward, 3 beds.	28 Piggery.	42 Passage.

SOURCE 4

Sampson Kempthorne's design for a cruciform workhouse. One Poor Law union that adopted this design for its workhouses was the Watford (Hertfordshire) Union.

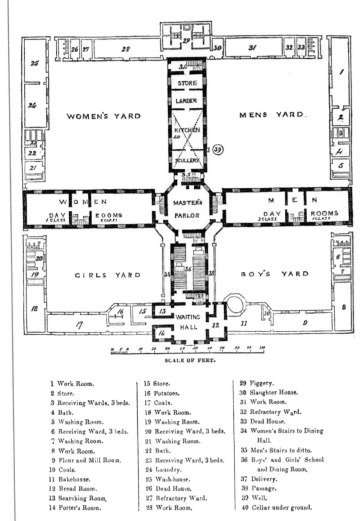

1 Work Room.	15 Store.	29 Piggery.
2 Store.	16 Potatoes.	30 Slaughter House.
3 Receiving Wards, 3 beds.	17 Coals.	31 Work Room.
4 Bath.	18 Work Room.	32 Refractory Ward.
5 Washing Room.	19 Washing Room.	33 Dead House.
6 Receiving Ward, 3 beds.	20 Receiving Ward, 3 beds.	34 Women's Stairs to Dining Hall.
7 Washing Room.	21 Washing Room.	35 Men's Stairs to ditto.
8 Work Room.	22 Bath.	36 Boys' and Girls' School and Dining Room.
9 Flour and Mill Room.	23 Receiving Ward, 3 beds.	37 Delivery.
10 Coals.	24 Laundry.	38 Passage.
11 Bakehouse.	25 Wash-house.	39 Well.
12 Bread Room.	26 Dead House.	40 Cellar under ground.
13 Searching Room.	27 Refractory Ward.	
14 Porter's Room.	28 Work Room.	

Workhouse regime: designed to demoralise?

Workhouses had to provide for the most vulnerable and needy members of society, both as transient and as long-term inmates. They had, too, to impose the workhouse test to ensure that the principle of less eligibility was being maintained. Inevitably, these demands and expectations conflicted as boards of guardians struggled to match their own prejudices and preconceptions with the demands of their localities and the requirements of the Poor Law commissioners.

Routine, rules and regulations

Every aspect of workhouse life was governed by a stream of rules and regulations laid down by the commissioners in London. The routine was designed to be unpleasant and was intended to deter people from seeking relief.

- On entry to a workhouse, the pauper family was given a medical inspection and then split up. Husbands were separated from wives and parents from their children, although mothers did usually stay with their children until they were about seven years old. The assumption was that the pauper had given up all responsibility for his family and so was separated from it.

- Children were sent to the workhouse school and, when they were nine or ten years old, apprenticed (often to the cotton mills of Lancashire) without their parents' consent and sometimes without their knowledge.

- Paupers had to wear a workhouse uniform that sometimes fitted them and sometimes did not. Guardians were allowed to add variety to the uniform clothing, but few of them did.

- Men were given razors to shave once a week and all paupers had a weekly bath. Workhouse staff watched while this happened. This was to prevent any attempt at self-mutilation or drowning and to add to the sense of loss of personal privacy.

- No personal possessions were allowed and there were no lockers or cupboards in which paupers could put clothes or shoes. This was to prevent any expression of individuality.

- The daily routine was designed to be boring and monotonous:

07.00–08.00	Breakfast
08.00–12.00	Work
12.00–13.00	Dinner
13.00–18.00	Work
18.00–19.00	Supper
20.00	Bedtime

Each day began and ended with prayers; the routine was set to start an hour earlier in the summer.

Work

It was essential that workhouse inmates worked. The primary aim of this work was to rehabilitate the paupers and restore them to the workforce outside. As an aim, this was laudable, but when it was translated into practice huge problems arose, both of an ideological and practical nature.

- The work had to be available in the locality of the workhouse, and it had to be possible to do it inside the confines of the workhouse.

- It could not diminish available employment outside the workhouse to the extent that the able-bodied working poor became paupers.

- The philosophical stance of the commissioners made the situation even more difficult. They held that work done inside the workhouse could not pay more than it cost the workhouse to maintain the pauper. If it did, they argued, there would be no incentive for the pauper to return to the labour market.

So, with these constraints, what work was done?

- Some paupers, mainly women and children, worked to help maintain the workhouse. They worked in the laundries, kitchens and sick rooms. They worked as cleaners, attendants, childminders and sloppers-out.

- If work that was economical and easy to perform within a workhouse could not be found, dispiriting and monotonous work was given to the paupers. They made sacks and unravelled ropes so that the fibres could be used again; they chopped wood and smashed limestone into small pieces to make roads; and they ground animal bones into dust to be used by farmers as fertiliser. Paupers were, by and large, doing the same work as convicts and with the same attendant degradation.

Dietaries

The supply of food to paupers, while it just about kept them alive, served also to degrade and to discipline. The Poor Law commissioners issued six model diets from which boards of guardians could choose the one, or ones, that best suited their pockets and inclinations. Here, again, the principle of less eligibility had to hold sway, as far as possible, but many urban and rural able-bodied poor were only just about existing on what amounted to a subsistence-level diet outside the workhouse. Not even the most badly disposed guardians would want to take their paupers right to the edge of starvation. So, the aim of the published dietaries was to sustain and maintain life, but to make mealtimes as boring and tedious as possible. Paupers were to get no pleasure from the food they ate.

The way in which meals were taken was designed to instil repressive uniformity. Until 1842, all meals were to be eaten in silence. Paupers had the right to have their food weighed in front of them; many workhouses used this regulation to delay the serving of food until it was stone cold, thus further adding to pauper humiliation.

There were, too, other ways to degrade. The meat, oatmeal, cheese and bread that formed the mainstay of pauper meals were of poor quality and often adulterated. The meals themselves were poorly and carelessly prepared and cooked. In the 1830s, some workhouses did not allow paupers to use cutlery, and they were forced to scoop up their food with their hands and drink from bowls.

SOURCE 5

The dietary used in the Stafford Union workhouse in the 1840s.

Dietary for able bodied Men and Women.

		Breakfast.		Dinner.					Supper.*		
		Bread.	Gruel.	Bread.	Cooked Meat.	Potatoes.	Soup.	Suet or rice Pudding.	Bread.	Cheese.	Gruel or Broth.
		oz.	Pints.	oz.	oz.	lb.	Pints.	oz.	oz.	oz.	Pints.
SUNDAY	Men	6	1½	4	5	½	–	–	6	–	1½
	Women	5	1½	3	5	½	–	–	5	–	1½
MONDAY	Men	6	1½	4	–	–	1½	–	6	1	–
	Women	5	1½	3	–	–	1½	–	5	1	–
TUESDAY	Men	6	1½	4	–	–	1½	–	6	–	1½
	Women	5	1½	3	–	–	1½	–	5	–	1½
WEDNESDAY	Men	6	1½	4	–	–	1½	–	6	1	–
	Women	5	1½	3	–	–	1½	–	5	1	–
THURSDAY	Men	6	1½	4	5	½	–	–	6	–	1½
	Women	5	1½	3	5	½	–	–	5	–	1½
FRIDAY	Men	6	1½	–	–	–	–	14	6	–	1½
	Women	5	1½	–	–	–	–	12	5	–	1½
SATURDAY	Men	6	1½	4	–	–	1½	–	6	1	–
	Women	5	1½	3	–	–	1½	–	5	1	–

OLD PEOPLE, of 60 years of age, and upwards may be allowed 1oz. of Tea, 5oz. of Butter, and 7oz. of Sugar per week, in lieu of Gruel for Breakfast, if deemed expedient to make this change.

CHILDREN, under 9 years of age, to be dieted at discretion, above 9 to be allowed the same quantities as Women.

SICK to be dieted as directed by the Medical Officer.

*SUPPER---The Gruel or Broth may be substituted for the Cheese, and vice versa.

H. BRADFORD, PRINTER, THAME.

SOURCE 6

A cartoon, published in 1840, comparing meals under the old and the new poor laws.

Discipline

Workhouses were often rowdy places. Staff and paupers frequently hurled verbal and physical abuse at one another. Disturbances ranged from full-scale riots to the swift exchange of foul language. Among the paupers themselves, there were frequent outbreaks of bullying and blackmail, and there are recorded instances of sexual abuse between staff and paupers and between pauper and pauper.

Workhouse staff used a complicated system of rewards and punishments to maintain order. Paupers could be punished for being in the wrong part of the building, making too much noise, working too slowly or cheeking a member of staff. On the other hand, paupers could be rewarded with food, 'clean' jobs or pocket money. Paupers were usually very clear as to which of them were favoured by the authorities and which were not. Often, systems of rewards and punishments had no legal backing and had grown up through custom. There were, however, specific punishments laid down by the Poor Law commissioners, and a standard punishment book was kept in which all punishments were formally recorded.

In some ways, many punishments were enlightened. Under the old Poor Law, paupers were very much at the mercy of the overseer, who could, and did, abuse paupers with impunity. Operating within the new system, the guardians and staff did at least know that there were limits to their powers and that these limits were determined and universally applied by the Poor Law commissioners. Girls and women, for example, could not be beaten; although the reduction of rations was a common punishment, there was a minimum below which they could not be reduced. Most workhouses had punishment cells, and paupers were shut up there for minor misdemeanours. Some workhouse masters developed their own refinements, such as forcing recalcitrant paupers to spend the night in the workhouse mortuary. For more serious crimes, the usual processes of the law came into play.

Part of the problem in trying to manage an orderly workhouse was that a proportion of the population of paupers was mobile. These transient, itinerant paupers – drifting in and out of relief – brought with them the tensions, stresses and petty crime of the outside world. Indeed, all paupers were free to come and go as they pleased: only three hours' notice was required if paupers wanted their own clothes returned so that they could leave. Workhouse staff could not prevent paupers from leaving; neither could they refuse to readmit them. Many paupers exploited this to the full. It was not until 1871 that an Act of Parliament gave guardians the power to limit the number of times a pauper could leave the workhouse.

SOURCE

Extracts from workhouse rules of conduct, laid down by the Poor Law Commission and published in their *Seventh Annual Report*, 1841.

WORKHOUSE (Rules of Conduct)

Any pauper who shall neglect to observe such of the regulations herein contained as are applicable to and binding on him:

Or who shall make any noise when silence is ordered to be kept; or shall use obscene or profane language; or shall by any word or deed insult or revile any person; or shall threaten to strike or to assault any person; or shall not duly cleanse his person; or shall refuse or neglect to work, after having been required to do so; or shall pretend sickness; or shall play at cards or other games of chance; or shall enter, or attempt to enter, without permission, the ward or yard appointed to any class of paupers other than that to which he belongs; or shall misbehave in going to, at, or returning from public worship out of the workhouse, or at prayers in the workhouse; or shall wilfully disobey any lawful order of any officer of the workhouse;

Shall be deemed DISORDERLY

Any pauper who shall, within seven days, repeat any one or commit more than one of the offences specified, or shall by word or deed insult or revile the master or matron, or any other officer of the workhouse, or any of the Guardians; or shall be drunk; or shall unlawfully strike or otherwise unlawfully assault, any person; or shall wilfully or mischievously damage or soil any property whatsoever belonging to the Guardians; or shall wilfully disturb the other inmates during prayers or divine worship

Shall be deemed REFRACTORY

It shall be lawful for the master of the workhouse to punish any disorderly pauper by substituting, during a time not greater than forty-eight hours, for his or her dinner, as prescribed by the dietary, a meal consisting of eight ounces of bread, or one pound of cooked potatoes and also by withholding from him during the same period, all butter, cheese, tea, sugar or broth.

A Level Exam-Style Question Section A

Study Source 7 before you answer this question.

Assess the value of the source for revealing paupers' experience of workhouse life and the attitudes of the Poor Law commissioners to paupers.

Explain your answer, using the source, the information given about its origin and your own knowledge about the historical context. (20 marks)

Tip
Remember that these are rules: they don't describe life in any one workhouse. However, the fact that these rules were deemed necessary means that some paupers in some workhouses behaved in these ways. In introducing these rules, consider how the Poor Law commissioners were attempting to uphold the principle of less eligibility.

What about the children?

The very act of entering a workhouse meant that a pauper child's parents had relinquished responsibility for that child. Children, it was believed, unlike their able-bodied parents, could not be held responsible for their own poverty. On the other hand, they were paupers and their situation, under the less eligibility rule, could not be made better than that of poor children outside the workhouse, but, in reality, it was better. Pauper children received a basic education in the workhouse, better medical attention than they could have hoped for outside and, when they were about nine years old, they were apprenticed to a trade.

However, the education was often rudimentary in the extreme and they could be apprenticed to any passing tradespeople and taken far away. Children, unlike pauper adults, could not leave a workhouse of their own free will; if they ran away and were caught, they would be returned. They quickly became institutionalised and unable to cope with life beyond the walls of the workhouse. It was the Education Act (Forster's Act) 1870 that placed the education of pauper children firmly within the elementary school system and so helped their integration into society.

Who were the new paupers?

Outdoor relief continued to be the main form of support for paupers, despite the best efforts of the commissioners. This means that any analysis of the types of people opting for, or forced into, indoor relief cannot be taken as typical of the pauper population as a whole. However, it is interesting to see just which people were given indoor relief and to bear this in mind when looking at workhouse provision, regimes and staff and evaluating them for fitness for purpose.

Workhouses provided both short- and long-term care, and at any one time around one-fifth of all inmates had been inside for five or more years. There were, of course, regional and local differences, but by and large pauper populations within workhouses were surprisingly similar in structure.

- Young people – for whom the workhouse provided a temporary shelter and a solution to a personal crisis – moved in and out of workhouses, maybe several times a year, depending on variables such as the seasonality of employment, the harshness of the winter or the severity of a local epidemic.

- Vagrants – who were considered less deserving than any 'settled' poor – were given overnight accommodation in a 'casual ward', to which they were not admitted until the evening, when they were fed a meal of bread and water. In the better workhouses, they were stripped, deloused and had their clothes disinfected. These people were considered to be the lowest of the low and believed to be beyond redemption: the only aim of workhouse staff was to get rid of them as soon as possible the following morning.

- The elderly – were provided with shelter and sustenance until death by the workhouse. In this group, old men were more prominent than old women. Women, when old, could more frequently be of domestic use to their families and so tended to be kept by their relatives rather than being sent 'on the parish'.

- Children – who made up between 25 and 40 percent of all admissions – were both long- and short-stay inmates. The offspring of the transient able-bodied poor went in and out with their parents. However, most workhouse children were abandoned, orphans or ill. Many were the illegitimate sons and daughters of other inmates and were likely to spend all their childhood and early adolescence in the workhouse.

- Single women – who could not claim outdoor relief – made up a significant proportion of any workhouse community and included widows, abandoned wives, single mothers and prostitutes.

- The mentally ill – grew from 1 per 100 to 1 per 8 inmates as the century progressed.

Workhouse staff: appointed to intimidate?

A workhouse, like any large institution, required staff for it to function at all efficiently. There had to be, for example, cleaners, porters, washerwomen, cooks, scullery maids and chimney sweeps. Some of this work was carried out by the paupers themselves; most by the poor who lived outside the workhouse and did menial work for long hours and low pay in order to keep themselves and their families out of the institution they helped to make function.

There were some key posts that were unique to the workhouse. The master and matron, for example, were the key individuals in a pauper's day-to-day life. The master was responsible for the discipline and economy of the workhouse; the matron for the female paupers and the domestic side of life. Cruel or kind, they both enjoyed tremendous power over staff and paupers, having enormous influence on the way the workhouse was run and on how it was perceived by the paupers inside and society outside. These people, and the staff they supervised, had it in their power to make a workhouse a place of grim terror and dread, or a place where the most vulnerable in society were given help when they most needed it. Three examples serve to exemplify the enormous range in skill, expertise and attitude.

- At Ashford (Kent), the union workhouse was run by a retired, and much decorated, naval officer and his wife. It was renowned for its efficiency and for its compassion, and held up by the commissioners as a model to which others should aspire. When the master retired, paupers wept.

- George Catch, an ex-policeman, moved from workhouse to workhouse in London, inflicting terror and cruelty wherever he went. Boards of guardians gave him excellent testimonials simply to get rid of him, and it was not until the 1860s when, after a career of depravity, corruption and murder, he finally threw himself under a Great Western train.

- The master of Cerne Abbas workhouse in Wiltshire lasted as master for just two weeks. He had little education and simply could not cope with the paperwork demanded by the commissioners. The guardians appointed the workhouse porter in his place.

SOURCE

Part of a letter written by Edwin Chadwick, to the clerk of the Board of Guardians, St Luke Chelsea, on 27 May 1843. Chadwick was secretary to the Poor Law Commission, and here he is criticising the way in which the Poor Law Amendment Act 1834 was being implemented in the Chelsea Union.

The poor Law Commissioners regret to learn that their Assistant Commissioner, Mr Hall, on visiting the Chelsea workhouse, found it in a very unsatisfactory state. There was throughout a want of order, cleanliness and ventilation, the heat in the female wards being excessive, in consequence of there being a number of unnecessarily large fires kept up. Some of the paupers were in their own clothes, Article 7 of the workhouse rules having been, in this case, neglected. Smoking was going on in several of the rooms, both bedrooms and day rooms. The Commissioners think the allowance of such a practice, particularly in the bedrooms, highly objectionable. The Commissioners also learn that extra articles of food are freely allowed to be brought into the workhouse. The Commissioners think it desirable that a dietary should be prescribed for the inmates of the workhouse. The practice of allowing provisions to be brought into the workhouse as presents cannot, in the opinion of the Commissioners, fail to produce Irregularities.

SOURCE

Part of a letter written by T.M. Loveland, clerk to the Board of Guardians, St Luke Chelsea, on 15 June 1843, to Edwin Chadwick in response to Chadwick's letter (Source 8). Here, Loveland rejects the complaints made by the assistant commissioner.

The guardians caused, on receipt of your letter, a minute inspection of the House to be made, and have to state, with the exception of the lack of a little whitewashing, and that only here and there, there is no lack of order, cleanliness or ventilation in the Chelsea workhouse, as erroneously stated in your letter.

As to the charge of 'the heat in the female wards being excessive', the guardians find that there has been for some time past but one fire, and that only a moderate one, in the infirm ward. As to some of the paupers wearing their own clothing, there are some who do; but they are of the elder class, and who have been allowed to wear their own clothes on account of their former respectability. The guardians find smoking is confined to five old infirm women, who smoke medicinally. Some old men also smoke, but which is allowed by the guardians. As to 'extra articles of food', these, the presents of friends, have been permitted, but it is only to a trifling extent.

A Level Exam-Style Question Section B

'The workhouse system in the years 1834–47 failed to uphold the principle of less eligibility.' How far do you agree with this statement? (20 marks)

Tip

Consider the ways in which the principle of less eligibility was met and the ways in which it could not be, and was not, met before reaching a judgement.

ACTIVITY
KNOWLEDGE CHECK

Implementing the Poor Law Amendment Act

1 Why did the Poor Law Amendment Act not forbid outdoor relief?

2 Look carefully at the two workhouse plans (Sources 3 and 4). In small groups, discuss the following questions:

   a) Which would be the more intimidating for paupers?

   b) Which would be the easiest to run for the workhouse staff?

   c) What criteria did you use when reaching your decisions?

3 To what extent was the workhouse regime designed to humiliate and depersonalise paupers? Use Sources 5 and 7 in your answer.

4 Look carefully at Source 6. What point is the cartoonist making? Discuss in your group whether the artist was for or against the new Poor Law.

5 Read Sources 8 and 9. How far do these sources, taken together, reveal the problems the Poor Law Commission had in implementing their directives?

THINKING HISTORICALLY   Change (8 a, b & c) (I)

Imposing realities

A women's yard in a union workhouse.

Answer the following:

1 Explain why the conversation in the illustration would not have happened.

The shape of history is imposed by people looking back. People who lived through the 'history' did not always perceive the patterns that later historians identify. For example, some people living through the Industrial Revolution may have understood that great change was taking place, but they would not have been able to understand the massive economic, social and political consequences of industrialisation.

2 Consider the implementation of the doctrine of Utilitarianism.

   a) Who would have made the decision that it should be implemented?

   b) Could anybody have challenged this decision?

   c) Explain why someone living in the mid-19th century would not have been able to make a judgement about the long-term consequences of the implementation of the doctrine of Utilitarianism.

3 Who living at the present time might regard the implementation of the doctrine of Utilitarianism as an important event?

4 What does this illustration tell us about the structure of history as we understand it?

HOW EFFECTIVE WAS OPPOSITION TO THE IMPLEMENTATION OF THE POOR LAW AMENDMENT ACT?

Out in the parishes, it was mostly fear and anger that greeted the Poor Law Amendment Act and the ways in which it was implemented, but this fear and anger were not universal and they found expression in different ways and at different times. In parts of Cumbria and north Yorkshire, for example, where there were few able-bodied male paupers, the Act was considered irrelevant and protest against it unnecessary. Indeed, the Carlisle Union continued to divide its applicants into deserving and undeserving poor and treated them accordingly. However, where communities were outraged by the changes in tradition and practice brought about by the Act, there was an almost universal coming together of the powerful and influential with the poor and dispossessed to protest jointly.

Rumour and propaganda

Fear thrives on rumour, and propaganda makes good use of both rumour and the fear that feeds it. This is common in all stressful situations and the period when the Poor Law Amendment Act was being implemented was no exception.

- Union workhouses were built some distance from the homes of most of those seeking relief. This fuelled the belief among the poor that they were extermination centres where paupers were helped effortlessly from life in an attempt to keep the poor rates low.

- The *Book of Murder*, widely circulated and erroneously believed to be the work of the Poor Law commissioners, contained suggestions that pauper children should be gassed.

- In Devon, many of the poor believed that bread distributed as part of outdoor relief was poisoned in order to reduce those claiming this form of relief.

- Rumours circulated that all children over and above the first three in a pauper's family were to be killed.

- Many anti-Poor Law campaigners believed that the new Poor Law was introduced specifically to lower the national wage bill. Workhouses, it was argued, were supposed to force people onto the labour market, no matter how low the wages. A variant on this theme was the belief that mill owners in the North wanted unemployed agricultural workers from the south to work for them, so deliberately limiting rising wages and bringing about a workforce that lived at subsistence level.

Genuine fears

People's fears were based on individual perceptions of the way in which society should be organised.

- Many attacked the centralisation implicit in the new Poor Law. The commissioners were seen as being London-based, with no real concern for, or understanding of, the ways of life outside the metropolis.

- Many feared the replacement of the old Poor Law by the new would break the traditional, paternalistic bonds between rich and poor, which resulted in a kind of social contract.

- Rural ratepayers realised that outdoor relief was cheaper than indoor relief and were worried that a programme of workhouse building would lead to higher, not lower, poor rates.

- Ratepayers in northern industrial areas, prone to cyclical unemployment, realised that to build a workhouse large enough to contain all those who might need relief in times of depression would be an enormously costly undertaking, if not an impossible one.

Protest in the rural south

In 1835, the commissioners began their work in the most heavily pauperised districts of southern England, which was where most of the evidence came from that supported the report of the Poor Law Commission. Even though the implementation of the Act began here in a period of economic recovery when employment prospects were good for most labourers and fear of want was retreating, there were still sporadic outbursts of opposition. Local magistrates and clergy, angered at what they saw as unnecessary centralisation and the removal of the traditional master–servant relationship with its attendant responsibilities, joined with those of the poor who were alarmed and fearful, to protest. Two examples of different kinds of protest exemplify, firstly, protest against centralisation and removal, and, secondly, protest against the regime and institutionalism of the workhouse.

- In Buckinghamshire, people took to the streets when paupers from the old workhouse in Chalfont St Giles were being transported to the new union workhouse in Amersham. Only when the Riot Act was read, special constables sworn in and armed yeomanry put on the streets was it possible for the paupers to be transported the three miles to Amersham.

- In East Anglia, newly built workhouses were attacked, the one at St Clements in Ipswich being particularly badly damaged, and relieving officers assaulted. While the poor themselves took to the lanes and market squares of rural England, the more influential citizens used their positions to, for example, refuse to apply the less eligibility rule strictly, continue to provide outdoor relief to the able-bodied poor and generally to find all possible ways of circumventing what they saw as an inhumane and destructive law.

However, the recent fate of the Dorset labourers (the **Tolpuddle Martyrs**), sentenced to transportation for swearing illegal oaths, had tended to depress rural protest. By and large, most farmers and landowners, aided by good harvests and a more or less quiescent workforce, enabled the Poor Law Amendment Act to be put into practice in the south of England.

Opposition in the north: industrial Lancashire and West Yorkshire

In the north of England, it was a different matter. Edwin Chadwick urged an early start on unionising the industrial regions of Britain, while times were relatively prosperous. The commissioners ignored him. It was not until 1837, during the onset of a trade depression, that they turned their attention to the north of England and, in particular, to industrial Lancashire and the West Riding of Yorkshire.

Many areas had already adapted their relief provision to meet the cyclical depressions with which industry was beset. Guardians, magistrates, mill and factory owners resented interference from Londoners who had little knowledge of industrial conditions and whose report and subsequent Act were based upon an understanding of the rural south and bore little relevance to them. Workshop, factory and mill workers, facing lay-offs and short hours, needed short-term relief to tide them over periods of temporary unemployment, not removal of whole families to workhouses.

Organised and fired up by the demands of the **Ten Hours' Movement**, they turned to oppose what many saw as yet another assault on working people. Anti-Poor Law associations sprang up, utilising the already established network of short-term committees, uniting Tory paternalists like Richard Oastler and John Fielden with radical printers like R.J. Richardson and socialists like Laurence Pitkeithly. Huge public protest meetings were held, at which the commissioners of Somerset House and their '**bastilles**' were roundly denounced.

For a while, there was insurrection, as these examples show.

- Armed riots in Oldham, Rochdale, Todmorden, Huddersfield, Stockport, Dewsbury and Bradford were put down by the local militia.

- In Huddersfield, the guardian George Tinker warned the commissioners in 1837 that in the present alarming state of the district, it would be dangerous to put the law into operation.

- In Bradford in 1838, the assistant commissioner Alfred Power was threatened by the mob and pelted with stones and tin cans. Troops were sent out from London to quell the riots.

- London troops were sent to quell the 1838 riots in Dewsbury.

KEY TERMS

Tolpuddle Martyrs
In 1834, six agricultural workers from Tolpuddle, Dorset, led by George Loveless, were sentenced to seven years' transportation for swearing illegal oaths. The oath swearing was part of a loyalty ceremony that bound the men into a trade union. Although trade unions were not banned at the time, the government feared that unions of agricultural workers would heighten the general rural unrest and so used this device to nip such unions in the bud. After a series of mass campaigns, the men were pardoned and finally returned home.

The Ten Hours' Movement
A sustained campaign in the 1830s for the reduction of hours worked in textile mills to ten per day. The campaign was led inside parliament by Lord Shaftesbury and John Fielden, and outside by Richard Oastler. As part of the campaign, short-term committees were set up in most industrial towns to press for factory reform.

Bastille
A prison in Paris stormed by the mob at the beginning of the French Revolution in 1789. It came to be a symbol of despotic rule.

- The Poor Law Amendment Act could not be implemented in Todmorden, a Lancashire mill town, until 1877, because of the fierce opposition of mill owners and their workers.

- In Stockport in 1842, the workhouse was attacked and bread distributed to the poor outside.

SOURCE 10

From the 10 March 1838 edition of the **Chartist** newspaper the *Northern Star*. It was a Leeds-based radical newspaper established by its owner, Feargus O'Connor, in November 1837 and was fiercely critical of the Poor Law Amendment Act.

Fellow Rate-payers,

The time has come for you to give a practical demonstration of your hatred of the new Starvation law.

The 25th March is the day for the election of the new Guardians for the ensuing year; therefore it will depend on your exertions, whether you will allow men to be elected who are the mere tools of the three Commissioners in carrying out their diabolical schemes for starving the poor, reducing the labourers' wages and robbing you, the ratepayers of that control you have hitherto exercised over your money and your township's affairs; or will you elect men of character and humanity, who will prefer death itself rather than sacrifice the rights of their neighbours and constituents at the bidding of three pensioned Lawyers residing in London, and living in princely splendour out of your hard-earned money.

Ratepayers, do your duty and select none who are in the remotest degree favourable to the hellish Act. Remember that the law is cruel, illegal and unconstitutional. The real object of it is to lower wages and punish poverty as a crime. Remember also that children and parents are dying frequently in the same Bastille without seeing one another, of knowing of one another's fate.

KEY TERM

Chartist
A member of a working-class movement that emerged in the mid-1830s (see page 123). The aim of the movement was to gain political rights for working-class people.

What roles did Richard Oastler and John Fielden play in resisting the new Poor Law?

Richard Oastler, by 1834 when the Poor Law Amendment Act was passed, had been working very successfully for 14 years as the steward of Fixby, a large estate outside Huddersfield in West Yorkshire. The absentee landlord, Thomas Thornhill, knew about Oastler's support for the Ten Hours' Movement and to some extent sympathised with the movement's aims and to Oastler's involvement. Indeed, he had introduced Oastler to several leading politicians, including the Duke of Wellington, with whom Oastler had a long correspondence. However, it was Oastler's involvement in the anti-Poor Law agitation that was to lead to the withdrawal of Thornhill's support and Oastler's downfall.

Opposing the new Poor Law from the position of a factory reformer, Oastler believed the Poor Law commissioners were too powerful. Specifically, it was their ability to supply factories with cheap labour in the form of pauperised agricultural workers to which he objected. He believed this would lead to a reduction in factory wages and the consequent deterioration of the living conditions of the industrial working class. This, in turn, would lead to an increase in pauperism in the manufacturing towns and cities of the Midlands and the north. Oastler was also concerned at the amalgamation of parishes into larger units, believing that this would do away with the personal interaction between the giver and the receiver of relief, with the consequent depersonalisation of the system. An avid promoter of opposition to the introduction of the new Poor Law into the industrial north, by 1838 Oastler was urging workers to involve themselves in strikes and sabotage. Unsurprisingly, he led workers in violently resisting attempts to impose the new Poor Law in his local township of Fixby. Word of his involvement reached the commissioners in London, and Frankland Lewis approached Thomas Thornhill with a request for help in calming the situation and enabling the new Poor Law to be introduced into Fixby and surrounding areas. Thomas Thornhill's reaction was to dismiss Oastler immediately. Using legitimate means to press for factory reform was one thing; to defy the law of the land was, in Thornhill's view, quite another. This didn't stop Oastler campaigning. Indeed, freed from the necessity to run an estate, he had more time to urge working people to protest in every way possible. However, without an income, two years later he ended up in a debtors' prison. Such was the regard in which he was held amongst working people that Oastler committees were formed to raise the necessary money to ensure his release, and after four years they were successful.

SOURCE 11

From Richard Oastler *Damnation! Eternal Damnation to the Fiend-Begotten Coarser Food New Poor Law*, published in 1837.

CHRISTIAN READER

Be not alarmed at the sound of the title. I cannot bless that which GOD and NATURE CURSE. The Bible being true, the Poor Law Amendment Act is false! The Bible containing the will of God, – this accursed Act of parliament embodies the will of Lucifer[1]. It is the Sceptre of BELIAL[2], establishing its sway in the land of bibles!! DAMNATION; ETERNAL DAMNATION to the accursed Fiend!!

I tell you deliberately, if I have the misfortune to be reduced to poverty, that the man who dares tear me from the wife whom God hath joined to me, shall, if I have it in my power, receive his death at my hand! If I am ever confined in one of those hellish Poor Law Bastilles, and my wife torn from me because I am poor, I will, if possible, burn the whole pile to the ground.

RICHARD OASTLER

[1]Lucifer: the chief rebel angel, Satan, who became the Devil

[2]Belial: an alternative name for the Devil

John Fielden entered the Commons in 1832, representing the northern industrial town of Oldham along with William Cobbett (see Chapter 3, page 70). In the elections of 1835, 1837 and 1841, Fielden was again returned to the Commons by the Oldham electors. Radical in his views, Fielden was very much his own man with his own ideas; he sat with the Whigs in the House of Commons because he thought they were more likely to support radical measures than the Tories. However, he didn't always vote with them. Indeed, he voted against the Poor Law Amendment bill, which was a Whig measure, at every stage of its passage through the Commons. For years he tried in vain to get the Act repealed. Fielden worked as a member of the Commons committee in the years 1837–38, investigating the working of the new Poor Law. When the committee reported favourably, Fielden was vociferous in his criticism, claiming that it had only taken evidence from commissioners and from guardians known to be favourably disposed to the new law.

Fielden used his power, not only as an MP but also as a mill owner in Todmorden, Lancashire, where the cotton mills he owned with his brother were the largest employers in the area. An active member of the anti-Poor Law movement, Fielden was the only MP to attend the huge Yorkshire anti-Poor Law meeting at Hartshead Moor in May 1837 and, indeed, addressed the crowd. When the Poor Law commissioners tried to implement the new Poor Law in Todmorden, Fielden threatened to close down the family mills unless the guardians of the Poor Law union resigned. They refused – and the mills closed, throwing nearly 3,000 people out of work. The violence that ensued did not end when Fielden opened the mills after a week (paying the workers for the week they had not worked) and his workers attacked the homes of local guardians, requiring troops to restore order. Although Fielden himself was not involved in the riots, he refused to co-operate with the authorities in identifying the ringleaders and refused to pay poor rates. The situation in Todmorden remained so volatile that the new Poor Law was not implemented in Todmorden until 1877, long after Fielden's death.

SOURCE 12

From Poor Law Commission *Fourth Annual Report* 1838, describing the resistance to the implementation of the Poor Law Amendment Act that took place throughout 1838 in Todmorden and Langfield, where the Fielden brothers had their mills. They were the largest employers in the area.

In Todmorden Union, immediately on the introduction of the new system, an attempt was made by the partners of the manufactory to prevent the peaceful operation of the law, by throwing the whole of their workpeople at once out of employment, and closing their works. This attempt to intimidate the guardians by endangering the peace of the neighbourhood, having been defeated by the promptitude of the magistrates, and the steady determination of the guardians, Messrs Fielden, on the 16 day of July 1838, reopened their works.

On the guardians proceeding to assume the administration of relief, and to demand from the overseers of the several townships the sums necessary for this purpose, the overseers of Todmorden and Langfield (the townships in which Messrs Fielden's works are chiefly situated) adopted a course of passive resistance and disobedience to the law, in which they have persevered up to the present time. The overseers of the other townships having supplied the necessary funds, the guardians at once assumed the administration of relief to the poor of those townships. The poor of Todmorden and Langfield have not been relieved by the Board of Guardians for lack of necessary funds.

In the meantime the powers of the law have been exerted against the overseers of the two townships making default. The overseers of Todmorden have been convicted of a first and second offence under the 98th section of the Poor Law Amendment Act, and the fines of £51 in the first instance and of £20 in the second, have been levied by distress upon the goods of one of them. On 16th November last, two constables from Halifax, who were employed in executing a warrant of distress upon the overseers of Langfield, were violently assaulted and overpowered by a concourse of persons, the first assembling of which was accompanied by the ringing of a bell in one of Messrs Fielen's factories, from which a large number of workpeople issued, and took part in a riot which ensued. The two officers were stripped of their clothes, and otherwise brutally treated, and had great difficulty in escaping with their lives.

A Level Exam-Style Question Section A

Study Source 12 before you answer this question.

Assess the value of the source for revealing the extent of opposition in the north of England and the problems facing the commissioners as they tried to implement the Poor Law Amendment Act.

Explain your answer, using the source, the information given about its origin and your own knowledge about the historical context. (20 marks)

Tip
Think about the provenance of the source and whether the commissioners are likely to report in a biased way; consider, too, the significance of the fact that this is a report relating to one town in the north of England, whereas the Act was implemented nationally. How typical was the Todmorden reaction?

ACTIVITY
KNOWLEDGE CHECK

Opposition to the implementation of the new Poor Law

1 Why were working people so afraid of the new Poor Law?

2 Why do you think the commissioners, against the advice of Chadwick, began implementing the Poor Law Amendment Act in the south of England?

3 Why was there so much opposition to the implementation of the Poor Law Amendment Act in the north of England?

4 Read Sources 10 and 11. Which method of persuasion do you find most effective? Why? Would contemporaries have agreed with you? Give reasons for your answer.

5 Look at the opposition of Oastler and Fielden. Why, ultimately, were they unsuccessful?

How effective was the anti-Poor Law movement?

The anti-Poor Law movement was well organised and, as has been shown, very effective in the short term. However, despite the best efforts of the campaigners, the government was not going to back down and repeal the Poor Law Amendment Act 1834. It was, however, prepared to make concessions. In 1838, the General Prohibitory Order was set aside for unions in Lancashire and the West Riding of Yorkshire. There, the guardians were allowed to administer relief according to the provisions of the Elizabethan Poor Law 1601, and a considerable amount of discretion was permitted to guardians in negotiating local settlements. Very few workhouses, for example, were built until the 1850s and 1860s, and in Todmorden one was not built until 1877.

EXTRACT

2 From Alan Kidd *State, Society and the Poor in Nineteenth Century England*, published in 1999.

The Poor Law Commission began its work in the mid-1830s, steadily at first, establishing the union structures and issuing orders and regulations. But the administrative history of the New Poor Law in its first twenty years is one of conflict and compromise. In part, the compromise between central and local control represented in the New Poor Law is characteristic of the approach to government responsibility in the nineteenth century. But equally there was a mismatch between the intentions of central authority and the interests of many localities, especially in the industrial north.

How did it all end?

The new Poor Law was established relatively easily in other urban areas. The Metropolitan Anti-Poor Law Association, founded in London by Earl Stanhope, had little effect; there were few problems in the industrial north-east of England; a strike in the Potteries and a major recession in the stocking industry in Nottingham failed to push working people into protest. However, absence of violent protest did not necessarily mean acceptance. It was still possible for local boards of guardians, with an eye on local feelings, to ignore, adapt and amend directives from the commissioners, and many of them did.

Opposition was short lived. In many places, it was a spontaneous reaction to unwelcome change and, because it was mostly unorganised, had no chance of success. Even where opposition was organised, as with the anti-Poor Law associations of Lancashire and Yorkshire, the unlikely combination of paternalistic Tories and working-class radicals was bound to fall apart eventually. Those who remained to protest turned to Chartism, seeing working-class representation in the Commons the only hope of improving their lot. It ended, too, because ratepayers in the parishes saw an immediate change in the rates they paid.

Were the commission's priorities successfully met?

The two important planks of Poor Law policy after 1834 were not implemented as the Poor Law commissioners wished. Firstly, the Poor Law Amendment Act was implemented unevenly, and was implemented and interpreted in different ways by different boards of guardians in different parts of England and Wales. These differences were the consequence of many factors: the degree of local resistance to the Act, long-established local customs, the vested interests of those with power and influence in the parishes (those who had been overseers of the poor before 1834 were frequently returned as Poor Law guardians afterwards) and the persuasive skills of assistant commissioners. Secondly, parishes were not insisting on the removal of paupers under the Settlement Laws, and they continued to prefer paying '**resident relief**' after 1834 for those for whom they were responsible but who lived elsewhere.

KEY TERM

Resident relief
The system whereby guardians would pay relief for paupers for whom they were legally responsible, but who were living in another parish. This saved the expense and trauma of moving whole families back to their parish of legal settlement.

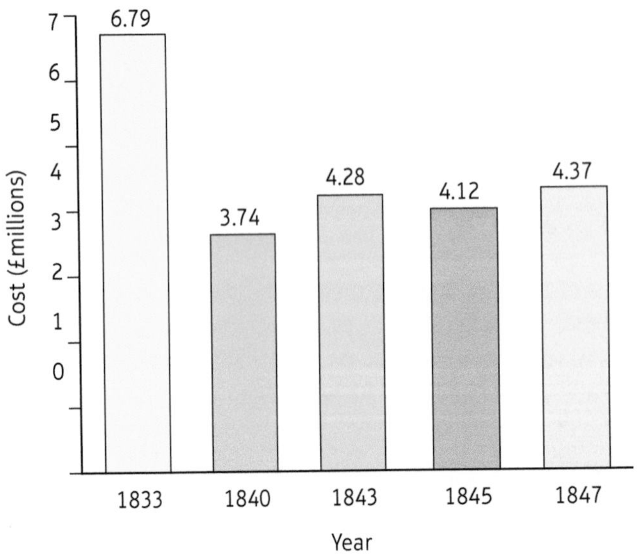

Figure 4.1 The cost of poor relief, 1833–47.

ACTIVITY
SUMMARY
The implementation of the Poor Law Amendment Act, 1834–47

1 To what extent did the able-bodied poor remain a problem in the years 1834–47?

2 How far were the workhouse test and the principle of less eligibility successful in their aims?

3 Consider Figure 4.1. Does the fall in the cost of poor relief indicate that parliament was right to pass the Poor Law Amendment Act?

4 Was flexibility in implementing the Poor Law Amendment Act indicative of strength or weakness on the part of the Poor Law Commission? Discuss this in your group.

WIDER READING

Brundage, A. *The Making of the New Poor Law*, Hutchinson (1978)

Crompton, F. *Workhouse Children*, Sutton (1997)

Crowther, M. A. *The Workhouse System 1834-1929*, University of Georgia Press (1982)

Englander, D. *Poverty and Poor Law Reform in 19th Century Britain 1834-1914*, Longman (1998)

Finer, S. E. *The Life and Times of Edwin Chadwick*, Methuen (1952)

Horn, P. *The Victorian Town Child*, Sutton (1997)

Longmate, N. *The Workhouse*, Temple Smith (1974)

Midwinter, E. *Victorian Social Reform*, Longman (1968)

Rose, M. E. *The English Poor Law*, David & Charles (1971)

Ward, J.T. (ed.) *Popular Movements 1830–59*, Macmillan (1970)

Wood, P. *Poverty and the Workhouse in Victorian Britain*, Sutton (1991)

3.5

The government, self-help and charity, 1847–80

KEY QUESTIONS

* To what extent did central government control of poor relief change in the years 1847–80?
* How significant were charity and self-help in dealing with the problem of poverty?
* How far did individuals develop, and also challenge, the prevailing orthodoxy concerning poverty and poor relief?

INTRODUCTION

The initial teething troubles caused by the assiduous implementation of the main principles of the Poor Law Amendment Act (see Chapter 4) had been largely dealt with by the mid-1840s. Commissioners and assistant commissioners had worked hard and with some measure of success. Opposition had, broadly, died down. Those seeking relief knew what to expect, and those paying for the relief knew what they were paying for. Observers might reasonably have expected a period of calm. This was not to be. The Andover workhouse scandal of 1845–46, although undoubtedly exaggerated, brought some of the worst abuses of the new Poor Law system to the attention of parliament and the public. The scandal provided the trigger for the abolition of the Poor Law Commission. It was replaced by the Poor Law Board, whose president was a cabinet minister and accountable to parliament.

The dominant 19th-century attitudes to poverty were clear. The poor had themselves created the poverty in which they lived. Their lifestyle – the drunkenness of men and the prostitution of women, the poorly nourished babies, the filthy children and the hovels in which they lived – was essentially their own choice. Only the destitute would be given relief, although some concessions were made for widows, orphans, the sick and the old. It was widely believed that, with a bit of effort on their own part, no able-bodied person need live in poverty. This is where the philosophy of self-help and the authoritarian Charity Organisation Society played their part through the latter half of the 19th century.

These commonly held beliefs about poverty and the poor were challenged in different ways and from individuals in very different positions in society. It was these mid-19th-century challenges that played a part in changing attitudes to the poor and which resulted in an easing of the strictures of the 1834 Poor Law Amendment Act.

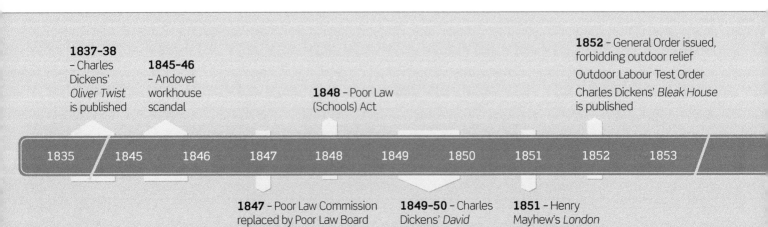

1837–38 – Charles Dickens' *Oliver Twist* is published

1845–46 – Andover workhouse scandal

1848 – Poor Law (Schools) Act

1852 – General Order issued, forbidding outdoor relief
Outdoor Labour Test Order
Charles Dickens' *Bleak House* is published

1835 | 1845 | 1846 | 1847 | 1848 | 1849 | 1850 | 1851 | 1852 | 1853

1847 – Poor Law Commission replaced by Poor Law Board that was accountable to parliament

1849–50 – Charles Dickens' *David Copperfield* is published

1851 – Henry Mayhew's *London Labour and the London Poor* is published

TO WHAT EXTENT DID CENTRAL GOVERNMENT CONTROL OF POOR RELIEF CHANGE IN THE YEARS ...?

...840s was generally eager to be excited, frightened, shocked and outraged by ... petrated in the nation's workhouses. Then, as now, the press was happy to oblige. ... were regularly reported in *The Times*, in provincial newspapers and in the ... incidents were investigated by the Poor Law commissioner assigned to the ...strict, and boards of guardians regularly denied any wrongdoing. Nevertheless, there was ... in some of the allegations. Of the 21 adverse reports carried in *The Times*, about 12 were ..., five were correct and the others were not, it seems, investigated. In at least one reported incident, it was found that Chartists (see page 123) had colluded with the paupers and a local paper to bring false charges of vermin-infested bedding and clothing against the guardians of the Basford Union in Nottinghamshire. However, it was the investigation into the reports of a scandal at the Andover workhouse in Hampshire that was to bring down the Poor Law Commission.

Why did the Andover workhouse scandal lead to the end of the Poor Law Commission?

For a long time, the Andover Union in Hampshire had been held up as being the model of post-1834 Poor Law administration. Outdoor relief had been abolished, and the strictest dietary was used in the union workhouses. Indeed, the union administration was praised in the annual reports of the Poor Law commissioners. In 1837, the guardians appointed Colin M'Dougal and his wife as the Andover workhouse master and matron. So confident were the guardians that they had the right people for the job that afterwards they made only cursory inspections. Reports began filtering out that all was not well. Thomas Wakley, who was MP for Finsbury and a strong opponent of the new Poor Law, asked a question in the House of Commons about the situation in the Andover workhouse. This was serious, and pointed to more than straightforward scaremongering by the press.

The Poor Law commissioners ordered Henry Parker, assistant commissioner with responsibility for the area, to investigate. Henry Parker discovered that the rumours were all true and that a range of dreadful abuses were being perpetrated in the Andover workhouse, ranging from sexual abuse of the female paupers by M'Dougal and his son, to serving even less food than laid down by the worst dietary and so forcing starving paupers to suck meat and marrow from the bones they were supposed to be crushing to make fertiliser. The Poor Law commissioners tried to extricate themselves from the situation by:

- sacking M'Dougal from his post as workhouse master

- blaming Parker for not uncovering the abuses sooner, conveniently forgetting they had reduced the number of assistant commissioners from 21 to nine, thus making his job impossible

1859 – Samuel Smiles' *Self-Help* is published

1864–65 – Charles Dickens' *Our Mutual Friend* is published

1867 – Metropolitan Poor Act – London organised into asylum districts to care for mentally ill paupers

Parliamentary Reform Act doubled electorate from 1m to 2m voters

1869 – Union Loans Act – Guardians permitted to take out loans for capital projects with repayments stretched over 30 years

Charity Organisation Society (COS) founded

1859 | 1863 | 1864 | 1865 | 1866 | 1867 | 1868 | 1869 | 1870 | 1871

1863 – Public Works Act allowed local authorities to borrow money for work schemes employing paupers

1865 – Union Chargeability Act

1868 – Poor Law Board allowed to combine small parishes in order to make the election of Poor Law guardians more democratic

1870 – Elementary Education Act (Forster's Act)

1871 – Poor Law Board replaced by the Local Government Board

- sacking Parker from his post of assistant commissioner
- issuing an Order forbidding bone crushing.

But it was too little, too late. Parker struck back by writing a well-argued pamphlet explaining his position, by gaining the support of Edwin Chadwick (see Chapter 4) who never lost an opportunity to undermine his superiors, and by precipitating an enquiry by a select committee of the House of Commons. The full report was extremely critical of the Poor Law Commission, and it was clear that a major shake-up in the administration of the poor laws was highly likely.

The Andover scandal was not the only problem that central government had with the commission, and the select committee's enquiry revealed more than the straightforward maladministration of one workhouse.

Problems with the Poor Law Commission

The apparent autonomy given by parliament to the three commissioners (see Chapter 4) was largely driven by the need to implement the Poor Law Amendment Act quickly and efficiently. It was always envisaged that the power given to the commissioners would be temporary, and the 1834 Act limited the life of the Commission to five years. After 1839, the Commission's powers were renewed on an annual basis. However, by 1842 opposition to the implementation of the Poor Law Amendment Act was waning. It looked as though parliament would not have to intervene and so it extended the commission's contract for a further five years to 1847. So why wasn't it extended beyond 1847?

- The Andover scandal (1845–46) revealed the worst abuses of the workhouse system and the apparent lack of willingness of the commission to detect and correct such matters.

- The way the commission itself pilloried the assistant commissioner responsible for the Andover workhouse, Henry Parker, alarmed those who knew how administrators should be treated in problematical situations.

- The select committee revealed that there were considerable tensions within Somerset House, where the commission worked. Edwin Chadwick, for example, had never reconciled himself to the 'lowly' position of secretary and used the Andover scandal to attack his superiors.

SOURCE 1
A cartoon published in the *Penny Satirist*, published in September 1846.

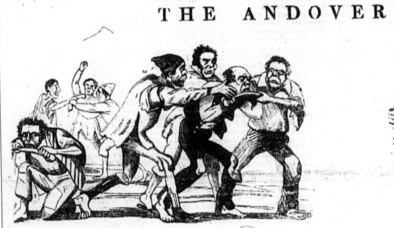 

THE ANDOVER BASTILE.

THE POOR PICKING THE BONES TO LIVE
See our Leader.

THE COMMISSION OF INQUIRY DISCUSSING THE SUBJECT OVER A GOOD DINNER.

(From the Newspapers.)

WORKHOUSE ATROCITIES.—Just before the Prorogation of Parliament, Mr. Wakley asked Sir James Graham if he had heard " that the paupers of a Union in Hampshire were employed in crushing bones, and that while so employed they were engaged in quarrelling with each other for the bones, in extracting marrow from them, and in gnawing off the meat from the extremities." With regard to the immediate case before us, it appears, from the investigation (observes the *Times*) which has taken place into this truly shocking affair, that the paupers are employed in crushing bones collected from various sources, including frequently the bones of horses as well as of other animals, and " occasionally" some from churchyards.

" They must have been ground down by hunger to a condition as low as that of the very dogs, for we have it in the words of the paupers themselves that they are ' ready to fight over the bones,' and, ' as soon as one sees a good bone which is unobserved by the rest, he contrives to steal it away, and hides it till he gets an opportunity of gnawing it.'"—DISPATCH.

ACTIVITY
KNOWLEDGE CHECK

The Andover workhouse scandal

1 Consider Source 1. What point is being made by the *Penny Satirist*?

2 How could Source 1 be used by opponents of the new Poor Law to criticise the Poor Law Commissi[on] and the principle of less eligibility?

3 Do you think that the Poor Law Commission had too much power, or too little? How would making i[t] answerable to parliament change the situation?

The Poor Law Board, 1847–75

Gradually, parliament became convinced that the Poor Law Commission had served its purpose and had to go.

SOURCE

From *Hansard*, May 1847. Sir George Grey, the home secretary, explains why he wants to replace the Poor Law Commission with a Poor Law Board.

In 1834 it was thought that the persons who were to be invested with the discretionary powers to be exercised by a central authority [the Poor Law Commissioners] ought not to form any part of the Executive Government; that they should be free from popular pressure. It was at that time thought better, also, that no political changes should be allowed to affect those who were to be entrusted with these powers. Upon these grounds, the Poor Law Commission was separated from the Executive Government.

Looking at the results of that arrangement and experience, I think I may assert that it has not been as successful as was anticipated. The responsibility of the Poor Law Commissioners to parliament was indirect and imperfect. The power they exercised was free from that check which is imposed upon those public officials who are obliged to listen in this House to charges made against them, and they [the Commissioners] were not able to answer their accusers. They have laboured under a major disadvantage in this respect.

Under the existing Poor Law Commission, what really happens? Complaints are made, and questions asked of the Home Secretary who is expected to give an answer; but his first answer has to be that he is entirely ignorant of the matter, but that he will enquire into the case and give a reply on a future day. Consequently, he obtains an explanation from the Commissioners, but still without a knowledge of all the circumstances, he is expected to give full information to the House on the subject. This, unquestionably, leads to a great inconvenience; and the administration of the Poor Law Amendment Act has been, to a certain degree, prejudiced by it.

The principle, therefore, of the bill which I have to propose, is that there should be a general superintending authority immediately responsible to Parliament and the existing powers of the Commission shall be transferred to a new Board.

A Level Exam-Style Question Section A

Study Source 2 before you answer this question.

Assess the value of the source for revealing the problems faced by the Poor Law commissioners and the reasons why changes were made to the administration of the Poor Law in 1847.

Explain your answer, using the source, the information given about its origin and your own knowledge about the historical context. (20 marks)

Tip

The source gives just one reason: accountability. What other reasons were involved? You might, for example, consider the impact of the Andover scandal on public opinion.

In 1847, the government replaced the Poor Law Commission with the Poor Law Board. It was intended, not only to rid the administration of the Poor Law of arrogance, rigidity and cant, but also to link it more firmly to government. Thus, while a president and two secretaries undertook the day-to-day work, several cabinet ministers sat on the Board *ex officio*. Furthermore, the president himself was invariably an MP. In this way, those who were responsible for the administration of the Poor Law were answerable to parliament and responsive to public opinion, but the switch from autonomy to parliamentary control did not signal an absolute break from the original administrators of the Poor Law Amendment Act. George Nicholls (one of the three original commissioners) was appointed permanent secretary to the Board; most of the assistant commissioners, renamed 'Poor Law inspectors', stayed on and their numbers were increased from nine to 13.

How far did the Poor Law Board achieve balance between indoor and outdoor relief?

By 1847, it had become clear that it was going to be impossible to abolish outdoor relief. Poor Law guardians regularly flouted orders prohibiting outdoor relief, applying pragmatic solutions to local difficulties. The irregular and infrequent visits of the assistant commissioners meant that local variations were not just possible, but became the norm. In 1846, the commission's last full year of operation, there were approximately 1,300,000 paupers in England and Wales. Of these, only 199,000 received relief inside union workhouses.

In 1852, the Poor Law Board made an attempt to incarcerate all the able-bodied paupers in workhouses by issuing a general order forbidding outdoor relief to the able-bodied. It failed. Many boards of guardians used all the loopholes possible (the most common one being sickness in the family) to continue giving outdoor relief. Indeed, aware that poor rates were again rising, cost-conscious guardians preferred the cheaper alternative of outdoor relief. For example, in East Anglia in 1860 it cost 3s 5½d a week to keep a pauper in a workhouse and 1s 9d if that same pauper was on outdoor relief. Similarly, in London in 1862, it cost 4s 8d a week to keep a pauper in a workhouse and 2s 3d if that same pauper was on outdoor relief. The superiority of outdoor over indoor relief was further endorsed in 1863. In the early 1860s, the American cotton crop failed, causing a crisis in the Lancashire cotton mills. Thousands of operatives needed short-term, outdoor relief. In order to ease the situation, the Public Works Act 1863 allowed local authorities to borrow money to set up work schemes to employ paupers. It did not really work because the crisis passed before it could come into play, but the point was that a basic principle of the Poor Law Amendment Act 1834 – the ending of outdoor relief for able-bodied paupers – had been breached, and breached by parliament.

SOURCE

3

Part of a letter from William Martin to the Poor Law Board written in 1850. He is complaining about his treatment by the Clitheroe Union. Across the letter is written 'State that the Board have no power to order relief, but will make enquiry of guardians as to his case'.

I beg permission to lay a case before you of one name of Wm Martin hawker by occupation; which has a wife and five children… who is reduced by five months sickness of his wife. The surgeon stated that she was in danger of losing her eyesight if she be not cautious. She asked him if moving to the seashore would help and he replied that he thought it would. So I appeared at the Board of Guardians the Tuesday following and I asked them if they would be so kind as to grant me a trifle of money to take her to the seashore. They asked me if I had got a certificate from the surgeon, I answered no sir, they answered if I had brought one they could have done better with me. So I prolonged the time one more week and I got a certificate from Mr Patchett the surgeon. So I appeared again at the Board, on the Tuesday following and they would not grant me one penny. So I resolved before she should lose her eyesight I would sell all my chattels. So on Sunday following I contrived for her to go down to Blackpool, and she remained there a few days, and returned home again much the better. And in a few days afterwards she was struck with the cholera.

On 13th December 1849 she went to the Relieving Officer and he gave her an order for the workhouse and she asked him for a horse and cart for it is twelve miles from my cottage and I am sure my children cannot walk such a distance, but he answered he would not.

How far had government action after 1847 changed the treatment of paupers?

The rigour and deterrent principles embodied in the Poor Law Amendment Act 1834 were directed at able-bodied men. It was never intended that boards of guardians apply them to the more vulnerable members of society: the elderly, the sick, the mentally ill and children. Indeed, the report of the Royal Commission published in 1834 (see pages 87–92) recommended the separation of different categories of paupers within a workhouse and that the paupers within each category should be treated differently. However, this ideal stumbled over the enormous cost implications. Initially, therefore, the 'general mixed workhouse' became the norm, something to which Chadwick, for one, was never reconciled. Nevertheless, after 1847, the Poor Law Board increasingly initiated different approaches to different categories of pauper.

The special needs of pauper children were almost universally recognised. It was generally considered undesirable, even before 1834, that children should mix freely with adult paupers and there was a growing belief that education was the way to ensure that pauper children did not return to the workhouse as pauper adults. After 1834, children under the age of 16 made up, fairly consistently, around one-third of all paupers in workhouses. So what was done and how did provision for children change after 1847?

- The Poor Law (Schools) Act 1848 allowed Poor Law unions to combine to provide district schools, where pauper children were educated in buildings often far distant from the workhouse in which they lived. Some progressive boards of guardians, such as those in Leeds and Manchester, set up industrial schools, where pauper children lived and learned a trade.

- In the 1850s, some boards of guardians abandoned district schools in favour of smaller, on-site schools where boys were taught a trade and girls learned domestic skills.

- In the 1860s, some boards of guardians began to experiment with boarding pauper children with working-class families.

- The Forster's Education Act 1870 set up **board schools** where there was no church provision, and guardians were encouraged to send their pauper children to these, enabling them to mix with children outside the workhouse.

Illness of the main breadwinner in a family was a major cause of poverty and eventually pauperism, yet the early Poor Law administrators paid little attention to the problem. It is true that the Poor Law Amendment Act allowed for the employment and payment of medical officers, but these were invariably poorly paid and were seen as being part of the disciplinary structure of the workhouse (see page 97). Boards of guardians frequently left their sick, injured and pregnant paupers to be treated in their own homes by Poor Law medical officers. Indeed, this was one of the major forms of outdoor relief after 1834. In this way, costs were kept to a minimum: in 1840, only £150,000 from a Poor Law expenditure of £34.5 million went on medical services. The change and development in Poor Law medical services happened, not in response to any plan or ideology, but in response to need and public opinion. For example, in the 1850s, Poor Law unions set up public dispensaries, which dispensed medicines to the general public as well as to paupers. From 1852, a poor person who could not pay for medical treatment or prescribed medicines automatically qualified for outdoor relief.

However, matters came to a head when Poor Law medical officers began complaining through the **Poor Law Medical Officers' Association** and through the **Workhouse Visiting Society** about the conditions in workhouse hospitals. Letters of complaint were published in *The Lancet*, which itself initiated an enquiry into conditions in London workhouse hospitals. Gradually, the public became aware that something had to be done. Indeed, in 1866, *The Times* embarked on a campaign intent on demonstrating that sickness and poverty were different and should be treated separately. Gathorne Hardy, then president of the Poor Law Board, agreed. In doing so, he signalled a major change of policy. Sick paupers were to be treated in hospitals that were separate from the workhouses. Thus began the separation of pauperism from illness. These 'pauper' hospitals were often the only places where ordinary working people could get medical help. This was particularly the case in London, where the Metropolitan Poor Act 1867 had organised London into 'asylum' districts, which provided general, specialist, isolation and mental hospitals. The Poor Law was thus beginning to provide a national, state-funded system of medical care for paupers and the poor. The move had been made from stigmatised, pauperised medicine to a basic medical service for the poor for which they did not have to pay. The connections between medicine and less eligibility were well and truly broken.

How far did government action improve the financial situation after 1847?

One of the driving forces for change in 1834 had been the rising cost of the Poor Rate. The Poor Law Amendment Act 1834 grouped parishes into unions, but each parish within the union had to pay for the maintenance of its own paupers. The result of this was that parishes with the most paupers had to levy the highest poor rates, and these were the parishes that were the least able to afford them. Conversely, prosperous parishes with few paupers levied a low Poor Rate and their prosperity was further enhanced. In some areas, the burden of the Poor Rate was so heavy that parishes could not meet their commitments.

The situation was resolved in 1865 by the Union Chargeability Act, which placed the financial burden of relief on the union as a whole. Each parish contributed to a common fund and its contribution was based upon the rateable value of properties in the parish, not the number of paupers for whom the parish was responsible. Thus, richer parishes subsidised the poorer ones, and those owning larger properties paid higher poor rates than those living in more modest dwellings. Even so, there was no uniform rating system in that, pound for pound, the owner of a property in, say, Hertfordshire would pay the same Poor Rate as the owner of a similar property in, say, Lancashire.

Most boards of guardians, too, were middle class and committed to keeping the rates as low as possible. These factors combined to lead some Poor Law unions to claim they could not afford to build, for example, the separate accommodation required by the 1834 Act for different classes of paupers. The Poor Law Loans Act 1869 attempted to ease the situation by allowing guardians to extend the repayments on loans from the Public Works commissioners to up to 30 years. Guardians could thus contemplate applying for the level of loan that would enable them to upgrade their facilities without adding too much to the Poor Rate they levied.

	Average expenditure (in £000s)	% increase or decrease on previous period	Cost per head of population
1844-48	5,290	+11	6s 2d
1849-53	5,198	−2	5s 10d
1854-58	5,791	+11	6s 0d
1859-63	5,880	+2	5s 1d
1864-68	6,717	+14	6s 2d

Figure 5.1 The Poor Rate, 1844-68.

ACTIVITY
KNOWLEDGE CHECK

The Poor Law Board

1 In no more than 150 words, summarise the reasons why the Poor Law Commission was closed down.

2 Why did the Poor Law Board fail to end outdoor relief?

3 To what extent was the government involved in improving the condition of paupers?

4 Study Figure 5.1. Despite the efforts of the Poor Law Board, why was the cost of maintaining paupers increasing?

What was the impact of the Parliamentary Reform Act 1867 on Poor Law policy?

The Parliamentary Reform Act 1867, by extending the voting qualification to include householders, doubled the electorate from one million to two million men. The 'respectable' working class could now vote; indeed, in several industrial boroughs (for example Oldham) the majority of the electorate was working class. This Act impacted on Poor Law policy in two main ways.

- There was increased pressure from radicals to democratise the election of guardians of the poor. Since 1834, the Poor Law franchise had favoured the well-to-do ratepayers by enabling plural voting: the greater the amount and value of property that a ratepayer owned, the more votes he could have in guardian elections. This system had the greatest impact in rural parishes, where the number of ratepayers was small and the dominance of the landed gentry was able to continue into the 1860s. The franchise took a small step towards democratisation in 1868 when the Poor Law Board was empowered to combine small parishes for the purpose of electing guardians. However, the Board moved slowly. In ten years they had only combined some 580 small parishes out of a total of 6,111 with a population of fewer than 300. Nevertheless, the facility for change was there, as was the increasing pressure for change.

- Increasing the franchise to include the better-off working class meant that government became increasingly aware of, and concerned with, the welfare of the people. The new legislation that affected, for example, housing and public health (see pages 40–43) was dependent upon the local authorities for enforcement. It no longer made any administrative sense to keep the Poor Law separate from this and so, in 1871, the Poor Law Board was replaced by the Local Government Board. However, the government still retained some control, as the president of the Board was invariably a cabinet minister.

The Local Government Board and relief

When the Local Government Board took over responsibility for the administration of the Poor Law in 1871, it tried desperately to reduce the number of paupers receiving relief.

- It issued a circular condemning outdoor relief on the basis that it took away from the poor all desire to save for bad times by offering relief to them in their own homes whenever they needed it.

- It supported local authorities when they took a harsh line with the able-bodied poor asking for relief. Poplar, in east London, for example, set up a deterrent workhouse that set the undeserving poor to harsh work. Others followed suit. They were able to do this because a growing number of charities were beginning to provide charity payments for the deserving poor (see pages 116-17).

- It authorised boards of guardians to take part in emigration schemes, whereby groups of paupers (either whole families or specific categories of poor and paupers) were sponsored to emigrate.

However, one factor remained constant. Although the ratio of paupers relieved inside the workhouse to those receiving outdoor relief changed over time, the greater number of paupers were always relieved *outside* the workhouse.

Year	Total number of paupers relieved	Number receiving indoor relief	Number receiving outdoor relief
1840	1,199,592	169,232	1,030,297
1850	1,008,700	123,004	885,696
1860	844,633	113,507	731,126
1870	1,032,800	156,800	876,000
1880	792,499	215,377	577,122

Figure 5.2 From the Local Government Board's 31st Annual Report, showing the number of paupers receiving indoor and outdoor relief, 1840-80.

EXTRACT

1 From M.A. Crowther *The Workhouse System*, published in 1981.

The Poor Law Commissioners had been active policy makers, prejudiced in their approach to the problem of poverty, but not inert. The reputation of the Poor Law Board, in contrast, was one of inactivity, and the Local Government Board's little better. The work of charitable reformers stands out in contrast to that of official bureaucracy. In Poor Law matters the Board was indeed conservative, tending to concentrate on the able-bodied pauper; and neither its structure nor its finances enabled it to take a firm lead. The very unpopularity of the first commissioners made succeeding authorities more cautious in their dealings with the localities. They preferred to work through private pressure, steady attrition, unpublicised bargains. The Poor Law Commission had been designed to deter paupers, not to offer them free hospital treatment or specialised care in institutions, and the central authority was slow to shed Chadwick's influence. During the nineteenth century it devised no long-term policy for the large and expensive institutions which were arising, and was reluctant to accept that many workhouses were turning into hospitals. The Local Government Board insisted that official responsibility extended only to the destitute, not the poor.

ACTIVITY
KNOWLEDGE CHECK

From Poor Law Board to Local Government Board

1 Why do you think the democratisation of elections to boards of guardians happened at such a slow rate?

2 'The replacement of the Poor Law Board by the Local Government Board was designed to tidy up administration; it had nothing to do with improving the lives of paupers.' Do you agree?

3 Does Figure 5.2 prove that the Local Government Board was better at administering the Poor Law than the Poor Law Board? Explain your answer.

A Level Exam-Style Question Section B

How accurate is it to say that little changed, concerning the Poor Law, between 1846 and 1872? (20 marks)

Tip

Consider the transitions between Poor Law Commission and Poor Law Board, and Poor Law Board and Local Government Board. What differences were there, for example, in accountability of those administering the Poor Law, and in the ways in which paupers were treated?

HOW SIGNIFICANT WERE CHARITY AND SELF-HELP IN DEALING WITH THE PROBLEM OF POVERTY?

To the poor, the availability of support to keep them from destitution was of paramount importance. As explained previously, from 1834 the state was trying to reduce the cost, and therefore the services available, via the Poor Law. The problems of obtaining relief were coupled, for the poor, with a growing dread of the workhouse that was reinforced by the stigma associated with the status of pauper. An alternative to Poor Law relief was help from one of the many charities that sprang up in the 19th century. These, however, were often an expression of the enthusiasm and interests of those who set them up, and not necessarily directed to the specific needs of the poor. Unsurprisingly, those facing poverty or the fear of potential poverty, tended to turn first to family, friends and the resources established by the working class.

What was the significance of the work of the Charity Organisation Society?

The Charity Organisation Society (COS) was founded in 1869 with the practical aim of co-ordinating the work of the many private charities that had been founded. From the beginning, the COS was a powerful organisation supported by influential people. Members of the House of Commons, the aristocracy, the armed forces, the professions and the Established Church attended the inauguration meeting. They all supported, and used their extensive influence to promulgate, the three main aims of the society:

- co-operation with the Poor Law authorities at a local level in order to establish a clear division between the work of the Poor Law authorities and voluntary charities

- organisation of the work of other charities, to better co-ordinate their efforts and ensure charitable relief was appropriately given

- ensuring only the deserving were in receipt of charitable relief by supporting the use of casework, whereby only those categorised as 'deserving' would be helped.

SOURCE

4 From the Charity Organisation Society's *Eighth Annual Report,* published 1876.

> The working man does not need to be told that temporary sickness is likely now and then to visit his household; that times of slackness will occasionally come, that if he marries early and has a large family, his resources will be stretched to the uttermost; that if he lives long enough, old age will render him more or less incapable of work – all these are the ordinary circumstances of a labourer's life, and if he is taught that as they arise they will be met by state relief or private charity, he will assuredly make no effort to meet them himself. A spirit of dependence, fatal to all progress, will be engendered in him, he will not concern himself with the causes of his distress or consider at all how the condition of his class may be improved; the road to idleness and drunkenness will be made easy to him, and it involves no prophesying to say that the last state of a population influenced after such a fashion as this will certainly be worse than the first.

Members of the COS were opposed to indiscriminate giving as they believed that charity was not a right but a gift, given at the discretion of the giver. It should only be given, they believed, to the 'deserving' poor, who would be offered limited charity to help them get back on their feet. The benefits for those selected for relief had to be both moral and material, and the relief was intended to reform the behaviour of the recipient as well as to put food on the table. Relief was to be temporary and designed to be of permanent benefit to the recipient, whose lifestyle would be forever changed.

COS branches were founded in a number of provincial towns and cities, but it would be a mistake to think of it as a national organisation. Its federal structure meant that local branches tended to work in a fairly autonomous way. The Liverpool branch, for example, continued to give direct relief to the poor of Liverpool, while the District Provident Society in Manchester made little effort to co-ordinate the work of different charities in their area. Even in London, the headquarters of the COS, there was considerable variety in the work of the various offices.

The COS's publicity and propaganda emphasised its success in working with the new Poor Law and its ability to target relief to those who deserved it. Indeed, most of those applying for relief were turned down as being 'undeserving', which was seen by COS supporters as being indicative of rigour. However, the organisation was not without its difficulties and its critics.

- Provincial branches often failed to recruit sufficient volunteers or raise enough funds.

- The rigorous investigative methods of the COS volunteers were resented by the poor.

- Many charities became alienated by what they saw as the overbearing attitude of the COS to themselves as providers of relief, and preferred to raise their own funds and dispense their own monies as they thought fit.

- Boards of guardians frequently had strained relationships with their local COS branches as the guardians regarded them as interfering in the ways in which they chose to administer the Poor Law.

What, if anything, did the COS achieve?

- It is certain that the views of its intellectual supporters were listened to in the corridors of power, and that it had an influence on official thinking that was out of all proportion to its actual charitable activities. Regarded as experts on poverty and charity, members of the COS readily gave evidence to enquiries on social problems (see Chapter 6).

- By 1880, the COS had established practices and procedures that it used when visiting poor families, collecting information in a systematic way, enabling comparisons to be made between different applicants. This was to form the basis of later social work and social work training.

ACTIVITY
KNOWLEDGE CHECK

The COS

1 Read Source 4. What can be learned from this source about the motives of those who formed the COS?

2 The COS claimed to be working well with various boards of guardians. In what ways could it be seen to challenge the work of those administering the Poor Law?

3 In your view, what were the strengths and weaknesses of the COS?

EXTEND YOUR KNOWLEDGE

The Goschen Minute (1869)

In 1869, George Goschen, the last president of the Poor Law Board, issued a Minute to Poor Law guardians in London. In this, he urged a division of responsibility between Poor Law guardians and the providers of charity in order to avoid duplication of relief. The intention was for guardians to provide for the destitute, while charitable giving to the needy would be the province of other organisations. In this, he was greatly encouraged by the establishment of the COS.

How effective were friendly societies?

Friendly societies date from the 17th century and were originally simply groups of friends, neighbours or fellow workers joining together to provide for themselves in time of need. For a weekly subscription, members would be entitled to payment in times of sickness, death or unemployment. There was a surge in the number and membership of friendly societies at the beginning of the 19th century, as workers tried to protect themselves against the uncertainties thrown up by the Industrial Revolution, a mobile population and the decline of traditional occupations. There was a further surge after 1834, as people anticipated a more rigorous Poor Law and increased problems in obtaining state relief. This signalled a significant change in the organisation of friendly societies. No longer independent and local, by 1847 the friendly society movement had become an organisation with central bodies to which individual societies (sometimes called lodges) could affiliate. This meant that risk was spread over several branches and benefits could be provided over a wider geographical area.

Of the 3,074 lodges affiliated to the Manchester Unity of Oddfellows, which was the biggest friendly society in the 19th century, nearly half were founded after the Poor Law Amendment Act 1834; by 1870 the Oddfellows had 434,100 members and the next biggest, the Ancient Order of Foresters, had 361,735 members. After 1846, societies were required to register and submit accounts to the office of the Registrar of Friendly Societies. This gave them certain benefits, such as legal protection of their funds. By 1877, registered membership of friendly societies throughout Britain topped 2.7 million.

SOURCE

5

An advertising hand bill issued by the South London branch of the Odd Fellows' Friendly Society, c1885. The advertisement shows that the contribution required from members amounted to 7s per quarter, in addition to entrance fees. Hence, it would be unlikely to attract poorer workers.

IMPORTANT NOTICE TO WORKING MEN!

INDEPENDENT ORDER OF

Odd Fellows' Friendly Society

SOUTH LONDON UNITY.

REGISTERED UNDER THE FRIENDLY SOCIETIES ACT, 1876.

THE

STAR of TEMPERANCE LODGE

HELD AT

LOCKHART'S COCOA ROOMS,

161, WESTMINSTER BRIDGE ROAD,

EVERY THURSDAY EVENING.

Healthy Men under 40 years of age, who prudently desire to make a provision in case of affliction, and wish to join a really substantial Society, are invited to join this Lodge, which, although not confined to Teetotalers, is opened under Temperance principles and not held at a Public House, which is often a temptation to Members, sometimes causing them to spend more money in attending the Lodge than the actual amount of their contributions ; it is also a branch of a vast and flourishing Unity having an accumulated capital as a guarantee of its stability. Particular attention is called to the following low scale of ENTRANCE FEES :—

18 to 21 Years of Age, 2s. 6d. ; 21 to 25, 4s. ; 25 to 30, 6s. ; 30 to 35, 8s. 35 and under 40, 10s.

Not less than 2s. 6d. must be paid on or before Initiation, the balance (if any) within three months.

CONTRIBUTIONS, 7s. PER QUARTER,

Which may be paid weekly or otherwise, to suit the convenience of Members. No Fines for Stewards.   No Levies or any other Extras.

BENEFITS IN SICKNESS—

12s. for 26 Weeks and 6s. for 26 Weeks, and 3s. as long as illness lasts,

With Medical Attendance and Medicine.

Member's Death,   Wife's Death,

£15.   £7 10s.

Members travelling in search of employment will receive travelling checks. FREE IMMEDIATELY to Medical Attendance and Medicine ; Funeral Benefit in Six Months ; to Sick and Travelling Benefits in Twelve Months.

Medical Attendant—Dr. COPPIN, 138, Westminster Bridge Road.

Any further information can be obtained at the above Cocoa Rooms any evening in the week ; or of the Secretary, P.G.P. ARTHUR IMHOFE, 39, Auckland Street, Vauxhall.

WILKES & Co., Printers, 63, Newington Butts, S.E.

Membership of a friendly society gave the promise of security freed from the process, procedures and shame of pauperism. Membership also gave companionship on a regular basis. Lodge members knew each other and meetings were generally held in the local pub, so there were ample opportunities for the exchange of advice and the giving and receiving of small acts of kindness. In joining friendly societies, working-class people were fulfilling one of the aims of the Poor Law Amendment Act, namely that self-help institutions should be the main source of relief for the poor and so numbers taking the workhouse test would fall. Any assistance given by a friendly society to its members was given as a right because of contributions that had been made. This was different from charities (see pages 116–17), which were institutions founded by one group of people to give assistance to a different group.

However, not all working people were able to benefit from membership of a friendly society for the following reasons:

- Many societies charged an entry fee and all expected a weekly contribution to funds. About 6d a week was the norm. This was simply beyond the means of the poorest workers, who frequently suffered from irregular employment.

- Some societies fined members who missed a payment, adding to debt from which the individual was already suffering.

- Some societies refused membership to people who had a history of illness or who were over 40 years old. Those in dangerous occupations, such as mining, were rarely if ever accepted as members.

- Fully paid-up members were not always assured of benefits when they needed them. Some friendly societies were badly managed and collapsed. Some were guilty of encouraging workers to join in the full knowledge that they would not be able to keep up the weekly payments, whilst others were unable to pay out the full benefits when they were needed because of bad financial management.

Those who could not afford to join a friendly society turned to burial societies.

Burial societies

Many friendly societies offered death or burial benefits, sufficient to cover the cost of a funeral. This was not, of course, available to those who could not afford to join a friendly society. It was the fear of a **pauper funeral** that drove many to contribute to burial societies. For a payment as little as 1d a week, the Blackburn Philanthropic Burial Society, for example, would provide a burial

KEY TERM

Pauper funeral

Here, the principle of 'less eligibility' was imposed, which meant that a pauper was not entitled to the same sort of funeral that a non-pauper could expect. A pauper's body was wrapped in a paper shroud, placed in a flimsy wooden coffin and interred in a mass grave. Mass graves could accommodate as many as 20 coffins. Quicklime was used to speed up decomposition so that the same graves could be used over and over again. The graves were unmarked.

allowance of £4, sufficient for a funeral. Burial societies started as local affairs, but the market soon became dominated by larger enterprises. The Royal Liver Friendly Society, formed by Liverpool workers in 1850, 20 years later had over 550,000 members. By 1880, the three largest burial societies (the Royal Liver, the Liverpool Victoria and the Royal London) together had over four million members. These societies, with their armies of part-time collectors of weekly contributions, focused on the poorest members of society.

The welfare work of unions and co-operatives

Trade unions

In a similar way to the friendly societies, the trade unions expanded rapidly in the mid- and late 19th century. Industrialisation was well established and workers were ready to combine to negotiate, or fight, for improved working conditions and higher pay. Many trade unions were trade or skill based, such as the Amalgamated Society of Joiners and Carpenters. Others, such as the Amalgamated Society of Engineers (ASE), which was formed in 1851, were amalgamations of a number of smaller unions. Members of these unions could afford a weekly subscription of around 1s and as a consequence were eligible for a range of benefits. The ASE, for example, offered pensions, and benefits for sickness and death. Other unions were able to offer unemployment pay, a benefit not available from friendly societies.

SOURCE

A report of benefits paid by the Colchester branch of the Amalgamated Society of Joiners and Carpenters. From *The Colchester Mercury*, published on 29 March 1879.

Each member subscribed 1s per week and for that he received 10s per week when out of employment and 12s per week when sick; and during the time such relief was paid, the weekly subscription was not called for, a feature novel in Benefit Societies. Any member meeting with an accident, which permanently incapacitated him from following his trade as a carpenter and joiner, received £100; and for partial disablement, a sum of £50 was paid. The subscription also covered insurance of tools; and on the occasion of the fire at Mr Dobson's premises at Colchester, some men who were members had their tools replaced at a cost of £50. Any person being a member for 19 years was entitled to a superannuation allowance of 7s per week. On the death of a member his widow or relatives received £12.

Not all unions were able to be as generous as the Amalgamated Society of Joiners and Carpenters. The Brickmakers Society of London, for example, had no sickness fund. Even so, it was only the skilled workers who could afford the weekly subscription that would yield the sort of benefits when they hit hard times that would keep them from pauperism and the shadow of the workhouse.

Co-operative societies

The co-operative movement was another self-help movement that was managed by working people for themselves. In 1844, a group of Rochdale weavers started the Rochdale Society of Equitable Pioneers with just 28 weavers paying £1 each by way of a subscription. The money was used to rent a shop in Toad Lane and to buy in, and then sell on, good-quality goods to working-class families. Co-operative (co-op) shops were owned by their members, who were paid a dividend on every purchase they made. In just seven years, there were 130 shops spread throughout the north of England; by 1880, there were close to a million co-op shareholders. It was the prospect of regular dividends that explains the popularity of co-op shops – that and the knowledge that the foodstuffs they bought were not **adulterated**. The quarterly payment of dividends was most frequently used by working families to pay their rent, while those who could afford it left their dividends with the co-op where they accrued interest. Co-operative societies gave many working-class families some ability to plan their finances, even if they were simply given the reassurance that the rent could be paid and they would be able to keep a roof over their heads.

KEY TERM

Adulterated food
Food and drink that was spoiled by adding something to it. For example, adding chalk to bread to make it look white.

The concept underpinning the co-operative movement was a simple one: working-class people were to be weaned off the credit readily provided by commercially run shops, and the **truck shops** run by some employers. Co-operative shops, therefore, would not give credit: everything had to be paid for, in cash, at the time of purchase. This limited membership of the co-operative movement to the skilled and semi-skilled members of the working class. Furthermore, because co-op dividends were based on the amount of money people spent, the poorer the people were, the less they had to spend and the lower their dividend. This was the theory. There is evidence that during downturns in trade and in times of sickness and temporary distress, co-operative societies did give limited credit to their members. They were, after all, in competition with other retail outlets. Even so, the co-operative movement was not for the feckless and those living close to the edge.

KEY TERM

Truck shop
Some employers operated a system whereby their workers were paid partly in tokens that could only be exchanged in the firm's truck shop where the employers controlled the prices of the goods.

SOURCE 7 A 19th-century co-operative grocery shop.

ACTIVITY
KNOWLEDGE CHECK

By the poor, for the poor?

1 Why were friendly societies popular with the poor?

2 What were the strengths and the weaknesses of ways in which trade unions and co-operative societies tried to help working people when they fell on hard times?

3 What were the differences between the COS and the other organisations – trade unions, friendly and co-operative societies – in the ways in which they approached caring for the poor?

EXTEND YOUR KNOWLEDGE

The role of mothers

A lot of attention has been paid by historians to the wages earned by working-class men and to the benefits they might, or might not, receive if they fell on hard times. The ways in which the money earned by the main wage earner, usually the man, was used were crucial to the survival of families if they were to escape pauperism. However, it was invariably the mothers in a family who managed that money and frequently supplemented it with casual earnings.

Some charities appreciated the significance of the role of mothers. Indeed, the COS condemned some charities for providing free meals, claiming that to do this undermined the role of the mother. Even so, some charities continued to provide free meals, especially for children.

Mothers struggling to manage a family budget would have appreciated an injection of cash to spend as they thought fit. However, this was rarely given, either by charities or by the Poor Law authorities providing outdoor relief. All organisations preferred to provide relief in kind, believing that in this way the recipients would use it 'correctly'. So boots and clothes for the children, and tickets for coal merchants enabling the poor to 'buy' coal, for example, would be given. But mothers living close to the edge of pauperism found ways round these gifts in order to exchange them for cash. For example, coal tickets could be sold on and well-made middle-class clothes and boots could be taken to the **pawnshop** in order to generate immediate cash. Free meals were too good an opportunity to miss, and the recipients would frequently come away with pies, biscuits and slices of bread and butter hidden in pockets and wrapped in shawls and aprons in order to feed family members. The middle class gave what they thought the poor needed. The poor turned the gifts into what they really needed.

KEY TERM

Pawnshop
A place where the poor could go to get an immediate cash loan in exchange for one, or some, of their possessions. The possession(s) could be reclaimed when the loan was repaid. If it was not repaid within a certain length of time, the pawnbroker could sell the item and keep the money from the sale. Pawnshops still exist today in many towns and cities.

THINKING HISTORICALLY Interpretations (6a)

A Level Exam-Style Question
Section B

'Charitable organisations failed to meet the needs of the poor.' How far do you agree with this statement? (20 marks)

Tip
Challenge the implication that 'the poor' were a single group of people. Consider the ways in which the poor who were just about able to manage were lifted out of poverty, whereas those living on the edge could not benefit – and why.

Ever-changing history

Our interpretations of the past change as we change. This may be because our social attitudes have changed over time, or perhaps a historian has constructed a new theory, or perhaps technology has allowed archaeologists to discover something new.

Work in pairs.

1 Make a timeline that starts with the Andover workhouse scandal and ends 50 years in the future. Construct reactions that illustrate the point that time changes history. How might people's reactions to the scandal change over time? In the future box, you can speculate how people might react to the event in 50 years' time. Below is an example. It shows how people's views about an event (in this case the outbreak of the First World War) might have changed over time. Now create your own time boxes, starting with the Andover scandal.

1914	1917	1932	1968	2066
Event: The outbreak of the First World War	German patriot: 'The start of Germany's greatest war' Farmer in northern France: 'A disaster'	British diplomat: 'The start of Britain's greatest colonial war' Unemployed German: 'A disaster'	Farmer in northern France: 'The pity of war. I keep finding bullets.' British diplomat: 'The beginning of the end of the British Empire' An Indian historian: 'A major step on the road to independence'	?

Answer the following questions:

2 Identify three factors that have affected how the Andover workhouse scandal is interpreted over time.

3 If a historian was to write a book proposing a radically new interpretation of the Andover workhouse scandal, how might other historians react? What would affect their reaction?

4 How will the future change the past?

HOW FAR DID INDIVIDUALS DEVELOP, AND ALSO CHALLENGE, THE PREVAILING ORTHODOXY CONCERNING POVERTY AND POOR RELIEF?

The **prevailing orthodoxy** throughout most of the 19th century, and certainly in the period 1847–80, was that:

- poverty was necessary, and even desirable, if people were to strive to improve their lot

- indigence, the inability of individuals to provide for themselves and their families even at the most basic level, was the fault of the poor themselves.

It was this prevailing orthodoxy that led to the workhouse test and the principle of less eligibility (see Chapter 4), and to the crude division of paupers into the 'deserving' and the 'undeserving'. It was the work of Samuel Smiles that reinforced and developed this prevailing orthodoxy, whereas that of Henry Mayhew and Charles Dickens challenged it and that led ultimately to investigations into the causes of poverty at the end of the 19th and beginning of the 20th centuries (see Chapter 6).

KEY TERM

Prevailing orthodoxy
Beliefs or practices that are commonly held.

SOURCE
8

From Patrick Colquhoun *On Destitution*, published in 1806. Colquhoun was a friend of Jeremy Bentham (see page 82), whose thinking influenced 19th-century social policy. Here, Colquhoun describes the orthodoxy that prevailed throughout most of the 19th century.

Poverty is a most necessary and indispensable ingredient in society, without which nations and communities could not exist in a state of civilisation. It is the lot of man – the source of wealth, since without poverty there would be no labour, and without labour there could be no riches, no refinement, no comfort and no benefit to those who may be possessed of wealth. The natural source of subsistence is the work of the individual. While that remains with him, he is called 'poor'. When it fails in whole or in part, he becomes indigent.

SOURCE
9

Work painted by Ford Madox Brown in 1865. Ford Madox Brown (1821–93) was an English painter of moral and historical subjects.

ACTIVITY
KNOWLEDGE CHECK

Prevailing orthodoxy

1 Read Source 8. What arguments could be made against the views expressed here?

2 Look at Source 9. In what ways does Source 9 support the views expressed in Source 8?

3 How far do Sources 8 and 9, taken together, demonstrate the nature of the 19th-century prevailing orthodoxy regarding poverty and pauperism?

Samuel Smiles (1812–1904): author and political reformer

Samuel Smiles began writing articles on parliamentary reform when he was a medical student at Edinburgh University, which were published by the progressive *Edinburgh Weekly Chronicle*. Smiles' interest in reform continued after he had qualified as a doctor in 1832 and was working in his home town of Haddington in East Lothian, 20 miles east of Edinburgh. His admiration for the radical politician and MP for Leeds, Joseph Hume – also a Scottish doctor who qualified from Edinburgh University – was to have a profound influence on him, and Smiles began contributing articles on parliamentary reform to the *Leeds Times*.

In 1838, Smiles was invited to become editor of the *Leeds Times*. The proprietor, a Mr Hobson, had been impressed by the quality of the articles Smiles had written and thought he had the necessary skills to improve circulation figures. These had fallen off badly because of competition from the radical Chartist newspaper, the *Northern Star*. Here was the opportunity for Smiles to make a complete change of career – but it was risky as there was no guarantee of continued employment in the highly charged world of journalism. He took a chance and moved to Leeds, giving up medicine. Smiles was to hold the post of editor until 1845, using his newspaper to campaign for the reform of parliament, women's suffrage, free trade and factory reform.

Smiles didn't confine his radical activities to the *Leeds Times*. He was a strong supporter of the co-operative movement in Leeds, and in particular of the Leeds Mutual Society and the Leeds Redemption Society. In 1840, he became secretary to the Leeds Parliamentary Reform Association. The association supported the six points of the People's Charter that embodied the demands of the Chartist movement. Although originally a supporter of **Chartism** and of the six points of the Charter, Smiles became alarmed by the growing militarism of some of the leading Chartists. Of particular concern to him was Feargus O'Connor, proprietor of the *Northern Star*, who advocated the use of physical force. Smiles began to distance himself from Chartist activities. He left the *Leeds Times* and became secretary to an innovative development: the newly formed Leeds and Thirsk Railway.

In the 1850s, Smiles became disappointed with the lack of progress towards parliamentary reform, and turned to writing. He had come to believe that parliamentary reform, by itself, would not be enough to lift people out of poverty and give the poor a voice. What was needed in addition to parliamentary reform, he believed, was individual reform: individuals had to change their own attitudes and practices. Arguing that self-help provided the best route to success, his book *Self-Help* was published in 1859. It became an instant bestseller, presumably amongst the middle classes. Through self-help, Smiles argued, it was possible to accumulate wealth without having to show concern for your neighbours because the opportunity to exercise self-help was open to them, too. Everyone, no matter how humble, could raise themselves and their families to a position of prosperity. There was no need, either, to pay vast amounts in poor rates because most of the poor could raise themselves out of poverty. Only the genuinely destitute needed help. In support of his belief in the ability of individuals to improve their lot, Smiles wrote several biographies of famous men, including George Stephenson and Josiah Wedgwood, all of whom had achieved success through hard work. The year 1875 saw the publication of his book *Thrift*, in which he argued that thrift and the correct use of money was the basis of self-help. Five years later came *Duty*, full of examples of great deeds done by men, and some women, who he believed set shining examples to the rest of the population. Interestingly, Smiles' final book *Conduct* was never published. In 1896 and 1898, his publisher refused to publish it. When Smiles died in 1904, the manuscript was found in his desk. On the orders of his publisher, it was destroyed. No known copies exist.

KEY TERM

Chartism
A radical movement that began in the 1830s, after the 1832 Parliamentary Reform Act had failed to give the vote to working-class people. Chartists supported the six points of the People's Charter: annual elections; equal electoral districts; payment of MPs; universal manhood suffrage; the secret ballot; and the abolition of a property qualification for MPs. Chartism as a movement died out in the 1850s.

SOURCE

 10 From Samuel Smiles *Self-Help,* published in 1859.

'Heaven helps those who help themselves' is a well-tried maxim, embodying the results of vast human experience. The spirit of self-help is the root of all genuine growth in the individual and, exhibited in the lives of the many, it constitutes the true source of national vigour and strength. Help from without is often enfeebling in its effects, but help from within invariably invigorates. Whatever is done *for* men or classes, to a certain extent takes away the stimulus and necessity of doing for themselves.

National progress is the sum of individual industry, energy and uprightness, as national decay is of individual idleness, selfishness and vice. The highest patriotism and philanthropy consist, not so much in altering laws and modifying institutions, as in helping and stimulating men to elevate and improve themselves by their own free and independent individual action.

Samuel Smiles

1 How likely would Samuel Smiles' ideas, as expressed in Source 10, be viewed sympathetically by the COS? Explain your answer.

2 Samuel Smiles makes out a case for self-help. What would be the counter-arguments? Set up a debate in your group.

3 In your view, does Samuel Smiles challenge or support the prevailing orthodoxy?

EXTRACT

2 From Alan Kidd *State, Society and the Poor in Nineteenth-century England*, published in 1999.

It seems ironic that moralists and charity reformers spent so much time preaching 'self-help' to the masses in the face of overwhelming evidence of self-reliance and mutual assistance arising from within the working class itself. Despite the repeated and routine condemnations of working class fecklessness and improvidence throughout the century, there is ample indication of self-help and mutual aid amongst the poor, although it was often in forms which the propertied classes did not understand or suspected of being subversive. In times of hardship, unemployment, sickness, childhood, old age and death, a majority of the working class drew on their own resources or the support of their relatives and neighbours before they considered asking for poor relief or charity. In a large part, their self-help and mutual-aid strategies arose from the experience of life during an era of rapid social and economic change.

Henry Mayhew (1812–87): investigative journalist

The fourth of seven sons and with ten sisters, Henry Mayhew was destined, like his brothers, for a career in law. Also like his brothers, he was disinherited by his father when they all dropped out of law and pursued their own interests. Deciding to become a writer, Mayhew contributed to, and edited, the comic magazine *Figaro in London* from its founding in 1831 until its collapse in 1838. He also wrote a play *The Wandering Minstrel* in 1834 and briefly managed a theatre. Returning to England from France, where he had fled to escape his creditors, in 1841 Mayhew co-founded the satirical magazine *Punch* with his friend Mark Lemon. It was an unexpected success, selling 6,000 copies a week in the 1840s. Severing his connection with the magazine in 1845, Mayhew wrote articles for the *Illustrated London News* and eventually worked mainly as a journalist for the *Morning Chronicle*.

In 1849, Henry Mayhew wrote a series of articles for the *Morning Chronicle* in which he described the lives of the poor in London. Later, these were gathered together and published in a book, *London Labour and the London Poor*. The articles and the book captured the imagination of the reading public. Although this series was primarily concerned with London, Mayhew did place his findings for London in a wider national context. The point about Mayhew was that he visited the homes and workplaces of the poor and wrote about what he saw, heard, smelled and felt. Mayhew's innovative and unemotional investigative journalism revealed the extent to which London's economy depended on unskilled and casual labour. He, like many Victorians, was interested in classification. He divided the labouring poor, whose lives he was investigating, into 'Those who will work, those who cannot work and those who will not work.'

Those who will work

These were the able-bodied poor, who undertook an enormous range and variety of jobs. The elite of this group, Mayhew found, were the skilled artisans. These ranged from the cabinetmakers and jewellers of London to the machine-tool engineers and textile-mill overlookers in the Midlands and north. They were manual workers, but they had specific skills that they could sell. Similarly, there were craftsmen like masons and bricklayers, mule spinners, weavers and ironworkers who, when the demand was there, could command a reasonable wage. Finally, there was the largest group of all: the labourers. In an age only just becoming mechanised, most of the lifting and blasting, reaping, mowing, carrying, sweeping and scrubbing had to be done by hand. This was casual work and readily available when times were good, but virtually non-existent in times of slump.

Those who cannot work

Some of the able-bodied poor could not work because there simply was no work for them to do. In bad weather, house painters and bricklayers could not work. A failed cotton crop in the USA meant that mill workers in England were laid off. The skilled artisans could, possibly, have been able to save some money against bad times. But, in an age when there was no redundancy money and no unemployment benefit, most of the labouring poor had to do the best they could. Pawnbrokers flourished and corner shops gave credit, but when these possibilities were exhausted, many took to begging or were forced to seek help from charities or the guardians of the poor. Labouring work brought with it its own dangers, from working with unfenced machinery to living in cramped, wet conditions. Many labourers could not work because of smashed limbs, cracked skulls, broken backs, ripped scalps and diseases like pneumonia, tuberculosis, bronchitis and arthritis. The elderly, with neither the strength nor the health to work, fell into this group too. In an age with no state or occupational pensions, the childless elderly faced a desperate old age.

Those who will not work

In every society and at all times, there are people who choose not to work. It was no different in Mayhew's time. Beggars and vagrants (Mayhew noted they were nearly always men and boys) were a common sight. He calculated that there were between 40,000 and 100,000 destitute men and boys tramping the roads and begging where they could.

SOURCE

11 From the *Morning Chronicle*, 6 November 1849. Here, Henry Mayhew describes the living and working conditions of a female shirt-maker.

The woman lived over a coal and potato shed, occupying a small close room on the second floor back. It did not require a second glance either at the room or the occupant to tell that the poor creature was steeped in poverty to the very lips. In one corner of the apartment was rolled up the bed on the floor... beside the window was an oyster tub set upon a chair. At this she was busy washing, while on the table a small brown pan was filled with the newly washed clothes; beside it were the remains of the dinner, a piece of dry coarse bread and half a cup of coffee.

In answer to my enquiries she made the following statement: 'I'm only in the shirt line. Do nothing else. These (she said, taking a cloth off a bundle of checked shirts) is 2d a piece. I have had some at 2½d and even 3d, but them has full linen fronts and linen wristbands. It takes full five hours to do one. I have to find my own cotton and thread. I gets two skeins of cotton for 1d, because I am obliged to have it fine for them, and two skeins will make about three to four shirts. If I was to begin very early here, about six in the morning and work till nine at night, I can't make above three a day in them hours. But when there's a press of business, I work earlier and later. I often gets up at two and three in the morning and carries on till the evening of the following day, merely lying down in my clothes to take a nap of five or ten minutes. Average all the year round I can't make more than 4s a week, and then there's cotton and candles to buy out of that. The candles will cost about 10d or 1s a week in the depth of winter, and the cotton about 3d or 4d a week, so that clears 2s 6d a week. Yes – I reckon that's about it! I know it's so little I can't get a rag to my back.'

ACTIVITY
KNOWLEDGE CHECK

Henry Mayhew

1 How helpful do you find Henry Mayhew's classification of the labouring poor?

2 Compare Mayhew's classification to the simpler one of dividing the poor into 'deserving' and 'undeserving'. Which classification would a Poor Law officer find a) easier and b) fairer when administering poor relief?

3 Read Source 11. In what ways could the female shirt-maker described by Mayhew be helped by any of the agencies described in this section?

4 To what extent did Henry Mayhew challenge the prevailing orthodoxy relating to the poor?

Charles Dickens (1812–70): novelist and social critic

Novelists both reflect and direct the attitudes of the society within which they are working. Dickens, in particular, had a tremendous impact on Victorian attitudes to the poor, to poverty and to welfare. This was partly because of the way his work was presented to the public, and partly because of the power of his writing. He consistently emphasised two points: the poor were people, with hopes and desires like everyone else; and the workhouse system was a mindless, cruel institution that dehumanised clients and carers alike.

Born in Portsmouth in 1812, Dickens experienced poverty at first hand. The whole Dickens family was plunged into poverty when his father, John Dickens, was thrown into the Marshalsea prison for debt to a baker. When he was 12 years old, Charles was taken out of school and sent to work in the appalling conditions of a blacking factory where polish was made. After three years, Dickens was able to return to school as his father's debt had been repaid, but they were experiences he never forgot. They provided the background to the early chapters of *David Copperfield* (1849–50) and *Great Expectations* (1861).

Dickens' literary career began with journalism, contributing initially to *The Mirror of Parliament* and *The True Sun* before becoming a parliamentary journalist for the *Morning Chronicle*. Dickens wrote a series of pen sketches under the pseudonym 'Boz' and married Catherine Hogarth, the daughter of the editor of *Sketches by Boz*. Publishing in short instalments, rather like the brief 'sketches', became Dickens' hallmark and, because of the quality of his writing, guaranteed success. The publication of his novels in weekly, or monthly, instalments enabled Dickens to gauge his readers' reactions and modify the plots accordingly, thus ensuring their popularity. By ending each instalment on something of a cliff-hanger, Dickens was able to hold his readers' attention, leaving them eager for the next instalment. His novels weren't only popular with the middle classes, there is evidence that the illiterate poor gathered together to have episodes read to them.

While *Oliver Twist* (1837–38) is perhaps Dickens' most damning indictment of the workhouse system, other novels contain telling cameos. *Bleak House* (1852), although a bitter satire on the Courts of Chancery, contains pen portraits providing insight into the plight of the poor. Jo, the crossing sweeper, for example, describes how he feels excluded from normal human life and contact. *Little Dorrit* (1855–57) tells of Amy Dorrit, whose father was imprisoned for debt so complex that no one could work out how he could be released from the Marshalsea. In *Our Mutual Friend* (1864–65), Betty Higden reacts with intensity to the very idea of the workhouse.

Keenly aware of the plight of the poor, Dickens provided a voice for them in a manner that captured the interest and the concern of the middle classes. But he was not the only novelist to draw attention to the poor. Elizabeth Gaskell in *Mary Barton* (1848) and Benjamin Disraeli in *Sybil, or The Two Nations* (1845), for example, focused on poverty and the problems faced by those living close to the edge. This was pressure for change of a more subtle, but nonetheless pervasive, kind.

SOURCE

From Charles Dickens' *Oliver Twist*, published in 1838. When he was a boy, Dickens and his family lived in lodgings in Norfolk Street, London. This was close to a workhouse.

'Boy', said the gentleman in the high chair, 'listen to me. You know you're an orphan, I suppose? Well! You have come here to be educated, and taught a useful trade. So you'll begin to pick oakum, tomorrow morning at six o'clock.'

The members of the Board were very wise men. So they established the rule, that all poor people should have the alternative of being starved by a gradual process in the house, or by a quick one out of it. With this view, they contracted with the waterworks to lay on an unlimited supply of water; and with a corn factor to supply the periodically small quantities of oatmeal; and issued three meals of thin gruel a day, with an onion twice a week and half a roll on Sundays. They made a great many other wise and humane regulations, kindly undertook to divorce poor people, and instead of compelling a man to support his family, took his family away from him and made him a bachelor!

The system was rather expensive at first, in consequence of the increase in the undertaker's bill, and the necessity of taking in [altering] the clothes of all the paupers, which fluttered loosely on their wasted, shrunken forms, after a week or two's gruel.

The room in which the boys were fed was a large stone hall, with a copper [stove] at one end, out of which the master, dressed in an apron for the purpose and assisted by one or two women, ladled the gruel at meal-times. Each boy had one porringer [bowl] and no more – except on occasions of great public rejoicing, when he had two ounces and a quarter of bread besides. The bowls never wanted washing. The boys polished them with their spoons till they shone again. Oliver Twist and his companions suffered the tortures of slow starvation for three months.

Oliver remained a close prisoner in the dark and solitary room to which he had been consigned by the wisdom and mercy of the Board. 'If the parish would like him to learn a right pleasant trade, in a good 'spectable chimbley-sweepin bisness,' said Mr Gamfield, 'I wants a 'prentis, and I am ready to take him.'

A Level Exam-Style Question Section A

Study Source 12 before you answer this question.

Assess the value of the source for revealing attitudes to poverty and the ways by which attitudes were changed.

Explain your answer, using the source, the information given about its origin and your own knowledge about the historical context. (20 marks)

Tip

Consider the irony in the Dickens extract: what is he really saying about workhouses? How likely was it that novels played a part in changing attitudes?

SOURCE

13 *Oliver Twist asks for more.* An illustration, drawn by George Cruikshank, for Charles Dickens' novel *Oliver Twist*, published in 1838.

Charles Dickens

1 In your view, would the fact that Dickens had experienced poverty as a child mean he could not be objective when writing about the poor?

2 'Novels have no impact on people's attitudes.' Debate this in your group, with reference to Dickens' novels depicting the poor.

3 How far did Dickens' novels challenge the prevailing orthodoxy?

4 Whose writings presented the greatest challenge to the prevailing orthodoxy: Dickens, Mayhew or Smiles?

EXTRACT 3 From T.S. Ashton 'The Standard of Life of the Workers in England 1790–1830', published in the *Journal of Economic History*, Supplement IX, 1949.

During the period 1790–1830 factory production increased rapidly. A greater proportion of the people came to benefit from it, both as producers and consumers. The fall in the price of textiles reduced the price of clothing. Government contracts for uniforms and army boots called into being new industries, and after the war the products of these found a market among the better paid artisans. Boots began to take the place of clogs, and hats replaced shawls, at least for wear on Sundays. Miscellaneous commodities, ranging from clocks to pocket handkerchiefs, began to enter into the scheme of expenditure, and after 1820 such things as tea and coffee and sugar fell in price substantially. The growth of trade unions, friendly societies, savings banks, popular newspapers and pamphlets, schools and non-conformist chapels – all give evidence of a large class raised well above the level of mere subsistence.

EXTRACT 4 From Peter Mathias *The First Industrial Nation: An Economic History of Britain 1700–1914*, published 1969.

There are two sorts of calculations by which to approach the question of the standard of living [in the years 1700-1914] on a systematic basis. One is from 'national income' calculations to work out the annual total value of goods and services produced over time, divided by population numbers. The other is by looking at wages and prices, and trying to find out how much a man or a family could buy with his wage packet at different times.

The figures do not prove that the standard of living was going up. That depended in large part on how the national income was being distributed. We know that rates of investment were rising with industrialisation, but only gradually to something like 10 percent of the national income by the 1840s. No firm data exist about how the proportion of the national income which was going to consumption was divided between rents, profits, salaries and wages. However, the national income was rising steeply enough to make a rise in living standards a reasonable hypothesis.

EXTRACT 5 From E.J. Hobsbawm *Industry and Empire*, published 1968.

When workers lost their employment they had nothing to fall back on except their savings, their friendly society or their trade union, their credit with local shopkeepers, their neighbours or friends, the pawnbroker or the Poor Law, which was still the only public provision for what we now call social security. When they grew old or infirm, they were lost, unless helped by their children, for effective insurance or private pension schemes covered only a few of them.

When the first serious social surveys were made toward the end of the century – by Booth in London and Rowntree in York – they suggested that about 40 percent of the working class lived in what was then called poverty.

THINKING HISTORICALLY Change (8 a, b & c) (II)

Judgements about change

If two professionals were asked to track a patient's health over time, one might approach this task by measuring heart rate, weight and cholesterol, while the other professional might assess the patient's mental well-being, relationships and ability to achieve their goals. Both are valid approaches, but result in different reports. What is true in this medical case is true in historical cases. Measuring change in something requires: (a) a concept of what that something is (e.g. 'What is "health"?' 'What is an "economy"?'); (b) judgements about how this thing should be measured; and (c) judgements about what relevant 'markers of change' are (how we distinguish a change from a temporary and insignificant fluctuation).

Historians have differed in their accounts of economic change and development in England in the 18th and 19th centuries and debated the appropriateness of the term 'condition of England' to characterise the story of the economy in this period.

Look at Extracts 3–5 about the standard of living during this time and answer the following questions:

1 Do all three accounts agree that the standard of living of people at this time underwent a change?

2 Do all three accounts agree that the pace of change was the same – that it happened at the same time and at the same pace?

3 Do all three accounts agree in characterising change as a) rapid, b) dramatic and c) impacting on society as a whole?

4 Do the historians all think of the 'condition of England' question in the same way? For example, do they all focus on wages and investment, or on the life patterns of individuals?

ACTIVITY SUMMARY

Helping the poor, 1847–80

1 How far was government control of the Poor Law increased in the years 1847–80?

2 Why did charity not reach all of those struggling with poverty?

3 To what extent was Samuel Smiles a supporter of, or a challenge to, the poor laws?

4 Would those running the various charities be likely to welcome the writings of Samuel Smiles, Henry Mayhew and Charles Dickens?

WIDER READING

Brundage, A. *The English Poor Laws 1700–1930*, Palgrave (2002)

Crowther, M.A. *The Workhouse System 1834–1929*, University of Georgia Press (1982)

Dickens, C. *The Adventures of Oliver Twist* (1838)

Evans, E.J. (ed.) *Social Policy 1830–1914*, Routledge & Kegan Paul (1978)

Kidd, A. *State, Society and the Poor in the Nineteenth Century*, Macmillan (1999)

Murray, P. *Poverty and Welfare 1830–1914*, Hodder & Stoughton (1999)

Smiles, S. *Self-Help* (1859)

Thompson, E.P. (ed.) *The Unknown Mayhew*, Pelican Books (1973)

3.6 Social and welfare reforms: pressure and action, 1880-1914

KEY QUESTIONS

* Why was there pressure for social reform in the years 1880–1914?
* What was the significance of the Royal Commission on the Poor Laws, 1905–09?
* To what extent were the Liberal government reforms, 1906–14, effective in relieving poverty?

INTRODUCTION

The late 18th century and most of the 19th century were characterised by large numbers of reports and surveys, commissions and enquiries. There was a hunger for information about the poor and about poverty, and a need to answer the questions 'How many?' 'Where?' and 'What does relief cost?' These were, as you have seen, characterised by the use of anecdotal, qualitative material, usually to support previously held beliefs about poverty. Emphasis was placed, too, on the individual's character and lifestyle in bringing them to, and keeping them in, poverty. The increasing attraction of the doctrine of utility in managing policy, particularly when applied to pauperism, meant that all forms of administrative activity tended to be evaluated by their tendency to enhance the lives of the greatest number of people. As the 19th century progressed, there was a gradual shift in the way in which society viewed the problem of poverty. By the early 20th century, poverty had come to be seen as a problem that could be solved, and solved by increasingly expensive intervention on the part of the state. Investigators began using quantitative measurements and analysis, and redefined poverty as a failure to reach an accepted minimum standard of living. Evaluation of all forms of administrative activity was measured by the tendency it had to attack the causes of poverty, not reform the paupers. The doctrine of utility was challenged and eventually died as a philosophy underpinning the treatment of the poor.

WHY WAS THERE PRESSURE FOR SOCIAL REFORM IN THE YEARS 1880-1914?

Henry Mayhew (see Chapter 5) was one of the first investigative journalists. He sorted and sifted, analysed and categorised all the interviews with the poor that he had logged in the *Morning Chronicle*. Ever since the publication of *London Labour and the London Poor*, there have been criticisms of Mayhew's methodology, his findings and his conclusions. In general, the criticisms point out that his investigations were not systematic and his statistics were unreliable; that his focus on marginal

1880-81 – First Boer War

1893 – Royal Commission on the Aged Poor

1900 – Trades Union Congress sets up the Labour Representative Committee
Fabian Society sends delegates to the Labour Party Foundation Conference

1902 – End of second Boer War

1903 – Charles Booth's *Inquiry into the Life and Labour of the People of London* completed

1880 / 1885 / 1893 / 1899 / 1900 / 1901 / 1902 / 1903 / 1904

1885 – Mansion House Enquiry into Unemployment

1899 – Start of second Boer War

1901 – Death of Queen Victoria
Benjamin Seebohm Rowntree's *Poverty: A Study of Town Life* is published

1903-4 – Interdepartmental Committee on Physical Deterioration set up
Debate about national efficiency begins

occupations skewed his findings and gave an exaggerated picture of the extent of poverty in London; that his journalistic leanings and his need to make a living led him to be less scrupulous with the truth and he went for the more lurid and colourful descriptions of the plight of the poor. While all of these criticisms contain an element of the truth, they must not be allowed to detract from the very real contribution Mayhew made to the perception of poverty. Perhaps most importantly of all, Mayhew challenged the accepted idea that the poor were responsible for their own poverty, and he warned of the consequences of inaction. It was Mayhew who laid the basis of the investigations of Charles Booth and Benjamin Seebohm Rowntree.

SOURCE 1

It was conditions like these in Providence Place in Islington, London that Booth was recording in his study of the poor in the late 19th century.

1905 | 1906 | 1907 | 1908 | 1909 | 1910 | 1911 | 1912 | 1913 | 1914

1905–9 – Royal Commission on the Poor Laws established

1906 – Liberal Party wins General Election
Labour Representative Committee renamed the Labour Party and wins 29 seats

1908 – Campbell-Bannerman dies; Herbert Henry Asquith becomes prime minister

1909 – Royal Commission on the Poor Laws publishes majority and minority reports
Old Age Pensions Act
Labour Exchanges Act
Trade Boards Act

1910 – January: General election: Liberal Party returned to power with a reduced majority
April: House of Lords accepts the Budget
December: Second general election: Liberal Party returned to power

1911 – MPs receive salaries for the first time
Parliament Act removes power of Lords over finance bills and restricts powers over other bills
December: National Insurance Act

1914 – First World War breaks out

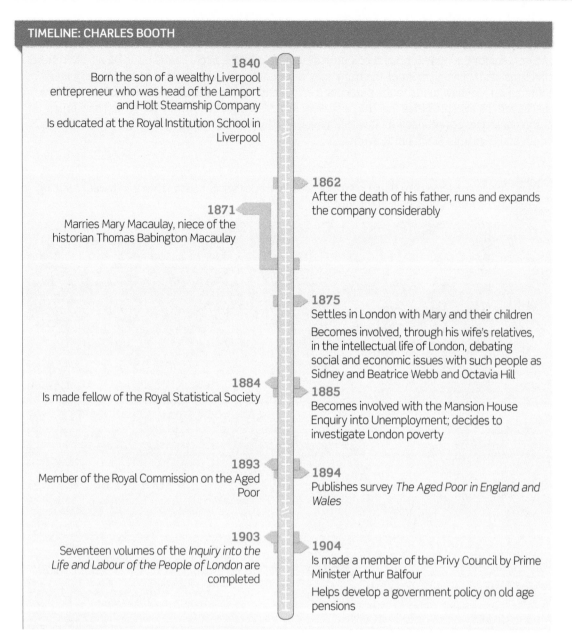

TIMELINE: CHARLES BOOTH

1840
Born the son of a wealthy Liverpool entrepreneur who was head of the Lamport and Holt Steamship Company
Is educated at the Royal Institution School in Liverpool

1862
After the death of his father, runs and expands the company considerably

1871
Marries Mary Macaulay, niece of the historian Thomas Babington Macaulay

1875
Settles in London with Mary and their children
Becomes involved, through his wife's relatives, in the intellectual life of London, debating social and economic issues with such people as Sidney and Beatrice Webb and Octavia Hill

1884
Is made fellow of the Royal Statistical Society

1885
Becomes involved with the Mansion House Enquiry into Unemployment; decides to investigate London poverty

1893
Member of the Royal Commission on the Aged Poor

1894
Publishes survey *The Aged Poor in England and Wales*

1903
Seventeen volumes of the *Inquiry into the Life and Labour of the People of London* are completed

1904
Is made a member of the Privy Council by Prime Minister Arthur Balfour
Helps develop a government policy on old age pensions

Charles Booth (1840–1916)

Charles Booth was a wealthy, serious-minded entrepreneur, whose social conscience drove him to investigate the nature of poverty in London. He employed a team of up to 35 co-workers over a period of some 17 years to undertake a detailed study of the poor in London. Their findings moved the debate forward in that Booth was convinced that most of the poor were in distress through circumstances beyond their own control.

Booth's enquiries

Charles Booth's involvement in the intellectual and socially aware radical circles in London led him to reject the hard line of the COS (see Chapter 5) that poverty was the fault of the poor. On the other hand, he was not, as a successful entrepreneur, prepared to go as far as some thinkers and blame the capitalist system itself for creating poverty. After some involvement with the 1885 Mansion House Enquiry into Unemployment, Booth was ready. He was not content, as Mayhew had been, simply to describe the conditions in which the poor lived, but wanted to explore why they lived as they did. He wanted to explore the idea that there might be structural explanations for poverty, not just moral ones.

EXTEND YOUR KNOWLEDGE

The Mansion House Enquiry into Unemployment (1885)

In 1884, the lord mayor of London opened his annual relief fund for the poor, and asked the Royal Statistical Society to advise him on how the money should be best spent. An enquiry based on the 1881 census was organised and kept in the Mansion House. Booth offered to help and seconded one of his assistants, Jesse Argyle, to the work. The enquiry demonstrated the sort of information that could be extracted from the census and combined this with the results of various questionnaires that were sent to a range of different agencies in the City of London. This combination of existing statistics (the census) and specifically gathered information (the responses to the questionnaires) was to become the chief characteristic in Booth's great survey of the *Life and Labour of the People in London*.

Booth's investigation was originally intended to last for three years, but although his findings were published on a regular basis, the whole enquiry took closer to 17 years to complete. Obviously, the same team of investigators couldn't work on the project for that length of time. Booth was the one constant factor – the lynchpin of the whole exercise – but at any one time he had a team of upwards of 35 men and women working with him. Where Booth differed from other project managers was that his team, mostly university educated, were more fellow-collaborators and, while Booth controlled their work, he expected them to contribute ideas and take responsibility for writing sections of the final work.

Booth and his team divided the population into classes. Although he acknowledged that the classes overlapped each other and no sharp distinctions were really possible, he firmly believed that an appreciation of the differences between the classes was fundamental to understanding the causes of poverty. Booth found the following.

- Class A consisted of about 0.9 percent of the population who were at the bottom of any social hierarchy: semi-criminals, loafers and idlers, and people who sometimes took on occasional work. Booth believed that people were born into this class and rarely escaped from it. This class was the residuum – the very dregs of society.

- Class B consisted of about 7.5 percent of the population who were casual, low-paid workers. Most of them were dockers, who were employed on a daily basis and had no security of employment. Booth believed these people were, because of their mental, moral or physical state, incapable of bettering themselves.

- Class C were slightly better off than Class B (here there is the problem of the shading of boundaries) but the irregular nature of their work meant that life was a constant struggle for survival.

- Class D had low incomes but their work was regular and so they were able to budget for survival.

- Class E and Class F together made up about 51.5 percent of the population who were in regular employment that paid enough to enable them to lead comfortable lives.

- Class G and Class H were the lower- and upper-middle classes who made up 17.8 percent of the population.

SOURCE

2 From Charles Booth *Life and Labour of the People of London*, Vol. 2, published in 1892.

By the word 'poor' I mean to describe those who have a sufficiently regular though bare income, such as 18s to 21s per week for a moderate family, and by 'very poor' those who from any cause fall much below this standard. The 'poor' are those whose means may be sufficient, but are barely sufficient, for decent independent life; the 'very poor' those whose means are insufficient for this according to the usual standard of life in this country. My 'poor' may be described as living under a struggle to obtain the necessities of life and make both ends meet; while the 'very poor' live in a state of chronic want, the labourers of class B do not, on average, get as much as three days' work a week, but it is doubtful if many of them could or would work full time for long if they had the opportunity. The idea of such persons is to work when they like and play when they like; these it is who are rightly called the 'leisure class' amongst the poor – leisure bounded very closely by the pressure of want, but habitual to the extent of second nature.

How reliable were Booth's findings?

Despite the mass of detail and careful analysis provided in Booth's 17 volumes, and the very obvious thoroughness of his approach, there were contemporary criticisms. Booth himself supplied the basis of modern criticisms in that he openly admitted he relied on observation only. Thus, Booth did not take into account income when defining poverty. This subjective and unreliable measure can lead to criticism that his investigation was flawed.

The most strident contemporary criticism came from Helen Bosanquet of the COS (see page 143). She objected to the social survey method developed by Booth because it had no underpinning philosophy or principle. She believed that his '**poverty line**' was flawed because she disputed the 'facts' on which it was based as they were produced by the, to her, dubious survey method; she condemned the false impression of definiteness it conveyed. She attacked the statistical basis of Booth's findings, claiming that it underestimated the income level of poor families. She, of course, championed the family case-work approach of the COS and criticised Booth's workers who, although they did spend time living in poor quarters, tended to rely on primary research findings of such people as school board members and teachers. This does tend to shed some doubt on the reliability of Booth's findings, a view that was developed further by historians in the last decades of the 20th century.

EXTEND YOUR KNOWLEDGE

The later interpretation of Booth's findings
Later historians and sociologists have been lucky; Booth's original notes and those of his fellow investigators have survived. It is therefore possible to go back to the beginning, rework his figures and reconsider.

The view that Booth's defined classes were an uneasy mix of the economic and the moral is represented by J. Brown, who argues strongly that Booth's moral preoccupations influenced his work. He shows that, by dividing the working classes into various strata, and by focusing on classes A and B, Booth is reflecting a common fear of contemporary politicians and social reformers that the respectable poor would be infected by contact with classes A and B during periods of social distress.

Karel Williams approached Booth's work from a slightly different perspective, pointing out that as part of his investigation Booth surveyed schoolteachers for their views on how many children were in poverty. This suggested a figure of 45 percent, much higher than the 30.7 percent projected by school visitors. Yet, Booth provided no evidence for this and other apparent discrepancies in his evidence.

ACTIVITY
KNOWLEDGE CHECK

Charles Booth

1 a) Draw a pie chart showing Booth's eight classes.

   b) Using the definitions in Source 2, label the different parts of the pie chart.

   c) What is helpful and what are the problems with Booth's analysis of poverty?

2 Look back to Henry Mayhew's definitions on pages 124-25.

   a) What is the difference between the way in which Mayhew classified the poor in the mid-19th century and Booth's classifications, 50 years later?

   b) How far are these differences indicative of a change in attitude to the causes of poverty?

Benjamin Seebohm Rowntree (1871–1954)

Benjamin Seebohm Rowntree (usually known as Seebohm Rowntree) was a devout Quaker all his life; this tended to dominate his attitude to society in general and his own workforce in particular. Believing that healthy, contented workers were also efficient workers, he championed democracy in the workplace, a minimum wage, family allowances and old age pensions.

TIMELINE: BENJAMIN SEEBOHM ROWNTREE

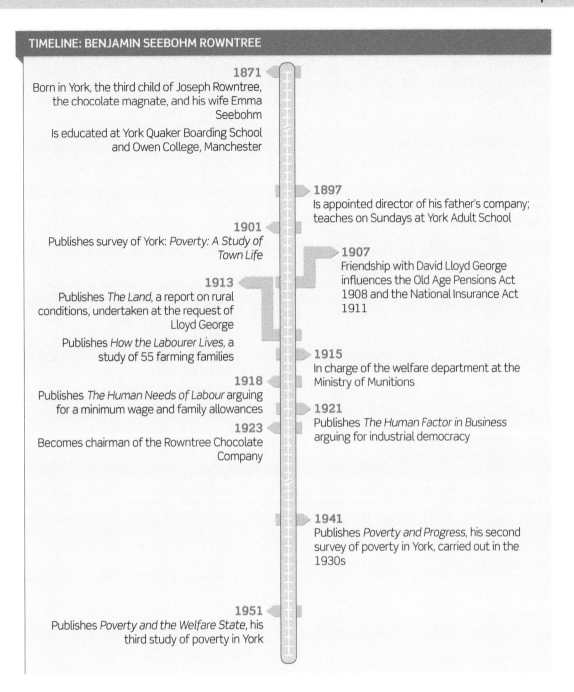

1871
Born in York, the third child of Joseph Rowntree, the chocolate magnate, and his wife Emma Seebohm
Is educated at York Quaker Boarding School and Owen College, Manchester

1897
Is appointed director of his father's company; teaches on Sundays at York Adult School

1901
Publishes survey of York: *Poverty: A Study of Town Life*

1907
Friendship with David Lloyd George influences the Old Age Pensions Act 1908 and the National Insurance Act 1911

1913
Publishes *The Land*, a report on rural conditions, undertaken at the request of Lloyd George
Publishes *How the Labourer Lives*, a study of 55 farming families

1915
In charge of the welfare department at the Ministry of Munitions

1918
Publishes *The Human Needs of Labour* arguing for a minimum wage and family allowances

1921
Publishes *The Human Factor in Business* arguing for industrial democracy

1923
Becomes chairman of the Rowntree Chocolate Company

1941
Publishes *Poverty and Progress*, his second survey of poverty in York, carried out in the 1930s

1951
Publishes *Poverty and the Welfare State*, his third study of poverty in York

Rowntree's enquiries

Seebohm Rowntree conducted three surveys of poverty in York that provided a wealth of statistical data and which supported the findings of Charles Booth in London. Rowntree made it clear that his aim was to find out both the numbers of people living in poverty and the nature of that poverty. He set out to conduct an enquiry into the poor in the city of York in much the same way as Charles Booth was doing in London. He hoped to build on Booth's work and give more precision to Booth's idea of a 'poverty line'. Rowntree was to complete three surveys on poverty in York in all: the second in 1941 and the third in 1951.

Rowntree's first general survey of York was carried out in 1899 and his findings published in 1901. He used one full-time investigator who made house-to-house visits, and relied, too, on information from clergymen, teachers and voluntary workers. Rowntree was focusing on the working classes in York, whom he defined as those families where the head of the household was a wage earner and no servants were employed. Altogether, some 11,560 households were visited (almost all the wage-earning households in York) and information obtained from about 46,754 people, exactly two-thirds of the total population of the city.

Rowntree found that about 28 percent of the population of York were in obvious need and living in squalor. Using the information he could gather about their wages, he worked out that the minimum wage that would be necessary for a family to live in a state of physical efficiency was 21 shillings a week. At this level, he drew his 'poverty line', and was able to demonstrate that around ten percent of the population of York lived below this poverty line and were living in what Rowntree defined as '**primary poverty**'. There was no way in which they would ever make ends meet. The remaining 18 percent, Rowntree determined, were living in what he defined a '**secondary poverty**'. These people were teetering on the brink of primary poverty, with the bare necessities of life but without any leeway for emergencies and certainly no savings. The death of the main wage earner, a trade slump leading to lay-offs, or even a child's illness could throw the family into primary poverty. Rowntree began to uncover, too, what he defined as a 'poverty cycle'. He found that childhood was a time of poverty; conditions improved when the children grew and became wage earners and continued into their early married years. As soon as children were born, couples slipped below the poverty line and remained there until their children began to earn. After a period of relative prosperity when their children were grown, couples fell below the poverty line again when they were old and could no longer work.

KEY TERMS

Primary poverty
People cannot obtain even the basic necessities of life (food, shelter and clothing) no matter how well they organise their budgets. This is absolute poverty.

Secondary poverty
People can obtain the basic necessities of life (food, shelter and clothing) provided there are no extra calls on their budget.

SOURCE 3
From B.S. Rowntree *Poverty: A Study of Town Life*, published in 1901.

Let us clearly understand what 'mere physical efficiency' means. A family living upon the scale allowed for in this estimate must never spend a penny on railway fare or bus. They must never go into the country unless they walk. They must never purchase a halfpenny newspaper or spend a penny to buy a ticket for a popular concert. They must write no letters to absent children, for they cannot afford to pay the postage. They must never contribute to their church or chapel, or give any help to a neighbour, which costs them money. They cannot save, nor can they join a sick club or Trade Union, because they cannot pay the necessary subscriptions. The children must have no pocket money for dolls, marbles, or sweets. The father must smoke no tobacco, and must drink no beer. The mother must never buy any pretty clothes for herself or for her children, the character of the family wardrobe as for the family diet, being governed by the regulation, 'nothing must be bought but that which is absolutely necessary for the maintenance of physical health, and what is bought must be of the plainest and most economical description'. Should a child fall ill, it must be attended by the parish doctor; should it die, it must be buried by the parish. Finally, the wage-earner must never be absent from his work for a single day.

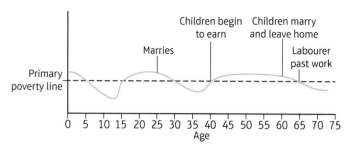

Figure 6.1 Rowntree's poverty line and poverty cycle, from B.S. Rowntree *Poverty: A Study of Town Life*, published in 1901.

SOURCE 4
Menus collected by Rowntree in York, 1901.

	Breakfast	Dinner	Tea	Supper
Friday	Bread, butter, tea	Bread, butter, toast, tea	Bread, butter, tea	
Saturday	Bread, bacon, coffee	Bacon, potatoes, pudding, tea	Bread, butter, shortcake	Tea, bread, kippers
Sunday	Bread, butter, shortcake, coffee	Pork, onions, potatoes, Yorkshire pudding	Bread, butter, shortcake, tea	Bread and meat
Monday	Bread, bacon, butter, tea	Pork, potatoes, pudding, tea	Bread, butter, tea	
Tuesday	Bread, bacon, butter, coffee	Pork, bread, tea	Bread, butter, boiled eggs, tea	Bread, bacon, butter, tea
Wednesday	Bread, bacon, butter, tea	Bacon, eggs, potatoes, bread, tea	Bread, butter, tea	
Thursday	Bread, butter, coffee	Bread, bacon, tea	Bread, butter, tea.	

How reliable were Rowntree's findings?

Helen Bosanquet of the COS immediately attacked Rowntree's findings in much the same way as she attacked those of Charles Booth. As with Booth, she claimed he had overestimated the level of poverty by setting the poverty line too high. Rowntree himself was aware of the shortcomings of his survey, recognising that it was based mainly on observation. He does, too, describe how he arrived at the number of people who were living in primary and secondary poverty, and this can be open to criticism as being too subjective.

Subjective though his criteria and analyses were, at least they were more or less consistent. It must be remembered, too, that the distinction between 'primary' and 'secondary' poverty was not designed to identify the poor. That had already been done. It was intended to use the terms to describe the nature of that poverty. It should also be noted that the criteria used by Rowntree to identify the poor did not here include income. Poverty was identified by that which was visible to the investigators. Thus, a family of poor managers with a higher income than a family of good managers on a lower income would be classed as 'poor' when the latter would not. In this, Rowntree's criteria were similar to those used by Booth and so their findings can, with some justification, be compared. They both found that around 30 percent of a total urban population were living in poverty at the end of the 19th century. And both investigators suggested that poverty was a state that was beyond the control of the poor.

EXTEND YOUR KNOWLEDGE

Later interpretations of Rowntree's findings

While it is clear that Rowntree's survey covered all the identifiable working-class families in York, it is equally clear that there are some problems with the ways in which he arrived at his conclusions and these have been identified by historians and sociologists (for example, M. Brown and N. Madge and K. Coates and R. Silburn). Certainly, precise statements about numbers, percentages and income levels must be treated with caution. Rowntree was unable to ascertain the exact wages of many workers and estimated them: 'In the case of skilled workers, the earnings were assumed to be the average wage which obtains in the district for the particular trade.' Thus, his frequent use of two decimal places cannot be justified by the crude nature of his data.

EXTRACT

From the historian Donald Read *Edwardian England 1901–15*, published in 1972.

The social revelations of Booth and Rowntree undermined the Victorian assumption that poverty was more often than not the outcome of individual character failings. Booth still accepted that a substantial proportion of those in distress must be weak or corrupt; but he argued that it was their environment, and especially their struggle for work, not inherent weakness, which had degraded them. This was a halfway position. Rowntree explicitly stated that though many unskilled workers lacked ideas they did not lack good moral qualities. Poverty, he concluded, was in large part 'the result of false social and economic conditions'. Why should honest workmen be expected to struggle against these conditions unsupported except by charity or by the Poor Law, each with their attendant stigma of inadequacy? Here was an approach to the poverty problem conflicting markedly with that of the Charity Organisation Society, which into Edwardian times assumed that poverty involved a failing not so much in society as in individual character, and that relief should be dispensed only with the careful purpose of forcing individuals back into self-support. The main weakness of Booth's description of poverty and unemployment was his failure to take account of the trade cycle. His picture of poverty was largely static. Rowntree's was more dynamic, allowing for variations both in general economic and family circumstances.

SOURCE

A poor family, living in one room, at the beginning of the 20th century.

A Level Exam-Style Question Section B

How accurate is it to say that the revelations of Booth and Rowntree undermined Victorian assumptions about the nature of poverty? (20 marks)

Tip

Make sure you are clear about what the Victorian assumptions were about the nature of poverty. Be certain, too, to tease out the differences between Booth and Rowntree when considering how far they undermined Victorian assumptions about the nature of poverty.

ACTIVITY
KNOWLEDGE CHECK

Seebohm Rowntree

1 How helpful do you find Rowntree's concept of the cycle of poverty?

2 Study Source 4. This dietary would probably be quite filling – but how nutritious would it have been?

3 Study Sources 3, 4 and 5. Which source would be the most reliable for a study of poverty at the beginning of the 20th century?

4 Booth and Rowntree both made an analysis of poverty.

   a) What were the similarities and the differences between their analyses? Use Source 2 and Figure 6.1 in your answer.

   b) Which analysis do you consider the most useful when trying to determine the amount of poverty in 19th- and early 20th-century Britain?

5 Does the fact that Booth's and Rowntree's surveys were statistically flawed mean that they should be ignored?

The Fabian Society: a think tank

KEY TERM

Socialism
A political and economic ideology which advocates that the means of production should be owned and democratically controlled by the community as a whole.

The 1880s saw an upsurge of socialist activity in Britain and the Fabian Society was both part of that upsurge and one of its leaders. Founded in London in January 1884, the Fabian Society had as its object advancing the principles of **socialism** in a gradual, non-confrontational way. It grew out of an older society, 'The Fellowship of the New Life', whose members were dedicated to transforming society by setting an example of good, clean and simple living for others to follow. Increasing pressure from some members to politicise their approach led to the formation of a separate society, the Fabian Society, which absorbed 'The Fellowship of the New Life' in 1898.

The Fabian Society became the pre-eminent Edwardian left-wing academic and intellectual society, attracting a range of prominent movers and shakers of the day: George Bernard Shaw, H.G. Wells, Annie Besant, Ramsay MacDonald and Emmeline Pankhurst, for example. The society held public meetings, published numerous pamphlets and lobbied politicians on a wide range of topics from Poor Law reform to international alliances, but all having at their core the need to advance national and international socialism. All the early Fabians were united in their rejection of violent upheaval as a way of bringing about change, preferring to utilise the power of local government and trade unions. Key members were Sidney and Beatrice Webb, who were prodigious authors on a range of subjects but primarily important for their range of studies of industrial Britain and for developing a thorough research methodology. Indeed, it was their *Minority Report to the Commission of the Poor Law* (see page 141) that contributed much to the basis of the modern welfare state.

EXTEND YOUR KNOWLEDGE

Beatrice Webb (1858–1943)
Beatrice Webb was an indefatigable social investigator, reformer and pioneer socialist. The eighth daughter of Richard Potter, a wealthy railway entrepreneur, she had little formal education but read widely and travelled extensively with her parents. In her early twenties, she joined the COS and it was whilst working amongst the poor that she came to realise that charity was not enough: the causes of poverty had to be tackled.

In 1886, Beatrice went to work as a researcher for Charles Booth on his survey of London poverty, where she was assigned to investigate the lives of London dockers. It was at this time that she wrote articles on dock labourers and the sweated trades that were published in the journal *The Nineteenth Century,* and as a result was invited to testify before the House of Lords. In 1892, she married Sidney Webb, who was by then a leading Fabian, and together they worked on several books including *The History of Trade Unionism* (1894) and *Industrial Democracy* (1897). Using money left to the Fabian Society by Henry Hutchinson, a wealthy Derby solicitor, they founded the London School of Economics and Political Science in 1895 and the journal the *New Statesman* in 1913. They both served on the Royal Commission on the Poor Laws, and were instrumental in the production of the minority report.

During the First World War, Beatrice served on several government committees, and continued writing pamphlets for the Fabian Society. In 1918, when Sidney was a member of the executive of the new Labour Party, Beatrice wrote its policy statement 'Labour and the New Socialist Order'. In the 1923 general election, Sidney was elected MP for Seaham and was appointed president of the Board of Trade by Prime Minister Ramsay MacDonald. Elevated to the Lords as Baron Passfield, Sidney served as secretary of state for the Colonies – Beatrice refused the title of Lady Passfield as a matter of principle. Beatrice and Sidney visited Russia in 1932 and were enthusiastic about what they saw, writing *Soviet Communism: A New Civilisation?* The question mark disappeared in later editions. Beatrice had a lasting influence on the early Labour Party and on socialist thinking.

KEY TERM

Boer War
The first Boer War (December 1880 to March 1881) was more of a skirmish between the British and the Boers living in the Transvaal. It was caused by the British attempt to impose a system of confederation over their colonies in southern Africa.

The second Boer War (October 1899 to May 1902) is the one most people mean when they refer to the 'Boer War'. It was fought between soldiers of the British Empire and the two independent Boer republics of the Orange Free State and the Transvaal Republic. The war resulted in the loss of about 75,000 lives and ended in defeat for the two independent republics, which were absorbed into the British Empire.

The first Fabian Society pamphlets were aimed at promoting social justice and were generally more radical in their policies than the early 20th century reforms of the Liberal government would suggest (see pages 143–49). In 1906, Fabians lobbied for the introduction of a minimum wage in order to stop British companies trying to remain competitive by lowering wages, and in 1911 for the creation of a universal health service that would enable the British to be sufficiently physically fit to defend and develop their Empire.

This latter lobbying was a development of the Fabian view of imperialism. In 1900, the Fabians produced a pamphlet *Fabianism and the Empire*, which maintained that imperialism should be the basis of British foreign policy as the pursuit of Empire would enable Britain to become the centre of a worldwide empire instead of a collection of islands off the north-west coast of Europe. This led Fabians to support the British in the **Boer War**, believing that small nations had no place in a world of empires. Shocked at the poor physical state of recruits to the army (see page 139), Fabians advocated the formation of a citizen army to replace the professional one. This citizen army would, Fabians maintained, be full of fit and healthy men. This would come about if government accepted their proposals for a universal health service and the extension of the Factory Acts so that those in half-time employment could be subjected to extensive physical training, education in citizenship and training in the use of modern weapons.

In 1900, Fabians were active in the formation of what was to become the Labour Party, sending delegates to the Labour Party Foundation Conference. This resulted in the emergence of the Labour Representative Committee (LRC), to which left-wing and socialist societies, including the Fabian Society, were affiliated. Six years later, 26 LRC sponsored candidates won seats in the election and set up as a separate party in the Commons – the Labour Party. This election success reflected a growth of interest, in the country at large, in socialism and socialist ideas. Unsurprisingly, during this period membership of the Fabian Society tripled, numbering some 2,500 by 1908, half of whom lived and worked in London. A student section was established in 1912, which had more than 500 members by 1914.

EXTEND YOUR KNOWLEDGE

The emerging Labour Party

The electoral changes of 1867 and 1884 had almost doubled the electorate and, in several industrial parliamentary constituencies, the majority of voters were working class and were clamouring for change. In 1900, the Trades Union Congress set up the LRC, intending it to be the political voice of the working class. The LRC (in 1906 renamed the Labour Party) aimed, first, to make the trades unions legally secure because they were the first line of defence for working people. It then turned its attention to social reform, calling for the abolition of the Poor Law, help for the unemployed, old age pensions and free education for all. Here was challenge to both the political parties.

The 1906 House of Commons contained 29 Labour MPs who supported, in the main, the triumphant Liberal Party. But the Liberals, with their landslide majority, were wary of them. The Labour Party had a programme of reform that was attractive to the working classes. If the Liberals did not introduce a programme of major welfare reforms, and so steal Labour's thunder, then maybe, at the next election or the one after that, Labour would replace the Liberals as the main opposition party to the Conservatives. It was possible, too, that if the working classes did not get the reforms they sought from the Liberals, they would push Labour into an even more extreme, left-wing, political position. It was just possible that the Labour Party would be prepared to embrace a more radical form of socialism, dedicated to the overthrow of capitalism. This was no idle fantasy. In Germany, Chancellor Otto von Bismarck had been forced to introduce social reforms in order to limit the growth of radical socialism.

A bequest of £20,000 from a Derby-based Fabian, Henry Hutchinson, led to the foundation of the London School of Economics and Political Science (LSE) by Fabian Society members in 1895. The prime movers here were the Webbs and G.B. Shaw. Originally intended as a research institute to provide proof of the efficacy of the collectivist ideal, the LSE quickly developed into an institution encouraging the study of a wide range of subjects. Fabians' commitment to the promotion of socialist ideals led, in 1913, to the foundation of the *New Statesman*. This left-wing socialist magazine was the brainchild of Sidney and Beatrice Webb and sold over 2,000 copies of the first edition, indicative of the interest in radical ideas in the early years of the 20th century.

A Level Exam-Style Question Section B

'The Fabian Society was nothing more than a talking shop for intellectuals.' How far do you agree with this statement? (20 marks)

Tip

Establish first what the quotation means by a 'talking shop for intellectuals' and then consider the impact the Fabians had on, for example, the debate on national efficiency and the problem of amending the poor laws.

The impact of the Boer War

The second Boer War (October 1899 to May 1902) was not a conscript war. Young men volunteered in their thousands, and in their thousands they were rejected as unfit. In some industrial areas, two out of every three potential recruits did not pass the basic army medical examination. The investigations of Booth and Rowntree seemed to confirm the findings of the recruitment boards; indeed, Rowntree noted that of 3,600 volunteers seeking enlistment in York, Leeds and Sheffield between 1897 and 1900, 26.5 percent were rejected as unfit and a further 29 percent were only accepted as 'specials', in the expectation that army training could bring them up to standard. This reinforced a general concern that the British working people were somehow operating at a less than efficient level. There were immediate fears, both economic and military.

- The security of the British Empire depended on a fit, efficient army; an army that couldn't find sufficient fit recruits would be unlikely to be able to maintain the Empire.

- Britain had been the leading industrial nation in the world in the early years of the 19th century. The successful economies of Germany and the USA seemed to imply that Britain now had a somewhat inferior workforce with neither the stamina nor the intelligence and skills to compete.

Accordingly, in 1903, the government set up a commission of enquiry.

The Interdepartmental Committee on Physical Deterioration, 1903-4

The committee's brief was to investigate claims that the health of the population was, in fact, deteriorating. It found that fears of national deterioration were largely unfounded. However, the committee concluded that the health of large sections of the urban population was being undermined by poverty, ignorance and neglect. It made 53 recommendations that were focused on changing public health administration and improving the standard of public health provision, introducing new methods of monitoring the health of the people, and improving standards of personal hygiene. In practical terms, these involved recommendations regarding, for example, medical inspections and the provision of free school meals for the very poor.

The debate on national efficiency

The political elite, together with many influential contemporary figures, were conscious of the relative decline of the British economy when compared to the fast-developing economies of the USA and Germany, but were uncertain as to whether recovery was possible. In this climate of uncertainty, new solutions were sought. The work of Booth and Rowntree, coupled with the revelations about the physical health of the army, fuelled a debate about national efficiency. This debate cut across party lines. Indeed, for a brief period some of the more enthusiastic supporters of national efficiency looked for a realignment of British politics, floating the idea of a new political party under the leadership of the former Liberal prime minister, Lord Rosebery. Some supporters of national efficiency focused almost entirely on the needs of the military. Others linked economic recovery with social reform and amongst these were Sidney Webb, who argued strongly that a minimum standard of living was essential to national efficiency and imperial strength. In these ways, the idea of national efficiency became part of the debate as to the way forward, and many found it acceptable to express their support for social reform using the national efficiency argument. This gave social reform a political respectability. Men such as Herbert Asquith and Richard Haldane, who had been involved in the campaign for national efficiency, became members of the Cabinet in the new Liberal administration of 1906, with Asquith becoming prime minister in 1908. Whilst there were many pressures on the government at that time to introduce social reform, the early Liberal reforms can be linked to the campaign for national efficiency.

It can be argued that the debate on national efficiency influenced arguments about social policy in two main ways. Firstly, it focused attention on the importance of Britain's human resources as being fundamental to national power in the economic field as well as the military one. Secondly, building on this, it encouraged policymakers to look more closely at social and economic policies that were being implemented by Britain's competitors and to calculate which were the most effective and could be implemented in Britain.

SOURCE

6 British Army recruits in front of the recruiting depot at St George's Barracks, London, c1896. They were not considered to be fighting fit but with good food and training they would eventually be healthy enough to be soldiers.

Towards social reform

1 In what ways did the experience of the Boer War add to the pressure for social reform?

2 Which do you find the more persuasive argument for social reform: the empirical research of Booth and Rowntree, or the ideas of the Fabian Society and the campaign for national efficiency? Explain your answer.

WHAT WAS THE SIGNIFICANCE OF THE ROYAL COMMISSION ON THE POOR LAWS, 1905-09?

A Royal Commission to enquire into the workings of the poor laws and the best way to relieve the poor was set up by the Conservative government in 1905. The 20 members of the commission had a wide range of appropriate expertise: five were Poor Law guardians, six were members of the COS and four were members of the Local Government Board. Social researchers Charles Booth and Beatrice and Sidney Webb were appointed, too, along with religious and trade union leaders. Members of the commission were thus far better qualified to address the problem of poverty than those who had participated in the Royal Commission in 1832–34. Their enquiry was also far more detailed. They visited 200 Poor Law unions and 400 institutions, took evidence from 450 witnesses and read through and analysed 900 statements of written evidence. However, when they came to report in 1909, they could not agree on the way forward and so produced two reports.

The majority report

The findings of the majority of Royal Commission members were as follows.

- The origins of poverty were basically moral.
- The Poor Law should stay as the main vehicle for dealing with poverty.
- Boards of guardians allowed too much relief and they should be replaced by public assistance committees.
- General mixed workhouses did not deter the able-bodied poor.
- There should be greater co-operation between charities and those administering the Poor Law, and voluntary aid committees should be set up to enable this to happen.

However, some members of the Royal Commission wanted to sweep the Poor Law away and start again with something quite different.

The minority report

The findings of the minority of the Royal Commission members were as follows.

- The origins of poverty were basically economic.

- A Ministry of Labour should be set up which would introduce and oversee public work schemes, set up a string of national labour exchanges to help the unemployed find jobs, organise a schedule of training schemes and set up detention colonies for those who were deliberately idle.

- The Poor Law administration should be broken up into education committees to deal with child poverty, pension committees to deal with problems of the elderly poor and health committees to deal with problems of the poor who were sick or infirm.

Initially, the majority report was well received. This alarmed Beatrice and Sidney Webb, who were the driving forces behind the minority report. They were so convinced they were correct that they launched themselves into a campaign for the break-up of the existing Poor Law. In doing this, although they captured the imagination and support of the younger generation, they risked antagonising leading politicians in both the government and the opposition.

However, the two 'sides' of the commission had more in common than might at first seem the case. Both condemned the existing system of relieving poverty. Both criticised the failure of central government to ensure that local boards of guardians behaved in a uniform way when providing relief. Both condemned the continuation, in some unions, of general mixed workhouses, and both criticised the wasteful overlapping of services provided by the Poor Law guardians and the local government boards.

The problem in setting up a Royal Commission that then produces two diametrically opposed reports is that governments do not feel compelled to act on either set of recommendations. In this case, those who favoured 'no change' were greatly strengthened by the majority report, and the changes it did recommend tended to be overlooked. The boards of guardians, in particular, vehemently opposed the proposal that they should be dissolved, and their opposition was supported by the Local Government Board and its political chief, John Burns. The divided commission stood little chance of success. On a more positive side, the work of the commission over a period of some four years gave the problem of poverty, and investigations into the causes of poverty, a high profile. This in itself put the necessary pressure on the government to force it to come up with solutions. However, by the time the reports were published, the Liberal government had already embarked on its own programme of reform.

Principles for welfare reform

The Royal Commission established certain principles for welfare reform in the 20th century.

- Poverty as a condition was not always the fault of the poor.
- Government should take responsibility for improving the situation of the poorest members of society.
- Poor Law Unions and Boards of Guardians should be abolished and replaced by Public Assistance Committees that would work closely with local voluntary agencies.

SOURCE

7

From Helen Bosanquet *The Poor Law Report of 1909,* published in 1909. She wrote for the COS and during 1908–21 was its editor. She was a member of the Royal Commission on the Poor Laws where she was the chief advocate of organised voluntary action and was the main author of the majority report.

Unless a community is to become bankrupt it must keep steadily in view the importance of enforcing upon the individual the primary duty of being self-supporting.

It is this which constitutes one of the chief difficulties of any scheme of public assistance. The mere fact that a provision exists for those who fail in their primary duty causes many to fail who might otherwise have succeeded. It is difficult for anyone not intimately acquainted with poor law administration to realise that many of those who claim relief are suffering from sheer laziness. The workhouse inmate who declared that 'so long as I can get sixteen ounces of pie for my dinner and my children kept for life, and they don't ask me to do any more than polish the stair bannisters, I'm not going to work,' was perhaps more outspoken, but not more lazy, than many another of his kind. Nor is it widely enough known how many who are incapable are so through their dishonest breaking of the laws of sobriety and morality. It is not of course true that poverty is always a crime; the sternest judge has never thought or said so. But the poverty which is due to excess or self-indulgence is a crime, and should be more frankly recognised as such.

The population which comes within the scope of the Poor Law is made up of the most mixed elements. Individuals of every age, of every shade of character, of every degree of physical or moral incapacity, with every variety of disease or disability, are all brought together by one factor, that they demand to be maintained at the cost of the community. It has been argued by some members of the Commission that the differences are so great as to outweigh the common element, and that the responsibility for providing for each particular need should be assigned to a special authority, regardless of whether the people to be provided for were to be maintained by the ratepayers or not.

The majority of the commission holds, on the contrary, that the common element is so important as to justify – indeed, to necessitate – the existence of a special law to authorise and regulate the relief of these people, and of a special authority to administer that law. When an individual claims to be maintained at the cost of the community, it is clear that the claim cannot be an unconditional one. No State has every yet offered, or ever can offer, free maintenance to everyone who likes to apply for it, whatever his circumstances may be; and it become necessary that any claim should be immediately submitted to a judicial authority which will decide whether the applicant is entitled to receive public assistance.

SOURCE

8

From Sidney and Beatrice Webb *English Poor Law Policy,* published in 1910. Here, they comment on the minority report, of which they were the main authors.

There are those who see in this proposal to 'break up' the Poor law an ignoring of what they call the 'moral factor'. To speak of the prevention of destitution is, to such critics, equivalent to implying that all destitution is due to causes over which the individual has no control – thus putting aside the contributory causes of idleness, extravagance, drunkenness, gambling and all sorts of irregularity of life. But this is to misconceive the position taken up by the Minority Commissioners, and to fail in appreciation of their proposals. They do not deny – indeed, what observer could possibly deny or minimise? – the extent to which the destitution of whole families is caused or aggravated by personal defects and shortcomings in one or other of their members, and most frequently in the husband and father upon whom the family maintenance normally depends.

The Minority Commissioners certainly do not ignore the fact that what has to be aimed at is not this or that improvement in material circumstances or physical comfort, but an improvement in personal character.

Two considerations may make the position clear. However large may be the part in producing destitution that we may choose to ascribe to the 'moral factor' – to defects or shortcomings in the character of the unfortunate victims themselves – the investigations of the Royal Commission indicate that at least nine-tenths of all the paupers arrive at pauperism along one or other of three roads. These are the Road of Neglected Childhood, the Road of Sickness and Feeble-mindedness, and the Road of Unemployment (including Under-employment). If it can be said that it is to some defect of moral character or personal shortcoming that the sinking into destitution at the bottom of the road is to be ascribed, it is abundantly clear that the assumed defect or shortcoming manifests itself in, or at least is accompanied by, either child-neglect, sickness, feeble-mindedness, or unemployment. These are the roads by which the future pauper travels.

A Level Exam-Style Question Section A

Study Source 8 before you answer this question.

Assess the value of the source for revealing the problems involved in amending the poor laws and the ways in which attitudes to poverty had changed by the beginning of the 20th century.

Explain your answer, using the source, the information given about its origin and your own knowledge about the historical context. (20 marks)

Tip
Remember to use the content of the source, particularly where it refers to the attitudes of those who wrote the majority report. Use the context of the source, too, to address the ways in which attitudes had changed.

EXTEND YOUR KNOWLEDGE

Helen Bosanquet (1860-1925)

The eldest daughter of the Reverend John Dendy and his wife Sarah, Helen obtained a First Class degree in Moral Sciences from Cambridge University in 1889. Through her membership of the London Ethical Society she met, and later, in 1895, married the philosopher Bernard Bosanquet. Helen soon gained a reputation as a social theorist and, from her work with the COS where she edited their *Review* in the years 1908-21, as a social reformer. Diametrically opposed to the views and approaches to poverty and the poor of Beatrice and Sidney Webb, her portrayals of working-class life can be less than generous. Nevertheless, she was well regarded at the time for her work with the COS and served on the Royal Commission on the Poor Laws (1905-9), becoming the main author of the majority report. She wrote many articles and published some important studies on poverty and the poor. Strongly opposed to state intervention, favouring private charity over public welfare programmes and staunchly opposed to the Fabians, she denounced the Webbs' approach whenever she could, accusing them of using evidence selectively to fit in with their own theories. She was active in founding social work training programmes at Bedford College and the Women's University Settlement. The latter ironically become part of the London School of Economics that was founded by the Webbs.

ACTIVITY
KNOWLEDGE CHECK

Majority and minority reports

1 Read Source 7. In no more than 150 words, summarise the argument being made by Helen Bosanquet.

2 Read Source 8. In no more than 150 words, summarise the argument being made by Sidney and Beatrice Webb.

3 Whose argument do you find the more convincing? Why?

TO WHAT EXTENT WERE THE LIBERAL GOVERNMENT REFORMS, 1906-14, EFFECTIVE IN RELIEVING POVERTY?

The Liberal government, elected in 1906, managed to avoid the problem of whether or not to reform the Poor Law by ignoring it altogether. It set about building new institutions that were completely separate from the Poor Law system. The measures it passed fell into two main groups. The early legislation, concerning children and the elderly, was the culmination of discussions that had taken place over many years. The later legislation, involving sickness and unemployment, took the government into new and uncharted territory.

Some relatively uncontroversial legislation, involving the welfare of children (see pages 48–49) was carried out under the premiership of Henry Campbell-Bannerman. In 1908, when Herbert Asquith took over as prime minister, welfare reform speeded up. With progressive Liberals – David Lloyd George at the Treasury and Winston Churchill at the Board of Trade – radical change was bound to come. The two men made a powerful duo. Lloyd George, in his mid-forties, was the first cabinet minister to have been born into relative poverty; Winston Churchill, in his early thirties, was the son of Lord Randolph Churchill and an aristocrat by birth. Both had the knack of capturing the mood of the people and using it to produce results.

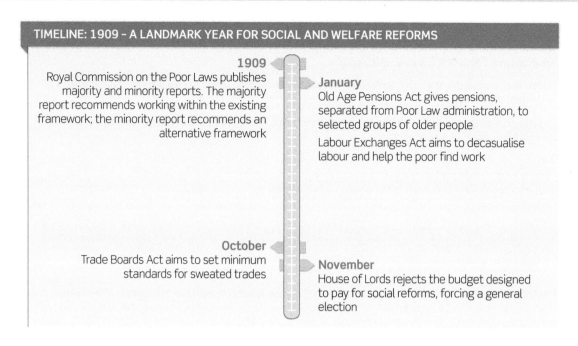

TIMELINE: 1909 – A LANDMARK YEAR FOR SOCIAL AND WELFARE REFORMS

1909
Royal Commission on the Poor Laws publishes majority and minority reports. The majority report recommends working within the existing framework; the minority report recommends an alternative framework

January
Old Age Pensions Act gives pensions, separated from Poor Law administration, to selected groups of older people

Labour Exchanges Act aims to decasualise labour and help the poor find work

October
Trade Boards Act aims to set minimum standards for sweated trades

November
House of Lords rejects the budget designed to pay for social reforms, forcing a general election

Old age pensions

The idea of providing old age pensions had first arisen as a serious proposal in the 1870s. Canon William Blackley, a relatively obscure rural clergyman, wrote an article in the 1878 edition of the journal *The Nineteenth Century* in which he proposed a compulsory contributory pension scheme. His suggestion was prompted by the failure of the friendly societies (see page 117) to provide for a wider group than the prosperous working class. This idea was developed in the 1890s by Charles Booth (see page 131) urging the introduction of a non-contributory pension scheme whereby the elderly would receive a pension by right, funded from taxation. In 1895, a Royal Commission on the Aged Poor reported that no fundamental alterations were needed to the existing system of providing relief for the aged poor, adding the rider that distinctions should be made between the respectable poor who had tried to provide for their old age, and the feckless poor who had become destitute as a result of their own lack of foresight. This unfortunate continuation of the categorisation of the poor into 'deserving' and 'undeserving' was to dog the debate and cloud decisions for several years. Equally strongly argued were the cases for contributory or non-contributory schemes. Contributory schemes were strongly favoured by the COS and all those who supported self-help, prudence and thrift. Why, it was argued, would people save for their old age if they could get a pension for nothing when they were old? Furthermore, it was argued that the cost of introducing such a scheme would be prohibitive: an estimated £16 million in the 1890s, more than was spent on poor relief. On the other hand, those favouring a non-contributory fund pointed out that the poorest members of society would hardly be in a position to contribute to a pension scheme from their meagre wages. The friendly societies supported this view, believing a contributory scheme would hit them, as people could not afford to pay into their schemes as well as a compulsory state one. The pension debate became widespread, and by 1908 there was a general consensus that some sort of pension scheme should be introduced. In 1909, the Liberal government's proposal was put before parliament.

The Old Age Pensions Act 1909
This Act provided for old age pensions as follows.

- Pensions were non-contributory and were funded from taxes.

- Pensions were paid to men and women over the age of 70, and they were to be paid through post offices.

- A single person received 5s a week and married couples 7s 6d, later raised to 10s.

- Full pensions were paid only to those with incomes of less than 8s a week; those with incomes of between 8s and 12s received a reduced pension on a sliding scale; over 12s a week, there was no pension at all.

- To qualify for a pension, men and women needed to have been British citizens resident in Britain for 20 years.

- Pensions were not paid to people who had continually failed to find work, who had been in prison in the last ten years, who had claimed poor relief in the previous two years, or who were drunkards.

The number of people claiming pensions was around 600,000, roughly the same number as the elderly claiming poor relief before the Act. The cost, too, was roughly the same. However, the Act did not reduce the number of elderly people receiving relief in workhouses, as many such people were too frail and vulnerable to be able to care for themselves even if they had an independent source of income. However, to thousands of older people, the shadow of the workhouse and the stigma of being in receipt of poor relief had gone. So, too, had the threat of an impoverished old age. Collections of local material are full of evidence of the gratitude of the elderly poor for the freedom from anxiety that pensions – nicknamed 'Lloyd Georges' by many – gave them.

SOURCE
9 A cartoon from the satirical magazine *Punch*, 6 January 1909.

PUNCH, OR THE LONDON CHARIVARI.—January 6, 1909.

THE NEW YEAR'S GIFT.

EXTRACT

2 From R. Roberts *The Classic Slum: Salford Life in the First Quarter of the Century,* published in 1971.

Ever since the German Parliament in 1889 had passed the model 'law of insurance against old age and infirmity' there had been much talk, but no action, in England about making similar provisions for the aged. At last, in 1908, the Liberal government allocated £1,200,000 for the establishment of a non-contributory old-age pension scheme and an Act was passed to become law on 1 January 1909. Pensions, however, would be withheld from those 'who had failed to work habitually according to their ability and need, and those who had failed to save money regularly.' Here was a means test with a vengeance. Paupers were not entitled to any pension.

There was to be no doling out of largesse under the scheme. Nevertheless, even these small doles meant life itself for many among the elderly poor. Old folk, my mother said, spending their allowance at the shop, 'would bless the name of Lloyd George as if he were a saint from heaven.' The government met with much opposition to the introduction of a pension scheme from both the middle and working classes. Free gifts of money, many urged, would dishearten the thrifty who had saved for their old age, and encourage the idle. Meanwhile, our elderly paupers still went to the workhouse.

ACTIVITY
KNOWLEDGE CHECK

Old age pensions

1 How successfully did Lloyd George resolve the conflicting arguments for contributory and non-contributory pension schemes?

2 How far does Extract 2 challenge the message of Source 9?

EXTEND YOUR KNOWLEDGE

Paying for Liberal reforms

Clearly the Liberal reforms cost money and, equally clearly, they were not self-funding, nor could they be funded by savings made on Poor Law costs. It seemed, initially, that around £16 million extra had to be raised in the budget of 1909. This came at a time when additional money was needed to fund the naval shipbuilding programme, intended to keep the Royal Navy abreast of the German one.

David Lloyd George, chancellor of the exchequer, found the money by, in the main, taxing the rich and better off. He increased taxes on tobacco and alcohol (always an easy moneymaker) and introduced a new tax on cars – a licence fee. Then he went for the big money. He raised income tax on a sliding scale, so that those with incomes of over £3,000 a year paid 1s 2d for every pound they earned, and those with smaller incomes paid 9d; people earning over £3,500 paid a super-tax of 6d in the pound. He increased death duties on estates worth more than £3,500 and introduced a new tax on profits gained from selling land.

This 'People's Budget' got through the House of Commons easily. It was a different matter when it came to the Lords. There was a tradition that the House of Lords never opposed a 'money bill', which is what the budget was. However, the Lords had an inbuilt conservative majority and many of them were large landowners. They felt threatened by Lloyd George's budget and threw it out. This precipitated an enormous constitutional crisis that was, eventually, resolved in favour of the House of Commons and the 'People's Budget'.

The Labour Exchanges Act 1909

The 19th-century attitude to unemployment was that, basically, it was the worker's fault. There was plenty of work available, and only the feckless or idle would fail to find it. For these, there was relief – but inside a workhouse. By the beginning of the 20th century, this attitude was changing, and gradually people were coming to understand that, within a capitalist economy, there were bound to be periods of trade depression when people could not find work. The problem, too, was one of underemployment, as men and women doing casual work competed with each other on an almost daily basis.

The Liberal government broke down the problem into two main parts: finding work; and insuring against the loss of that work due to illness and unemployment. Winston Churchill's principal adviser at the Board of Trade was William Beveridge. Beveridge had at one time been warden of Toynbee

Hall, the centre of Booth's researches, and was greatly influenced by his work and by Beatrice and Sidney Webb. He believed that workers needed help to find work and support when it was not available, rather than the 'punishment' of the workhouse.

The Labour Exchanges Act was clearly influenced by Beveridge and, aiming at the decasualisation of labour, passed through parliament without much dispute. It set up a series of labour exchanges that were intended to help the unemployed find any work that was available. In February 1910, 83 labour exchanges were opened, and by 1914 there were over 450 throughout England and Wales. Despite the fact that some employers were afraid that labour exchanges would provide a marvellous excuse for those who were unwilling to work because they were 'still looking', and some workers were afraid they would be used to recruit blackleg labour during a strike, they were a great success. Interestingly, the Webbs wanted to make labour exchanges compulsory, believing that if labour could only be hired through these exchanges, the government would be able to organise the labour market to the benefit of workers and the economy. Unemployment insurance on a voluntary basis would then be all that was necessary. Churchill and Lloyd George approached the problem the other way round, preferring to make labour exchanges voluntary but unemployment insurance compulsory in certain trades. In other words, they chose to tackle the problem of destitution by relieving the unemployed rather than attempting to prevent unemployment.

Labour exchanges were, however, only part of the story. Only by 'signing on' at a labour exchange would it be known that a person was unemployed and could qualify for unemployment payments, and so the Labour Exchanges Act was closely tied in to the National Insurance Act 1911.

SOURCE

10 From a speech by Winston Churchill, made in the House of Commons on 19 May 1909.

There are two general defects in the industrial position of this country, the lack of mobility of labour and the lack of information about all these questions of unemployment. For both defects the labour exchanges afford a remedy. Modern industry is national. Transport and communication knit the country together as no country has ever been knitted before. Labour alone has not profited by this improved organisation. The method by which labour obtains its market today is the old method, hawking labour about from place to place, and treating a job as a thing which places a man under an obligation when he has got it. The movement of labour when it is necessary should be effected with the least friction, the least suffering, the least loss of time and of status to the individual who is called upon by the force of economic conditions to move. The result of the policy will be to make it easy for him to move the moment the ordinary economic events arise which make movement necessary. Labour exchanges will not to any large extent create new employment. What they are going to do is to organise the existing labour by which we cannot help raising the general standard of economic life.

Labour exchanges are indispensible [sic] to any system of unemployment insurance, since it is not possible to make the distinction between the vagrant and the loafer on the one hand and the bona fide workman on the other, except in some elaborate and effective system of testing willingness to work such as is afforded by the system of labour exchanges. I shall tomorrow have an opportunity of asking the permission of the House to introduce this Bill, and we present it to the House as a piece of social machinery, nothing more and nothing less, the need of which has long been apparent, and the want of which has been widely and cruelly felt by large numbers of our fellow countrymen.

Trade Boards Act 1909

This was one of several Acts dealing with employment. It provided for the creation of boards in specific **sweated trades** – matchbox making, lace making and tailoring, for example – that could negotiate for, and set, legally enforceable minimum wage criteria. Although some 200,000 workers were involved, no attempt was made to define what was meant by a minimum wage. Nevertheless, an important precedent had been set: wages were no longer arrived at by a private agreement between employer and employee.

The National Insurance Act 1911

The illness of the main breadwinner was a major cause of poverty, and many families tried to insure themselves against this. In the early 1900s, between six and seven million people were insured against sickness. But many poorer people struggled to keep up the payments and, in times of financial stress, insurance payments of any kind were usually the first to go, and policies lapsed. Poor people, unable to afford to contribute even to friendly societies, faced a grave crisis when illness struck.

The Liberal government realised that the cost of funding any sort of health protection could not be carried by taxation. David Lloyd George, charged with spearheading the government's policies in Britain, impressed by the approach pioneered in Germany through its social insurance scheme, dispatched the senior civil servant W.J. Braithwaite to Germany in 1910 to find out in detail how it worked. The British system followed the German example insofar as the principle of compulsion was concerned and in making the system nationwide. However, the German system was imposed on a country that had experienced nothing like it, whereas in Britain there was a wide variety of institutions and organisations providing similar support. Friendly societies, trade unions and some commercial insurance companies had already developed the idea of offering safeguards against sickness, accident or death. Together, they formed a powerful vested interest group that could have derailed Lloyd George's plans. However, by careful negotiation on the part of Lloyd George, they were mollified by being designated approved societies through which payments were to be made, and any opposition they might have had faded.

SOURCE

11 From an article 'The Fabian Society and the Insurance Bill' published in the *Clarion*, a weekly socialist newspaper, on 10 November 1911.

Why the Fabian Society is Opposed to the Bill

First and foremost because it imposes upon the wage-earners what is in effect a poll-tax (ie a tax levied irrespective of ability to pay). To put the case in a nutshell, if Mr Lloyd George is not prepared to increase the super-tax, then he may as well give up at once all his great schemes of 'social reform', for it is the most elementary of economic truths that you cannot mitigate the evils of poverty at the expense of the poor.

If, as this Bill proposes, you deduct 4d a week from wages which are at present below the minimum necessary to maintain a family in mere physical efficiency, you are deliberately reducing their already insufficient nourishment, and therefore their power to resist disease.

In its sub-title the Bill is described as a measure for the 'prevention of sickness', but the mere fact that it excludes all non-wage-earning women and children is enough to deprive it of any claim to be taken seriously as a preventive scheme.

The Chancellor claims that he is giving 9d for 4d to every male contributor; but the truth is that the scale of 'minimum' benefits to be provided, although generous enough to the elderly, is only equivalent to what any well-managed friendly society can now offer to any young man or woman for 5d. 'But', it may be asked, 'is not this Bill after all better than nothing?' The answer to this question is, that as far as the better-off workers, who are already members of friendly societies or of strong trade unions are concerned, this bill is certainly better than nothing. It offers them solid financial advantages which the organised section will probably be able to retain. But for the others, the comparatively underpaid, underemployed, and unorganised, the equally emphatic answer is that the Bill is not worth having. From their insufficient incomes it will take 4d a week and in return it will give them no benefits worthy of the name.

If and when the bill comes into force, the problem of low wages will not only remain but will be intensified. Mr Lloyd George is the first Chancellor of the Exchequer who has conceived the plan of making the working classes themselves finance his measure of social reform. If he is successful, he will not be the last.

A Level Exam-Style Question Section A

Study Source 11 before you answer this question.

Assess the value of the source for revealing the nature of the opposition to the National Insurance bill, and to the arguments used by those opposing it.

Explain your answer, using the source, the information given about its origin and your own knowledge about the historical context. (20 marks)

Tip

In considering the nature of the opposition, look at the aims of the Fabian Society and whether those were typical of other groups, such as employers, who would also oppose it.

Part 1 of the National Insurance Act 1911 was an attempt to support the poor when ill-health struck the main breadwinner.

- The scheme applied to all workers earning less than £160 a year and all manual workers aged 16–60.

- Employees contributed 4d, employers 3d and the state 2d per week into the state insurance scheme.

- Insured people received 10s a week for up to 13 weeks and then 5s a week for a further 13 weeks in any one year.

- Payments were to be made through approved societies.

- Maternity care was provided, with a one-off benefit of 30s.

- Free treatment was given by a medical practitioner and all drugs and medicines were free.

Although £1.5 million was set aside for the treatment of TB, this was only available for contributors to the scheme; none of the benefits were available for their families.

This was probably the most unpopular of all the Liberal government's welfare reforms, even though it was arguably the most important. Most workers resented having to pay 4d from their wages and, in effect, because payment was flat rate, the poorer workers were hit the hardest. Many regarded it as a wage cut: there was no guarantee that they were going to be ill and would benefit from the scheme. Nevertheless, by 1913, 13 million workers had been insured in the scheme and an important safety net had been established.

Part 2 of the National Insurance Act 1911 dealt with insurance against unemployment.

- Employers, employees and the state each contributed 2½d to the scheme.
- Workers could claim unemployment benefit of 7s a week for up to 15 weeks in any one year.
- No claim could be paid if unemployment resulted from a person being dismissed for misconduct.

SOURCE
12 An election poster produced by the Liberal Party in 1911.

THE DAWN OF HOPE.

Mr. LLOYD GEORGE'S National Health Insurance Bill provides for the insurance of the Worker in case of Sickness.

Support the Liberal Government
in their policy of
SOCIAL REFORM.

The scheme at first applied to a small group of trades where people were generally well paid but which were prone to seasonal unemployment, such as shipbuilding and vehicle construction. Insurance was compulsory, and 2.25 million men were insured by the end of 1912. Because of high employment, it was not really possible to evaluate the scheme before the First World War broke out in 1914. However, it was important for what it represented: it established, as with pensions and health insurance, the principle that the relief of poverty was a national, and not a local, responsibility.

ACTIVITY
KNOWLEDGE CHECK

Dealing with poverty caused by unemployment and sickness

1 Read Source 10. Why does Churchill believe that labour exchanges are 'indispensible' to any system of unemployment insurance?

2 To what extent did the National Insurance Act break with the past?

3 Study Source 11. How valid were the claims being made?

Conclusion

The social and welfare reforms instigated by the Liberal governments established certain minimum standards, although these were by no means universal. It was clear, however, that the state was beginning to take over responsibility for its citizens, and it is tempting to regard these as the origins of the welfare state implemented 40 years later. True, there was some continuity of purpose and outcome. The Labour governments between 1945 and 1951 aimed to provide central, national support for all British citizens 'from cradle to grave'. It was based on the Beveridge Report of 1941 – the same William Beveridge who had been Winston Churchill's principal adviser in 1909. The range of reforms introduced by the Liberals was impressive, but it was not the result of a preconceived programme. It was no blueprint for change, as was the welfare state of the late 1940s and 1950s. Rather, it was a response to economic and political circumstances. There were, therefore, huge elements of compromise and a lot of Victorian moral attitudes present in the Liberal reforms. Most of the reforms used expertise already available and aimed to work with vested interests rather than antagonise them; beneficiaries of the two major schemes – health and unemployment – were expected to contribute to the schemes. Only pensions were funded solely by the taxpayer. Furthermore, the Liberal reforms did not apply to everyone, nor were they intended to do so. Thousands of people, for example, were deliberately excluded from old age pensions and the National Insurance scheme. Nevertheless, perhaps the most important factor attaching to the Liberal reforms was that they signalled a fundamental shift in attitudes to poverty and the poor, and in the responsibility the state had to assume for its citizens.

EXTRACT

3 From R.C. Birch *The Shaping of the Welfare State* (1974).

The outbreak of war in 1914 found the welfare state in its infancy. The Poor Law was still the basis for the treatment of poverty, and unemployment benefits were low and limited in time. Treatment for ill-health, outside the Poor Law, was given to the worker and not to his family, and little was done for hospitals, specialist services or preventative medicine. In the wider sense of welfare, education was compulsory only up to the age of fourteen, and of the 200,000 pupils in secondary schools, only a quarter occupied free places; three million children, of whom many deserved better, were confined to primary education. Housing still lagged behind even basic necessity, and social reform of all kinds was still inhibited by the old laissez-faire suspicion of state intervention and still governed by the convenient permissive idea. **Palliatives** rather than radical programmes of reform, had been applied.

KEY TERM

Palliative
A treatment that relieves symptoms rather than curing disease.

EXTRACT

4

From D. Fraser *The Evolution of the British Welfare State* (1973).

Lloyd George significantly pointed out, many of these [Liberal social policies] were actually provided for by the Poor Law, so that Liberal social policy was not just involved with extending state aid but with providing it on different, socially more acceptable, terms. A person who was sick, hungry, unemployed or old could in fact turn to the Poor Law for help. [For the Liberals it was] a deliberate act of policy to separate newer provisions from an all-embracing but socially unacceptable scope of the Poor Law, and the Local Government Board was clearly right in anticipating that the ultimate result of such a policy was that the Poor Law would not so much be killed as die away through neglect. When all its functions were appropriated by other social institutions the Poor Law would fall apart. Whatever historical perspective is used, one cannot escape the conclusion that Liberal social policy before the First World War was at once at variance with the past and an anticipation of radical changes in the future. The work of continuing these developments was not performed by Liberal hands, for the greatest of all Liberal governments turned out to be the last.

EXTRACT

5

From Bernard Harris *The Origins of the British Welfare State* (2004).

The Liberal reforms were a major watershed in the history of social policy development. Even though some have criticised the use of the insurance principle as a form of regressive taxation, the introduction of free school meals, the establishment of old age pensions and the creation of the unemployment and health insurance schemes marked the beginning of a new approach to the development of welfare policy which offered a genuine alternative to the deterrent and stigmatising policies of the Poor Law. As a result, the reforms undoubtedly played a major role in laying the foundations for the development of the welfare state in the twentieth century.

THINKING HISTORICALLY   Evidence (6b)

The strength of argument

Answer the following:

1 Read Extract 3.

  a) What is weak about this claim?

  b) What could be added to it to make it stronger?

2 Read Extract 4.

  a) Is this an argument?

  b) How might this argument be strengthened?

3 Read Extract 5.

  a) How is this argument stronger than that of Extract 4?

  b) Can you explain why this is the strongest claim of all three sources?

4 What elements make a historian's claims strong?

ACTIVITY
SUMMARY

Social reform, 1880–1914

1 To what extent did Booth and Rowntree challenge contemporary beliefs about the causes and extent of poverty?

2 How revolutionary was the Liberal government's social reform programme?

3 What was the impact of the Liberal reforms on the Poor Law?

4 Read Extracts 3 and 4.

  a) To what extent do the authors Birch and Fraser disagree about Liberal achievements by 1914?

  b) With which author do you agree, and why?

WIDER READING

Birch, R.C. *The Shaping of the Welfare State*, Longman (1974)

Brundage, A. *The English Poor Laws 1700–1930*, Palgrave (2002)

Englander, D. *Poverty and the Poor Law in 19th-century Britain, 1834–1914*, Longman (1998)

Fraser, D. *The Evolution of the British Welfare State*, Macmillan (1973)

Harris, B. *The Origins of the British Welfare State*, Macmillan (2004)

Hay, J.R. *The Origins of the Liberal Welfare Reforms 1906–1914*, Macmillan (1975)

Murray, P. *Poverty and Welfare 1830–1914*, Hodder (1999)

Read, D. *Edwardian England*, Harrap (1972)

Rose, M.E. *The Relief of Poverty 1834–1914*, Macmillan (1972)

3.7 Depression and the dole: poverty in the interwar years, 1920–39

KEY QUESTIONS

- What was the impact of the Depression on the British economy?
- How effective were the Jarrow march and the hunger marches of the 1930s?
- How far did government action relieve poverty in the 1930s?

INTRODUCTION

In the years immediately after the First World War, the British economy experienced a post-war boom. Technological developments made during the war meant that labour productivity improved after 1918 as semi-skilled labour could take on work previously undertaken by skilled workers. Between 1918 and April 1920, 2.9 million extra workers found jobs, although 500,000 women left the work they had taken on during the war. The stage seemed set for post-war prosperity for millions of families. But the boom was short lived. It collapsed in 1921, once the losses and shortages of the war years had been made good. It was then that Britain's dependence on the old staple industries of iron and steel, textiles, coal and shipbuilding became clear. These industries experienced persistent levels of high unemployment in the 1920s as British industry struggled to compete in international markets. High unemployment, of course, led to poverty for many families.

It is important to realise that high levels of unemployment were not seen throughout Britain. In the Midlands and the south of England new, light industries specialising in, for example, electrical goods, cars and chemicals, developed and flourished. However, the areas that supported heavy industries were in decline, and with decline came unemployment and poverty. Unemployment in these areas ranged between 40 and 80 percent and had a huge impact, not only on individuals but also on governments as they struggled to provide sufficient benefits in a time of worldwide economic decline.

The situation was exacerbated by the **Depression**. This began in 1929 with the **Wall Street Crash** in the USA, and affected nearly every developed country in the years 1929–39. There were two direct consequences for Britain. Firstly, there was a huge drop in the US demand for exports, which led to a fall in British industrial output with consequent unemployment. This mainly hit the staple industries that were already struggling. Secondly, this led to a flight of capital from Britain and a series of currency crises across Europe. This instability in the world's currency markets resulted in a

KEY TERMS

The Depression
A severe, sustained, worldwide downturn in economic activity. It began immediately after the Wall Street Crash and lasted, for some countries, until 1939.

Wall Street Crash (October 1929)
The ending of speculation on Wall Street, the American stock exchange. Thousands of Americans had borrowed money to invest in stocks and shares until there was more money out on loan than there was circulating in the economy. Banks crashed, many people lost all their money, as it had been invested in shares, and more than 13 million people became unemployed.

1918 - November: Armistice - end of the First World War

1921 - Safeguarding of Industries Act

Walter Hannington sets up the communist National Unemployed Workers Movement

1925 - April: Britain goes back on the gold standard

| 1918 | 1919 | 1920 | 1921 | 1924 | 1925 | 1926 |

1924 - Ellen Wilkinson elected Labour MP for Middlesbrough East

1926 - McKenna duties extended to include commercial vehicles

general decline in world trade. American markets for goods closed down and alternative markets for many types of manufactured goods could not be found. Countries raised tariffs to protect their own industries and world trade was seriously reduced. Poverty was the inevitable consequence. Many would argue that it was only the onset of war in 1939 that relieved the situation.

WHAT WAS THE IMPACT OF THE DEPRESSION ON THE BRITISH ECONOMY?

The 1920s and 1930s were, for many people living in Britain, years of reasonable prosperity. They experienced a rise in **real wages**, employment in new industries, improvements in health care, housing and education. Yet many others experienced the depths of desperate poverty. In the old industrial heartlands of South Wales, the west of Scotland, Lancashire, Tyneside and West Yorkshire, people were struggling.

KEY TERM

Real wage
The purchasing power of earnings when set against prices. If prices are high, money will buy less; if prices are low, money will buy more.

The decline of heavy industry

The British economy faced huge problems of adjustment after the First World War. It was not simply a question of shifting from a war-based economy to a peacetime one. It involved adapting a peacetime economy to a world of new technologies and changed markets. It was here that heavy industry failed to adapt, with consequent suffering for the labour force. These old, staple industries that were worst affected were coal mining, shipbuilding, iron and steel production, and textiles, particularly cotton.

Specific staple industries were affected in different ways. There was, for example, a brief boom in shipbuilding immediately after the war, and British yards managed to maintain 40 percent of the world's output in the 1920s. However, the Depression caused a collapse in world trade and there was no demand for new ships. In 1933, for example, British shipyards produced only seven percent of their pre-war output.

There was always a steady domestic demand for coal, but export markets fell from an immediate post-war output of 100 million tonnes per year to around 50 million tonnes by 1930. This was mainly due to European countries reviving their own coal industries, but it was due in part to poor management, under-investment and dreadful industrial relations within the coal industry itself.

Cheap iron and steel flooded in from Europe in the 1920s, causing the demand for British iron and steel to fall. The onset of the Depression caused British production of steel to fall by 45 percent and pig iron by 54 percent in 1929.

1934 – Special Areas Act
Unemployment Act

Incitement to
Disaffection Act

1936 – Rowntree's second study of poverty in York

Publication of Keynes' *General Theory of Employment, Interest and Money*

October–November: Jarrow march against unemployment

1937 – George Orwell's *The Road to Wigan Pier* is published

1939 – Second World War

1929	1934	1935	1936	1937	1938	1939

1929 – May: General election – Labour government elected

October: Wall Street crash

Depression

1935 – Public salaries restored to pre-1931 levels

Ellen Wilkinson returned as Labour MP for Jarrow

1938 – H.F. Tout publishes *The Standard of Living in Bristol*

Before the First World War, 75 percent of the British production of cotton goods was exported. After the war, cheaper cotton goods from the USA, India and the Far East flooded the market and undercut the British cotton industry. The situation was worsened during the Depression, and by 1938 the number of people employed in the British cotton industry had fallen by about 50 percent, and Britain's share of world trade had fallen from 65 percent in 1911 to 28 percent in 1938.

The impact of the decline of these old staple industries was heightened because of their geographical concentration. There were simply no other jobs because the traditional industries had been so dominant. When these industries declined, workers were laid off and became reliant on private or government schemes for relief. Many were thrust into long-term poverty.

	1924	1930
Coal	1,259,000	1,069,000
Iron and steel	313,000	287,000
Shipbuilding	254,000	205,000
Cotton	572,000	240,000

Figure 7.1 Total number of employees in traditional industries, 1924 and 1930.

	1924	1930
Coal	6.9	28.3
Iron and steel	20.4	32.6
Shipbuilding	28.3	31.7
Cotton	15.9	44.7

Figure 7.2 Percentage of people unemployed in traditional industries, 1924 and 1930.

SOURCE

1 An unemployed man, photographed in Wigan, Lancashire, in 1939 by Kurt Hutton and published in the magazine *Picture Post* in the same year.

The decline of Britain's staple industries was not a problem for the entire British economy. New industries and those that had developed during the war, such as motor vehicles and light industry, flourished. Their growth was helped by government action. The **McKenna duties**, intended to be temporary and imposed during the war, put a 33.33 percent tariff on the importing of commercial vehicles. This tariff remained in place until 1956 and gave considerable help to the British motor industry. The **Safeguarding of Industries Act 1921** was similarly intended to safeguard industries, such as those producing metallic tungsten, optical glass and synthetic chemicals, which were deemed by the government to be of strategic importance in any future war because they had been vital in the First World War. In these cases, a tariff of 33.33 percent was levied on foreign imports, and the tariff was to last for five years.

Heavy industry was consistently refused tariff protection. This meant that it was vulnerable to cheaper foreign imports. The steel industry, in particular, suffered from the practice of differential pricing. This was a system whereby producers could sell the same product to different customers at different prices. Foreign steel was sold in Britain at a price that consistently undercut the price of home-produced steel.

The refusal to give tariff protection to the staple industries was in part a result of Britain's long-held adherence to free trade (though with some exceptions) and the accompanying belief that the consumer would drive the markets. In the case of the staple industries, the consumer decided to buy cheap, and that wasn't British. Indeed, the immediate post-war boom of 1919–20 had resulted in considerable investment in the staple industries, in the hope that they would return to their pre-war level of success. They didn't – and cotton, iron and steel, and shipbuilding were heavily **overcapitalised** in a market where few wanted what these industries produced.

KEY TERMS

McKenna duties
Reginald McKenna was home secretary in September 1915 when he introduced a series of tariffs on luxury imports in order to fund the war effort. Originally, this excluded commercial vehicles because they were needed in wartime, but in 1926 it was extended to include commercial vehicles.

The Safeguarding of Industries Act 1921
An Act intended to protect strategic industries against foreign competition.

Overcapitalised
A situation where a company had issued more shares than its assets are worth.

EXTRACT

1 From Martin Pugh *State and Society*, published in 1994. Pugh is a professor of modern history.

For several years after the formation of the National Government, the slump grew even worse. But by 1934 clear signs of recovery manifested themselves, as unemployment began to fall and output exceeded the 1929 level. Indeed, between 1932 and 1937 unemployment fell from 3 million to 1.5 million, while industrial production increased by 46 per cent. This improvement has given rise to a much more optimistic view of the 1930s than has traditionally been held. The basis for the optimistic view rests on the evidence that, whereas national income increased by only 10 per cent from 1921 to 1929, it rose by 17 per cent from 1929 to 1937.

Of course this growth was rather patchy in geographical terms. It developed within a limited range of industries largely dependent on the domestic market for consumer goods rather than on recovery in exports. Indeed, in spite of the recovery, unemployment remained at nearly 11 per cent by the outbreak of war in 1939. The growth industries had failed to make a major impression on the worst of the problem. This was partly because growth was concentrated in the south-east and Midlands. Factors such as coal, iron or water that had influenced the original location of industry no longer applied. Electricity was available everywhere, and the London market made the south attractive to businessmen. Most of the jobs lost in the old industries were for skilled men, whereas the growth industries employers wanted women, and particularly young workers, for unskilled production line work because they would accept low wages and were unlikely to be union members.

The truth was that the growth industries flourished in the home market but were unable to compete abroad. The structural problems of British industry remained. There was simply less of it than in 1918.

SOURCE

2 From Wal Hannington *The Problem of the Distressed Areas*, published 1937. Walter Hannington was a founder member of the Communist Party of Great Britain and the national organiser of the National Unemployed Workers' Association from 1921 to 1939.

The present period of mass unemployment began in 1921. The worst effects of the slump have been felt in four of the basic industries of this country – industries upon which the power of Britain has been built – namely coal, iron and steel, shipbuilding and textiles. The unemployment which has affected these industries proves that the crisis within capitalism is deep and fundamental. It is not an unemployment occasioned by seasonal conditions in the whims and fancies of fashion, as might be said of certain of the minor trades. There is, in fact, evidence of the very deep breakdown of the capitalist order of society when the basic industries of the system are plunged into continuous slump; when the mines are sealed up and allowed to become flooded; when steel works are allowed to rust and crumble; and millions of valuable textile spindles are turned into scrap metal.

What more conclusive proof could be required to show that the condition of the masses of workers rendered idle by the failure of these industries presents not a problem which can work itself out but one which calls for far-reaching and fundamental changes in the system itself?

ACTIVITY
KNOWLEDGE CHECK

The decline of staple industries

1 Look at Figures 7.1 and 7.2.

   a) Which industries were in the most trouble before the Depression hit in 1930? Give reasons for your answer.

   b) Which industries were worst affected when the Depression hit in 1930? Give reasons for your answer.

2 Why was unemployment not evenly spread throughout Britain?

3 The photograph in Source 1 was posed. Does this mean it is not valid as evidence?

4 Read Extract 1 and Source 2.

   a) On what do they agree?

   b) Where do they disagree?

   c) How can these differences be explained?

Changing patterns of trade and finance

The First World War changed the structure of world trade. British exporters lost markets abroad because of the fighting and, in any case, their industries were geared up to war production. In the early years of the war, the USA took over many of these markets and continued to export to them in the 1920s. Japan, too, benefited from Britain's temporary withdrawal from world trade and began flooding the developing world with Japanese products. This was a field Britain had dominated before 1914. Countries such as India developed their own iron, steel and textile industries and, in 1919, introduced tariffs against British goods even though they were still part of the British Empire.

KEY TERM

Gold standard
The value of a currency defined in terms of the price of gold, for which notes and coins could be exchanged.

The structure of international finance was changed by the war. Britain's role as the centre of the financial world had been successfully challenged by the USA. Inevitably, the war disrupted the normal patterns of international finance. The **gold standard**, which prior to 1914 had been the basis of international finance, collapsed. After 1918, the world's financial markets struggled to get back to normal. For some, this meant going back to the gold standard that had provided such stability before the war. This was a time when exchange rates for currencies were fixed against the price of gold and therefore against each other. In April 1925, Britain went back on the gold standard. Unfortunately, this was done at a time when the price of gold was high and this made British exports expensive.

The Depression impacted on this shifting situation. Throughout the 1920s, the USA was the world's most economically powerful nation. Then, in 1929, the US stock market on Wall Street collapsed. This financial disaster quickly led to a severe economic depression. Determined to retrieve the situation, the US government erected high tariff barriers in order to protect home consumption, and recalled the loans it had made to foreign governments. The immediate effect of this was that world trade collapsed, unemployment rose sharply in all European countries and governments desperately tried to save their people from destitution.

Britain was one of the first countries to be affected by the USA's collapse.

- The USA was Britain's biggest trading partner. With American markets closed because of the high tariff barriers, there were very limited markets where British manufacturers could sell their goods. Some businesses were bankrupted; others had to lay off a large percentage of their workforce. Unemployment, already a problem, soared.

- The income from trade with the USA was the main way in which Britain raised money to repay debts incurred as a result of the First World War. With the collapse in trade came the huge loss of income and the government could not meet its debt repayments. To make matters worse, the USA called in all the loans made after the war, which meant that it expected its debtors to repay their loans in full, immediately.

- Britain was owed money by most of the First World War allies (Russia, Italy and France, for example) but they were in a similar situation and could not afford to make repayments.

- The situation was exacerbated by Britain's return to the gold standard.

SOURCE

3

Part of the budget speech made by Winston Churchill, Chancellor of the Exchequer, in the House of Commons on 28 April 1925.

A return to an effective gold standard has long been the settled and declared policy of this country. Every Expert Conference since the War – Brussels, Genoa – every expert Committee in the country, has urged the principle of a return to the gold standard. No responsible authority has advocated any other policy. No British government – and every party has held office – no political party, no previous holder of the Office of Chancellor of the Exchequer has challenged, or so far as I am aware is now challenging, the principle of reversion to the gold standard in international affairs at the earliest possible moment.

In our policy of returning to the gold standard we do not move alone. Indeed, I think we could not have afforded to remain stationary while so many others moved. The two greatest manufacturing countries in the world on either side of us, the United States and Germany, are in different ways either on, or related to, an international gold exchange. As far as the British Empire is concerned, there will be complete unity of action. Thus over the wide area of the British Empire and over a very wide and important area of the world there has been established at once one uniform standard of value to which all international transactions are related and can be referred. I believe that the establishment of this great area of common arrangement will facilitate the revival of international trade and of inter-Imperial trade.

Prosperity for some

The Depression affected different areas of Britain in different ways. Unemployment is generally taken as an indicator of prosperity, and here there were marked regional differences. Whereas the north and north-east, where heavy industry was concentrated, were hard hit, the Midlands and south-east were relatively prosperous. In those areas of Britain dependent on the heavy, staple industries, the Depression was severe and enduring. On the other hand, the south and south-east experienced remarkable growth and prosperity. How had this been possible? It was possible because the skills of the workforce were readily adapted to the new, light industries that were being developed after the First World War, and these, in turn, led to investment in these industries that led to growth and fuller employment. The shipyards, iron and steel industries and mines, for example, employed people with very specific and mainly non-transferable skills. When those industries declined to a point of collapse, there was nowhere for the workforce to go.

South-east England	5.6
London	6.5
South-west England	7.8
Midlands	9.4
North-west England	16.2
North-east England	16.6
Scotland	18.0
Northern Ireland	23.0
Wales	28.5

Shipbuilding	30.6
Coal mining	25.0
Shipping	22.3
Textiles	13.2
Engineering	8.3
Chemical industry	7.9
Skilled building crafts	6.3
Printing and paper	6.2
Commerce and finance	3.8

Figure 7.3 Percentage of unemployed by region in 1936.

Figure 7.4 Percentage of unemployed in specific trades and industries in 1936.

The new, light industries were readily able to meet the growing post-war demand for convenience and leisure goods, such as radios and cars, refrigerators and vacuum cleaners, newspapers and magazines. This demand stimulated the growth of the building industries, electrical engineering, chemical and printing trades. The car industry, for example, produced 33,000 cars in 1913, 95,000 in 1923 and 511,000 in 1937. After being run down during the war, the housing industry revived and in the early 1930s was responsible for the most rapid rate of house building in British history. Between 1924 and 1935, over one million houses were built for local authorities to rent out to council house tenants, and double that number of houses were built for private purchase.

A Level Exam-Style Question Section B

'The Depression created a country of two nations.' How far do you agree with this opinion of the British economy in the years 1924–36? (20 marks)

Tip

Consider how far the Depression was to blame for the division, and how far it was due to other factors, such as government reaction to the Depression by creating tariff barriers, or the lack of transferable skills in the workforce.

All these houses needed furnishing and equipping with consumer durables, which in turn stimulated demand in those industries.

It can be readily seen that there was a clear north/south divide in Britain, and one that was to lead to despair and mutual lack of understanding. This was exacerbated by having a London-based parliament that was struggling to manage the economy in turbulent national and international times.

ACTIVITY
KNOWLEDGE CHECK

Linkages

1 Work in a small group of between two and four people. Create a Venn diagram, mind map or flow chart showing linkages between all the factors that led to such massive unemployment in the traditional, staple industries in Britain.

2 Which factor do you consider to have been the most important? Write a paragraph to explain your choice.

3 Read Source 3. What arguments does Churchill put forward for Britain going back on to the gold standard? Why was he wrong?

4 Why was there prosperity for some and desperate poverty for others in Britain at this time?

HOW EFFECTIVE WERE THE JARROW MARCH AND THE HUNGER MARCHES OF THE 1930s?

In the years 1935–36, Seebohm Rowntree (see Chapter 6, page 135) carried out a second study of poverty in York. Using a slightly more generous 'poverty line', he concluded that a family of five (mother, father and three children) would need an income of £2 3s 6d (excluding rent) to be able to live above the poverty line. On this measure, 31 percent of families in York were living in poverty. Interestingly, Rowntree found that, while the main cause of poverty in 1899 was low wages, in the mid-1930s it was unemployment. H.F. Tout, investigating poverty in Bristol, one of the most prosperous cities in Britain, reached similar conclusions to Rowntree. He found that an unemployed man with a wife and three or more children, and any old-age pensioner living only on the state pension, would be living in poverty.

The key to poverty seemed to be unemployment, even in the towns of York and Bristol, which did not support heavy industry. However, a survey of 800 households in Stockton-on-Tees at the same time reached almost identical conclusions. It showed that the average income of families where the main breadwinner was unemployed came to £1 9s 2½d – well below the minimum income Rowntree found necessary to keep a family out of poverty. Indeed, **unemployment benefit** was usually between 45 and 66 percent of a man's previous wage. For those who had previously been living close to the edge, this was a disaster. It was against this background that people took direct action.

KEY TERM

Unemployment benefit
This was paid out of National Insurance and was intended to help working people get through a few weeks, originally 15, while they looked for a new job.

The Jarrow march, 5 October–1 November 1936

In October 1936, mass unemployment and extreme poverty drove 200 men to march 300 miles from the Tyneside town of Jarrow in the north-east of England to London. They carried a petition signed by 11,000 people which they intended to present to parliament, requesting the re-establishment of industry in Jarrow. Although this was the primary objective of the march, an important secondary objective was to generate sympathy for the unemployed and their plight by showing, as they marched south, that they were law-abiding, responsible citizens.

The trigger for the march had been the closure of Palmers shipbuilding yard, the main employer of labour in Jarrow. Admiralty orders for two destroyers kept the yard open until July 1932, but after that the order books were empty and the company went bankrupt. In the background was the National Shipbuilders Security (NSS) Ltd, a company created by the government to buy up failing yards and dismantle them so that production could be focused in a smaller number of profitable ones. In the early summer of 1934, Palmers was acquired by the NSS, and dismantling began.

An American investor, T. Vosper Salt, was convinced that Jarrow, with its existing rail network, docks and labour force, was the ideal place for a new steelworks. The feasibility study he financed was positive, particularly in view of the general opinion that steel prices would rise. However, the British Iron and Steel Federation was less than enthusiastic. Arguing that steel production could be increased by existing steelworks, the Federation put pressure on London's financial institutions not to back the scheme. No new steelworks were built in Jarrow. The town was in a desperate situation.

SOURCE 4

From Ellen Wilkinson *The Town that was Murdered*, published 1939.

On February 28 1930, the first public statement was made regarding National Shipbuilders' Security Ltd. Its purpose was defined as being to assist the shipbuilding industry by the purchase of redundant or obsolete yards. To ensure that the productive capacity of the industry was definitely reduced, the shipbuilding equipment was to be scrapped and the site of the yard was to be restricted against further use for shipbuilding.

With the scrapping of the shipyards, the trade unions were anxious to secure for their unemployed members either some compensation or alternative employment. Sir James Lithgow [Chairman of the NSS] produced as soothing syrup the optimistic claim that no men would be displaced. For, argued Sir James, the improved efficiency of the industry resulting from concentration would enable more work to be obtained when trade improved. On the point of attracting new industries to the cleared sites, Sir James assured the union leaders that the NSS directors were of course anxious to do this.

In the early summer of 1934 it was announced that Palmer's had been sold to NSS. The death warrant of Palmer's was signed. The reason for Jarrow's existence had vanished overnight.

Why was Palmer's yard sold? It was certainly not an obsolete yard. One of the biggest firms in the industry, and one which had invariably secured a fair share of competitive tenders, cannot be classed as obsolete. Financial weakness, and not technical inefficiency, decided the fate of the company. The rationalisation of the shipbuilding industry has been carried through in that way – with an eye on the balance sheet rather than on the efficiency of the particular companies. Palmer's was scrapped to safeguard the profits of some of the firms remaining in the industry.

Sold by National Shipbuilding Security to a demolition firm, work was commenced to clear the site. Oxy-acetylene burners made short work of steel girders. Cranes crashed to the ground, the machine shops were emptied, the blast furnaces and their numerous chimneys were demolished. The familiar overhead cranes vanished. Of the total unemployed in Jarrow 73 percent have been out of work for such long periods as not to be able to qualify for Unemployment Insurance benefit, 43.3 percent of the men have been continuously without work for over a year. Indeed, in Jarrow there are 251 who have never had a week's work in five years.

> **A Level Exam-Style Question Section A**
>
> *Study Source 4 before you answer this question.*
>
> Assess the value of the source for revealing the reasons why there was so much unemployment in Jarrow in the 1930s, and the effectiveness of steps taken to get people back to work.
>
> Explain your answer, using the source, the information given about it and your own knowledge about the historical context. (20 marks)
>
> **Tip**
> *Consider the attempts of the unions to gain reassurances and the assurances given by the NSS regarding safeguarding the workers.*

The idea of a march was enthusiastically backed by the Jarrow Borough Council, the local mayor Billy Thompson, the town's Labour MP, Ellen Wilkinson, and by local business, commercial and religious groups. It was decided that the march would be a strictly local affair, and would not be representative of any particular political persuasion. The march was meticulously organised. The route was planned, publicity organised and the overnight stops pre-booked. Medical students volunteered to accompany the marchers in case of problems – and 200 medically fit men were selected from over 1,200 volunteers to march. Women were not invited. A second-hand bus was purchased to carry cooking equipment, food and water, blankets and groundsheets. Over £1,500 was raised to meet costs, and after a blessing given by the Bishop of Jarrow, on 5 October 1936, the march set off.

Support for the march was mixed.

- At some stopovers on the way south, the marchers were greeted warmly and provided with good-quality accommodation, baths, spare clothes and food; at others, only beds in the local workhouse were on offer.

- Despite the nature of the official reception, the general public turned out to line the route of the march in their thousands.

- The Labour Party Conference, held in Edinburgh in October, was not supportive. Ellen Wilkinson was criticised by delegates for sending hungry and poorly clothed men on a march that would tax their strength with no appreciable outcome.

SOURCE

5   The Jarrow marchers on their way to London, October 1936. The photograph was printed in the *Daily Express* newspaper.

KEY TERMS

Trades Union Congress (TUC)
An umbrella group for the trades unions in Britain. While individual unions were not obliged to follow the advice of the TUC when it came to, for example, strikes, they usually did. The TUC represented a powerful voice for organised labour.

Dole
This was money that working people could claim if they had come to the end of their unemployment benefit.

- The **Trades Union Congress (TUC)** and the National Executive Council of the Labour Party advised Labour Party branches and trades councils along the route of the march not to offer any assistance or support to the marchers, although local branches often ignored this advice.

- The Bishop of Durham, Hensley Henson, sternly criticised his colleague the Bishop of Jarrow for apparently supporting the march by giving the marchers the church's blessing before they set out. Henson, severely critical of socialism and trade unionism, denounced the march for being nothing but revolutionary mob pressure designed to support the Labour Party.

On 1 November, the marchers reached London and joined a general rally against hunger held in Hyde Park by the Communist Party, where the size of the crowd varied between police estimates of 3,000 and 50,000 estimated by a journalist. The Jarrow marchers held their own well-supported public meeting two days later, although government ministers refused to attend. On 4 November, Ellen Wilkinson presented the Jarrow petition to the House of Commons; after a few minutes of ill-tempered discussion, the government moved on to other matters. It was over. The Jarrow marchers returned home by train, empty-handed. They found that, while they were away, the government had cut their unemployment benefit and **dole** money because they had not been available for work, even though there was no work to be had.

The overall effectiveness of the Jarrow march is difficult to quantify. Jarrow itself gained nothing in the short term, and yet at the same time the plight of unemployed workers in the staple industries was brought home in a vivid way to ordinary people living more comfortable lives in the Midlands and south-east. Many of the marchers themselves were of the view that the march was a waste of time; some, with hindsight, taking the view that it was the onset of war in 1939 that revived industry in Jarrow. Contemporary commentators like Kevin Maguire of the *Daily Mirror* agreed with them. Yet some historians take a more positive view, arguing that the march helped to form people's perceptions of the 1930s and, in doing so, paved the way for the post-1945 social reforms. Indeed, the Labour Party, having shunned the march in the 1930s, regularly invokes its memory in times of industrial distress.

The Jarrow march

1 The American tycoon T. Vosper Salt, Jarrow's MP and the workforce all wanted new steelworks to be built in Jarrow. Why weren't they built?

2 How might the NSS have justified its actions as they related to Palmers' yard and the shipyard workers in Jarrow?

3 The photograph of the Jarrow march (Source 5) was printed in a national newspaper that had a wide circulation. What point do you think the newspaper's editors were making when they decided to publish it?

4 Why was there such a mixed reaction to the march?

Hunger marches

The Jarrow march was essentially a one-off march against unemployment that has gained iconic status in the history of the Depression. Yet there were many other marches that attracted far less publicity. These were focused on hunger.

The role of the National Unemployed Workers Movement (NUWM)

In 1921, the communist tool-maker Walter (Wal) Hannington set up the National Unemployed Workers Movement, which was an effective arm of the British Communist Party. Indeed, Hannington was elected to the Central Committee of the British Communist Party in 1929. Ultimately, the aim of the NUWM was to destroy capitalism, but its immediate concern in the 1920s and 1930s was about the rights of the unemployed to jobs and a reasonable subsistence allowance (see Source 6). The NUWM was the driving force behind a series of hunger marches from a number of British industrial towns to London in 1922–23, 1929, 1930, 1932, 1934 and 1936. Many of these marches led to violent clashes between the police and demonstrators and had little, if any, effect on government policy.

The first Welsh hunger march provides an excellent example of the divided leadership and divided loyalties that characterised many of these marches. The march started as a protest against the limitations that the government had placed on unemployment relief and the impact this had on miners and their families. A meeting, organised by the Rhondda District of the South Wales Miners' Federation and the NUWN, was held on Penrhys Mountain on 18 September 1927. Miners were selected to march to London on 8 November, to coincide with the opening of parliament. However, by the time November came, the Executive of the Miners' Federation had changed their minds, partly because of opposition from the Trades Union Congress (TUC). The NUWM, unsurprisingly, remained steadfast in their support and 270 miners marched to London. Local trades councils along the route supported the miners, although the press, TUC and the government remained implacably hostile.

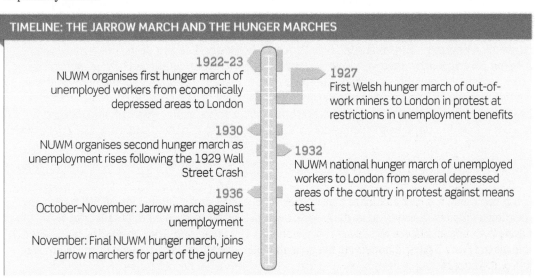

TIMELINE: THE JARROW MARCH AND THE HUNGER MARCHES

1922-23
NUWM organises first hunger march of unemployed workers from economically depressed areas to London

1927
First Welsh hunger march of out-of-work miners to London in protest at restrictions in unemployment benefits

1930
NUWM organises second hunger march as unemployment rises following the 1929 Wall Street Crash

1932
NUWM national hunger march of unemployed workers to London from several depressed areas of the country in protest against means test

1936
October-November: Jarrow march against unemployment

November: Final NUWM hunger march, joins Jarrow marchers for part of the journey

SOURCE

6 A poster advertising the Penrhys Mountain meeting on 18 September 1927.

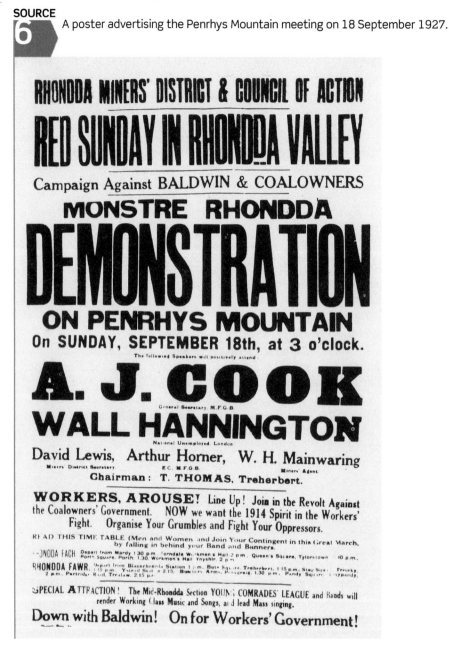

RHONDDA MINERS' DISTRICT & COUNCIL OF ACTION

RED SUNDAY IN RHONDDA VALLEY

Campaign Against BALDWIN & COALOWNERS

MONSTRE RHONDDA

DEMONSTRATION

ON PENRHYS MOUNTAIN

On SUNDAY, SEPTEMBER 18th, at 3 o'clock.

The following Speakers will positively attend

A. J. COOK

General Secretary, M.F.G.B.

WALL HANNINGTON

National Unemployed, London

David Lewis, Arthur Horner, W. H. Mainwaring

Miners District Secretary.   E.C. M.F.G.B.   Miners' Agent.

Chairman : T. THOMAS, Treherbert.

WORKERS, AROUSE! Line Up! Join in the Revolt Against the Coalowners' Government. NOW we want the 1914 Spirit in the Workers' Fight. Organise Your Grumbles and Fight Your Oppressors.

READ THIS TIME TABLE (Men and Women and Join Your Contingent in this Great March, by falling in behind your Band and Banners.

RHONDDA FACH. Depart from Mardy 1.30 p.m. Forndale Workmen's Hall 2 p.m. Queen's Square, Tylorstown 10 p.m. Porth Square, Porth. 1.30. Workmen's Hall Ynyshir. 2 p.m.

RHONDDA FAWR. Depart from Blaenrhondda Station 1 p.m. Bute Square, Treherbert, 1.15 p.m. Stag Squ. Treorky. 1.15 p.m. Ystrad Stat'n 2.15. Boachers Arms, Ponycraig 1.30 p.m. Pandy Squire Llwynypia. 2 p.m. Partridge Road, Treslaw. 2.15 p.m.

SPECIAL ATTRACTION! The Mid-Rhondda Section YOUNG COMRADES' LEAGUE and Bands will render Working Class Music and Songs, and lead Mass singing.

Down with Baldwin! On for Workers' Government!

Means test
Introduced as an emergency measure by the government in 1931, this was a 'household test' whereby all income coming in to a household was taken into account before benefits were given.

In 1932, angered by the imposition of the **means test**, the NUWM organised a national hunger march. This involved co-ordinating about 3,000 people, marching to Hyde Park in London from 18 starting points – mainly towns and cities in the depressed areas of South Wales, Scotland and the north of England – and ending in Hyde Park on 27 October. The aim of the marchers was to force the government, by their very strength of numbers, to reconsider the implementation of the means test. To this end they intended, after their rally, to present a petition to parliament, containing a million signatures. The government, alarmed by the possibility of a breakdown in law and order, drafted in 2,000 extra police. Serious violence broke out in and around Hyde Park and mounted police were used to disperse the demonstrators. Hannington was arrested and the police confiscated the petition. Although the marchers had received little publicity on their way to London, the rioting that continued for several days, during which a number of people were seriously injured, did hit the national press and generated questions in parliament. The NUWM had made its point.

The government, too, had a point to make. Spies were trained and infiltrated the NUWM, regularly reporting back to their handlers. In 1934, parliament passed an Incitement to Disaffection Act, making it a criminal offence to seduce any member of His Majesty's forces (this included the police) from his duty or allegiance, and giving the police greater powers of search. Many of those arrested during and after the hunger marches were arrested on the charge of incitement.

A much larger hunger march was organised by the NUWM for November 1936, when ten contingents of marchers converged on Hyde Park. This time, the Labour Party gave the demonstration its support, and Clement Attlee (leader of the Labour Party 1935–55 and prime minister 1945–51) addressed the crowd of some 12,000 from the same platform as Wal Hannington. This was the demonstration that was joined, for a short time, by the Jarrow marchers (see page 158). It was to be the NUWM's last demonstration; after 1936, it focused on helping thousands of individuals and their families find their way through the maze of benefit regulations.

EXTRACT 2
From the historian W.O. Simpson *Changing Horizons: Britain 1914–80,* published in 1986.

The revolutionary potential of the NUWM was exaggerated, both by Moscow and the British government. At its greatest, the NUWM claimed a membership of 100,000 with 386 different branches. It probably did more for unemployment than either the TUC or the Labour Party in terms of modifying the regulations governing the payment of benefit, but its leaders were very reluctant revolutionaries and such violence as the movement provoked owed as much to over-reaction by the police as to deliberate encouragement of disorder.

Ellen Wilkinson and Jarrow

Known as 'Red Ellen', partly because of her red hair and partly because of her left-wing politics, Ellen Wilkinson was a key individual in the north-east during the Depression. Elected as MP for Middlesbrough East in the general election of 1924, she found herself out of parliament following the general election of 1931 that returned a National Government (see page 167). Her selection as the Labour candidate for Jarrow inspired her to lead a deputation, early in 1934, of Jarrow's unemployed to meet with the prime minister, Ramsay MacDonald, in his nearby Seaham constituency. They were received with sympathy but no promise of help that was any different from that which was available nationally for any unemployed workers, and no assurances regarding any revival of heavy industry in Jarrow. Wilkinson was not impressed by the Special Areas Act (see page 170) that was passed late in 1934 and which was intended to help areas such as Jarrow, believing that it benefited the employers more than the workers. Unsurprisingly, Wilkinson was returned to the Commons as MP for Jarrow in the general election of 1935, with a majority of 2,350.

Once back in the Commons, Wilkinson was to fight hard to try to alleviate the plight of her unemployed constituents who were experiencing dire poverty that was caused mainly by the closure of Palmers shipbuilding yard. Initially, there were hopes that a steelworks would be built on the site of the shipyard, but these plans were not supported by the British Iron and Steel Federation. Horrified, on 30 June 1936, Wilkinson tried to persuade the president of the Board of Trade, Walter Runciman, to change the minds of the steel-masters who ran the Federation. Runciman would be moved neither by Wilkinson nor by the deputation from Jarrow's town council that urged him to sanction the building of a steelworks in the town. Runciman knew that the steel-masters were adamant that the most profitable way to increase production would be through existing iron and steel works and not by building new ones. The welfare of the unemployed was not their concern. Runciman refused to help Jarrow in the way Wilkinson wanted, asserting that Jarrow had to find its own salvation. These hollow words led directly to the Jarrow march. On 4 November, Wilkinson presented the petition, signed by 11,000 Jarrow people, to the House of Commons. It asked that the government and the Commons should recognise the plight of the unemployed in Jarrow, and provide work for them as a matter of urgency. Wilkinson was assured by Runciman that the employment position in Jarrow had improved, and the marchers were sent home by train. Both gestures were regarded by many MPs as acts of supreme complacency.

ACTIVITY
KNOWLEDGE CHECK

The hunger marches
1 Look carefully at Source 6. Who is it aimed at? What emotive words is it using to attract attention? Why might the authorities have found it worrying?
2 How well organised were the hunger marches when compared to the Jarrow march?
3 Why did the government react differently to the hunger marches than to the Jarrow march?
4 How important was Ellen Wilkinson's role in the Jarrow march?

A Level Exam-Style Question Section B

How accurate is it to say that the Jarrow march and the hunger marches achieved nothing? (20 marks)

Tip
As well as thinking about what didn't happen as a result of the marches, think about what they did achieve in terms of, for example, community solidarity and impact on the general public.

Ellen Wilkinson (1891–1947)

Ellen Wilkinson's role in British politics was not limited to Jarrow. Her first job after leaving Manchester University was in 1913 when she worked as a district organiser for the National Union of Women's Suffrage Societies. By 1915, she had moved on to trade union work, and became the first woman organiser of the Amalgamated Union of Co-operative Employees (AUCE). A lifelong pacifist, she supported the Non-conscription Fellowship during the First World War and joined the British Communist Party. In 1923, Ellen was elected to serve on the Manchester City Council and the following year was elected as the Labour Party member by Middlesbrough East to represent them in the House of Commons. In order to do this, she had to resign her membership of the Communist Party as Labour would not allow dual membership of both organisations. Following the 1929 general election, she was appointed parliamentary private secretary to the minister of health, but lost her seat in 1931.

The 1935 general election saw Wilkinson returned to the House of Commons as MP for Jarrow, and her involvement a year later in the Jarrow march, or crusade, against unemployment.

Despite the 1936 Labour Party Conference supporting the government's policy of non-intervention in the Spanish Civil War, Ellen Wilkinson and Clement Attlee travelled to Spain as observers, and witnessed the German bombing of Valencia and Madrid. On their return, they wrote in support of the International Brigades who were fighting General Franco's fascist forces.

In the wartime coalition government formed in 1940 by Churchill, Wilkinson was appointed parliamentary secretary to the minister of pensions. Later, she moved to work in the Home Office, where she was responsible for air-raid shelters. In the post-war Labour government of Clement Attlee, Wilkinson was appointed minister of education, the first woman to hold the post. Her time in office was marked by persuading parliament to pass the School Milk Act 1946, which gave free milk to all school children, improving the school meals service, and initiating the raising of the school-leaving age to 15.

Outside Britain, in October 1945, she visited Germany to report on reactivating their education system, and in November of that year she chaired an international conference in London that led to the formation of the United Nations Educational, Scientific and Cultural Organization (UNESCO).

Ellen Wilkinson's death in 1947 is generally attributed to lifelong bronchial asthma, exacerbated by overwork and pneumonia.

HOW FAR DID GOVERNMENT ACTION RELIEVE POVERTY IN THE 1930s?

The governments of the 1930s were facing unprecedented problems on a national and international level. They were fraught with internal divisions as senior members of political parties jockeyed for position and argued as to the best way to achieve economic stability. The relief of poverty was only one problem with which they had to deal, and some of the policy decisions that were made exacerbated the problem.

The second Labour government, 1929–31

The first Labour government of 1924 lasted for nine months and was brought down by a potential political scandal; the second Labour government lasted for longer, but was brought down because of cabinet divisions over cuts in government expenditure. The second Labour government, like the first, was dependent for its survival on the support of the Liberal Party.

Party	Votes	Percentage	Seats
Conservative	8,656,473	38.2	260
Labour	8,389,512	37.1	288
Liberal	5,308,510	23.4	59

Figure 7.5 General election results of 1929.

Initially, Prime Minister Ramsay MacDonald was optimistic. Registered unemployment had fallen between January and July, and unemployment benefits, brought in by the Liberal government before the First World War (see page 149) seemed to be sufficient to keep working people and their families from dire and desperate poverty. MacDonald was confident that more experience of government would convince the electorate of the competence of Labour to govern. He even took what was then a radical step and appointed Margaret Bondfield to be parliamentary secretary to the Ministry of Labour. But disaster, in the shape of the Wall Street Crash and the subsequent Depression, lay just around the corner.

EXTRACT

3 From Christopher Price 'Depression and Recovery' in *20th Century Britain: Economic, Social and Cultural Change* edited by Francesca Carnevali and Julie-Marie Strange, published in 1994.

The British government could do nothing to prevent or ameliorate a catastrophe. Despite its aspiration to global leadership, it faced a desperate struggle to put its own house in order. The British depression represented a worsening of the 1920s pattern of economic disappointment. The staple industries – steel, coal, shipbuilding and textiles – faced a sharp deterioration in their already miserable condition. Export markets collapsed and unemployment, heavily concentrated in these industries, went past 3 million.

The British depression was also geographically concentrated. The plight of the north of England, Scotland, Wales and Northern Ireland contrasted sharply with the relative prosperity of the south of England and the English Midlands, though pockets of poverty and well-being were randomly distributed throughout Britain. However, the burden of paying for unemployment fell nationwide. The heavy increase naturally strained public finances as tax revenues fell and the burden of unemployment benefit increased. The government faced difficulty in remaining on the gold standard, an aspiration requiring continued high interest rates and a balanced budget. By mid-1931 foreign credits were required to stay on gold and when the pound was forced off in September 1931, it seemed as if the British economy was on the verge of an inflationary collapse.

The 1931 crisis and the May Report

Struggling to cope with falling world markets and dislocation of trade, the government was faced with a double financial crisis.

- Foreign investors, frightened by the collapse of the giant Viennese bank, the Credit Anstalt, began making withdrawals from London banks. Between 15 July and 7 August, £33 million in gold and £33 million in foreign exchange was withdrawn from London – almost one quarter of the reserves.

- **Balancing the annual budget** was proving difficult, if not impossible. Increasing unemployment meant that more and more had to be paid out in benefits. Fewer people in work meant less being paid to the government in taxes. The only way to get the budget to balance was to reduce government expenditure, increase taxation, or both.

> **KEY TERM**
>
> Balancing the annual budget
> Governments work out budgets every year. In doing so, they must ensure that government expenditure in the forthcoming year will be balanced by the income the government expects to receive.

Forced by the Liberals to set up a committee to advise on what was to be done, the chancellor of the exchequer, Philip Snowden, set one up. It comprised largely businessmen and accountants, with just one trade unionist – Alan Pugh of the Iron and Steel Trades Federation – and was headed by Sir George May. Its terms of reference were to make recommendations to the chancellor of the exchequer for possible reductions in the national expenditure. In July 1931, the committee published its report. It calculated that £120 million was needed to balance the budget, and it recommended that £23 million should be found from increased taxation, and £97 million by cuts in government spending.

Areas for reduction in spending	Amount saved
Savings on unemployment relief	£67 million
Reductions in teachers' salaries	£14 million
Reductions in armed services' pay	£2 million
Reductions in police pay	£1 million
Postponement of road schemes	£8 million
Miscellaneous	£5 million

Figure 7.6 The May Report's recommendations for reducing government expenditure.

With the bulk of the proposed savings coming in reductions to unemployment relief, the poor were potentially going to be hit hard.

On 19 August, the Cabinet was in session for nearly 12 hours, arguing about where the cuts should fall.

- Snowden, chancellor of the exchequer, argued that unemployment benefit should be cut by ten percent, which would take it back to its pre-1924 level, arguing that this particular benefit could not be protected when all other areas of government expenditure were being slashed.

- Arthur Henderson, the foreign secretary, found himself the spokesman of nearly half of the Cabinet who could not accept cuts to unemployment benefit. Whilst agreeing to a raft of reductions in government expenditure, they insisted that the unemployed had suffered enough at the hands of capitalism and that to cut their unemployment benefit would victimise them further.

The Cabinet had its advisers.

- A delegation from the TUC lent considerable support to Henderson's plea not to touch unemployment benefit.

- The economist Maynard Keynes advised the government to think radically and follow an alternative strategy: Britain should come off the gold standard, causing the pound to drop in value. Britain's exports would then become cheaper and more competitive in the world's markets. This would lower the **balance of payments** deficit and ease the financial crisis. Furthermore, the Bank of England would not need to deplete its gold reserves supporting the pound. The only cabinet minister to support this strategy – which, with hindsight, was the correct one – was Ernest Bevin.

TIMELINE: 1931 – A FATEFUL YEAR

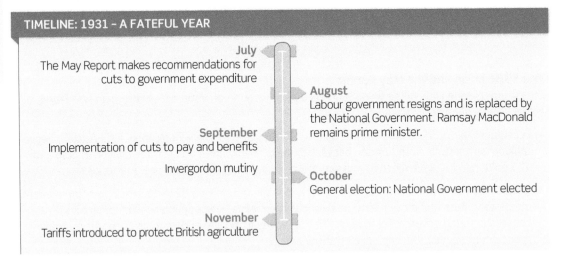

July
The May Report makes recommendations for cuts to government expenditure

August
Labour government resigns and is replaced by the National Government. Ramsay MacDonald remains prime minister.

September
Implementation of cuts to pay and benefits

Invergordon mutiny

October
General election: National Government elected

November
Tariffs introduced to protect British agriculture

EXTEND YOUR KNOWLEDGE

Keynesian theory of economics
John Maynard Keynes (1883–1946) was an English economist whose ideas changed the economic policies of governments. In the 1920s, he believed in the quantity theory of money. This was the belief that the money supply in any economy had a direct relationship with prices in that economy. For example, if the amount of money circulating was increased, prices would rise proportionately. This led him to advocate the end of laissez-faire and to propose state intervention in order to stabilise prices.

After 1929, as conditions worsened, Keynes realised that his quantity theory would not end unemployment. He began to develop his liquidity preference theory. Liquidity refers to the assets a company can quickly realise, and cash is always a company's best liquid asset. Firms fearing for the future would become risk averse. They would hold on to cash, refusing either to give or receive credit. Money would be hoarded, there would be no investment in industry and unemployment would soar.

In 1931, Britain came off the gold standard and laissez-faire was abandoned. Although Britain's economic position improved considerably, mass unemployment remained. Keynes came to believe that lack of demand lay at the root of the problem. If the demand for goods and services could be raised, then people would be fully employed, meeting that demand. The only way in which this could be done, Keynes argued, was by government-funded public works. This would put money into workers' pockets, demand for goods would increase and full employment in the companies, foundries, mills and yards would return.

In 1936, Keynes' *General Theory of Employment, Interest and Money* was published.

Ironically, it was rearmament that provided the catalyst for the regeneration of heavy industry along the lines suggested by Keynes.

Ramsay MacDonald did his utmost to bring about consensus. Eventually, the Cabinet agreed unanimously to cutbacks totalling £56 million. This was not enough. The key issue remained: should unemployment benefit be cut? MacDonald and Henderson each believed the other was betraying Labour ideals. When a vote was taken, the Cabinet was divided 11–9 in favour of a complete package of cuts in government expenditure, including unemployment benefit. A divided Cabinet could not function, and, on 23 August, Ramsay MacDonald offered his resignation and that of his government, to King George V. The following day, MacDonald met with the king, Stanley Baldwin (who represented the Conservatives) and Herbert Samuel of the Liberals. MacDonald was assured of their support and he agreed to the king's request that he form an all-party National Government.

On 24 August, MacDonald met with his colleagues in what was the final meeting of the Labour cabinet. They were dumbfounded, and accused him of treachery, betrayal and of plotting to retain personal power at the expense of the Labour Party. MacDonald's defence was that he was putting country before party. He was promptly expelled from the Party. Labour returned to the opposition benches and it seemed that all hope of alleviating the poverty of the unemployed was gone.

ACTIVITY
KNOWLEDGE CHECK

The second Labour government

1 Why did Sir George May's report in 1931 generate such controversy?

2 In what ways did tackling the effects of the Depression become a political matter?

3 How far do you agree with the first sentence in Extract 3 that 'The British government could do nothing to prevent or ameliorate a catastrophe'? Set up a debate where one side argues in support of the statement, and the other argues against it.

The National Government, 1931-40

Ramsay MacDonald put together a small cabinet of ten for his new National Government, comprising four Labour, four Conservative and two Liberal members. MacDonald remained as prime minister with Philip Snowden as chancellor of the exchequer, Stanley Baldwin as deputy prime minister and Neville Chamberlain as minister of health. The Liberal, Herbert Samuel, became home secretary.

One of the first acts of the new government was to implement the cuts to which the Labour cabinet, by a slim majority, had agreed. Snowden's package, which he put before the House of Commons on 10–11 September 1931, comprised cuts in government expenditure:

- teachers' pay reduced by 15 percent
- the pay of the armed forces, judges and MPs reduced by an average of ten percent
- police pay reduced by five percent
- a reduction in unemployment benefits by ten percent; a reduction in the time these benefits would be paid and a reduction in the dole by ten percent.

Additionally, there were tax increases that, it was estimated, would bring in about £51.5 million.

Initially, these moves seemed to work. International confidence in the pound was restored, the gold standard seemed secure and the Bank of England was able to negotiate a loan of £80 million from New York and Paris bankers. But trouble was brewing. When the sailors of the Atlantic fleet, based at Invergordon, learned that their pay was being reduced by ten percent while those of the admirals who commanded them were having pay cuts of only seven percent, they refused to put to sea. News of this 'Invergordon mutiny' was telegraphed around the world and the value of the pound plummeted. The government was unable to negotiate any more loans. Britain was forced off the gold standard and the value of the pound slipped even further. However, this meant that British goods could be sold abroad more cheaply: exports were encouraged and imports discouraged. The weaker pound made it easier to balance the budget. Maynard Keynes had been right.

The 1931 election

The National Government was unelected, and in order to get itself and its policies endorsed by the public, it called an election for October 1931.

SOURCE

7
A general election poster of 1931 asking voters to support the National Government.

The campaign was bitter and personal, but the result demonstrated nationwide support for the National Government. National Government candidates, 471 of whom were Conservative, polled 14.5 million votes that won them 556 seats. The Labour Party vote fell by 1.5 million to 6.6 million, leaving the Labour Party only 56 seats.

SOURCE

From H. Jennings *Brynmawr,* published 1934. This is part of a study made by Hilda Jennings of a South Wales mining village in the early 1930s.

While some effects of unemployment are general, individual men and their families of course react in different ways, and out of some six hundred families normally dependent upon unemployment benefit, probably no two have precisely the same attitude to life and circumstances. The unemployed man must register twice a week at the Exchange: he must draw his pay there on Fridays. If he has been out [of work] for some time, each Friday he will have a short period of sickening anxiety lest the clerk should single him out and tell him that he is to be sent to the 'Court of Referees', then will follow a few days of consequent dread lest his benefits be stopped and he be cast on to the Poor Law, have to do 'task work' for his maintenance, and to take home less to his family in return for it. Having received his 'pay', duly contributed his 'Penny' to the Unemployed Lodge of the Miners' Federation, and conversed with his fellow unemployed, he returns home. The wife awaits his return in order that she may do the weekly shopping, and in many cases almost all of his unemployment pay, with the exception of a little pocket money for 'fags', goes straight to her.

So far, there is similarity of practice, but beneath the surface this similarity does not reign. One man will approach the Exchange with impatience and bitterness at his dependence and impotency to help himself; one in a mood to find causes of complaint and irritation with the officials; one with growing apathy, and no conscious feeling except when his pay is threatened; one, again, with each visit feels the need for a change in the economic and social system; his political consciousness is inflamed, and he will fumble in his mind for an alternative, or shout the current formulae at the next 'unemployed' or 'party' meeting according to his mental outlook and capacity.

Towards recovery?

Recovery under the National Government was helped by factors that had little to do with the government itself. From the mid-1930s, there was a general recovery in world trade. This, along with the weak pound, meant that British goods were cheap to buy abroad. Exports began to rise and this created more jobs. Towards the end of the 1930s, still more jobs were created as all major countries in Europe began concentrating on armaments production as the Nazi threat grew. The National Government was greatly helped, too, by the lack of a strong opposition. The Liberal Party had been fatally wounded by a split between Asquith and Lloyd George in the early 1920s, and the Labour Party was smarting from the self-inflicted wounds of the summer of 1931. A further general election of 1935 confirmed the National Government in power, although with a reduced majority.

Neville Chamberlain, who took over as chancellor of the exchequer from Philip Snowden in November 1931, built on these advantages. He introduced import duties – a general tariff barrier of ten percent – in order to protect British industry. British agriculture was protected from foreign imports. Initially, wheat producers were guaranteed a minimum price of 10s per hundredweight. By 1939, farmers who produced hops, milk, bacon, oats, barley, meat and potatoes were all protected in the same way. Between 1931 and 1937, the agricultural industry increased its productivity by 15 percent. Low interest rates led to a housing boom, creating jobs and a 'feel good' factor among those able to buy their own home for the first time. Indeed, in 1935, Chamberlain was able fully to restore public salaries to their pre-1931 levels.

The plight of the unemployed

The problem of the unemployed remained like a festering sore – painful and refusing to go away. Although unemployment was falling from about 1933 onwards, it remained unacceptably high. For the unemployed, bad times continued.

- The Unemployment Act 1934 set up a national Unemployment Assistance Board which standardised dole payments, made when a person's 26 weeks' entitlement to unemployment benefit had run out, and paid them using a means test. This was fiercely enforced by district officers and deeply unpopular amongst the unemployed. Rates were set nationally and could not be varied according to local circumstances. Nationally enforced rates led to a storm of protest from unemployed workers, who found that the new scales were, in some regions, less generous than those being applied by their own local authority. This forced the government to agree that the new scales would not be introduced until July 1936.

- The National Government backed the Iron and Steel Federation, formed in 1932, to supervise the demolition of old, unprofitable works and build new ones, thus creating jobs.

- The Special Areas Act 1934 applied to regions of high unemployment: South Wales, Tyneside, west Cumberland and southern Scotland. Within these areas, the government financed projects (for example, the steelworks at Ebbw Vale). This went some way towards creating new jobs. However, by May 1939 only 273 factories had been established under the Special Areas scheme and these employed just 8,500 people. The total number of unemployed in the Special Areas in July 1939 was 226,193.

- In 1935, the government developed a scheme whereby shipowners could apply for government loans that would enable them to scrap old ships and buy new ones. This scheme enabled the Cunard–White Star line to order two new liners, the *Queen Mary* and the *Queen Elizabeth*, from John Brown's shipyard on the River Clyde, creating work for unemployed shipyard workers.

A Level Exam-Style Question Section B

How accurate is it to say that the National Government successfully steered the British economy through the problems created by the Depression? (20 marks)

Tip

When planning your answer, think about the criteria you would use to measure 'success' and then measure the National Government's actions against that.

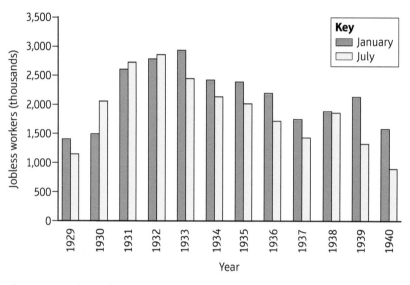

Figure 7.7 Registered unemployment, 1929-40.

A Level Exam-Style Question Section A

Study Source 9 before you answer this question.

Assess the value of the source for revealing the impact of the Depression and the effectiveness of the government's attempts to deal with the resultant unemployment.

Explain your answer, using the source, the information given about it and your own knowledge about the historical context. (20 marks)

Tip

Remember to consider the author of the source and think about his possible bias when addressing its reliability.

 SOURCE 9

From George Orwell *The Road to Wigan Pier,* published in 1937. Orwell's real name was Eric Arthur Blair. He wrote many novels, some non-fiction works of which *The Road to Wigan Pier* is one, and contributed articles to newspapers and journals. Left-wing in his politics, he hated totalitarianism and was keenly aware of the need for social justice.

When you see the unemployment figures quoted at two millions, it is fatally easy to take this as meaning that two million are out of work and that the rest of the population is comparatively comfortable. This is an enormous under-estimate, because, in the first place, the only people shown on unemployment figures are those actually drawing the dole – that is, in general, heads of families. An unemployed man's dependents do not figure on the list unless they, too, are drawing a separate allowance. A Labour Exchange officer told me that to get at the real number of people living on (not drawing) the dole, you have got to multiply the official figures by something over three. This alone brings the number of unemployed to around six million.

It will be seen that the income of a family on the dole normally averages around thirty shillings a week. One can write at least a quarter of this off as rent, which is to say that the average person, child or adult, has got to be fed, clothed, warmed and otherwise cared-for for six or seven shillings a week. Enormous groups of people, probably at least a third of the whole population of the industrial areas, are living at this level. The Means Test is very strictly enforced, and you are liable to be refused relief at the slightest hint that you are getting money from another source.

The most cruel and evil effect of the Means Test is the way in which it breaks up families. Old people, sometimes bedridden, are driven out of their homes by it. An old age pensioner, for instance, if a widower, would usually live with one or other of his children; his weekly ten shillings goes toward the household expenses, and probably he is not badly cared for. Under the means test he counts as a 'lodger' and if he stays at home his children's dole will be docked. So, perhaps seventy or seventy-five years of age he has to turn out into lodgings, handing his pension over to the lodging house keeper and existing on the verge of starvation. I have seen several cases of this myself.

SOURCE 10

From a letter to the editor of the *Times* newspaper, published on 22 February 1938, and the supporting statement from the editor, headed 'Idle and Content'.

Sir,

Both in the depressed regions (not now so depressed as they were) and in prosperous London there is a growing number of young men between 19 and 30 who are no longer trying to live independent lives. They have all refused offers of training by the Ministry of Labour, yet make no other effort at recovery on their own account. They have settled down and usually married. They often eke out the 25s to 35s a week, which they draw from the Unemployed Assistance Board, by a few undisclosed pickings in the market, the docks or the gambling industry. The fact is that under our existing policies there is nothing to disturb their complacent acceptance of this debilitating way of life, and their example is infectious. Relief scales and rules, which have been expanded and eased for the sake of the decent unemployed, have proved to be too easy going and tempting for the venal minority. What is now required for these thousands of parasitic young men is some new type of compulsory work centres, both residential and non-residential.

Ronald C Davison   London

IDLE AND CONTENT

Though it can be represented that in the distressed areas there have been predisposing causes to lethargy in a generation that grew up in a workless place, the excuse has no validity elsewhere. In a considerable number of the chronically or constantly unemployed young men, there is a slackness of moral fibre and of will as well as muscle. Mr R C Davison does not in his letter exaggerate the facts when he speaks of these young men no longer trying to live independent lives, but as having settled down to a permanent reliance on the Unemployment Assistance Board's allowances and casual supplements from odd jobs now and again.

SOURCE 11

A cartoon published in the *Daily Express* newspaper in 1936.

WORK AT LAST

The National Government

1 What were the strengths and the weaknesses of the package of cuts proposed by Philip Snowden, chancellor of the exchequer, and implemented by the government, in 1931?

2 What is the strength of the appeal of the National Government's election poster (Source 7)? Did it deliver on its promises, once elected?

3 Both Hilda Jennings (Source 8) and George Orwell (Source 9) wrote eyewitness accounts of life for the unemployed. How far do their accounts agree?

4 Read Source 10. How would a) Labour MP Ellen Wilkinson, b) Communist Wal Hannington and c) chancellor of the exchequer Neville Chamberlain have responded? You could work in groups of three, with each student taking on the role of one of the individuals and writing a response to the *Times* newspaper.

5 What is the 'message' of Source 11? In what ways is it correct?

Conclusion

The significance of the slump and Depression for Britain were far reaching. They impacted on the British economy, creating a north/south divide insofar as prosperity was concerned; they caused the collapse of Britain's staple industries and resultant mass unemployment, and they brought about the creation of a coalition 'National' Government to try to cope with the situation.

Meanwhile, storm clouds of a different nature were gathering over Europe. In 1937, Neville Chamberlain became Britain's prime minister, four years after Adolf Hitler became chancellor of Germany. Chamberlain's skills and interest lay in the fields of administrative and social reform. Yet his administration, of necessity, became preoccupied with the dreadful and terrifying threat Hitler's aggression was posing to the peace and fragile security in Europe. Ironically, it was in preparing to face that threat that Britain's unemployed returned to work.

SOURCE

From E. Wright Bakke *The Unemployed Man,* published in 1933.

There is evidence that the scheme [Unemployed Insurance] has alleviated the worst physical effects of unemployment. It has kept the diet from falling to unhealthful levels; it has kept workers from falling into arrears on their rent; it has made it unnecessary to dispose of home furnishings to the extent which would have been necessary without it; it has to some extent made it possible for men and women to keep up their associations with their fellows longer; it has kept unrest at a minimum, the failure of political agitation of Communist factions to flourish amongst those secure in the knowledge that the State is assisting them to help themselves. It has not relieved, however, and cannot by its very nature relieve, the mental and moral fatigue and discouragement which result from having no job. It cannot supply the loss of status and the sense of self respect which vanish with the job.

EXTRACT

4 From John Gorman *To Build Jerusalem,* published in 1980.

The unemployed continued to demonstrate against the cuts and inhuman conditions imposed by the National Government led by Ramsay MacDonald. The cuts had reduced the rate of adult benefit; the number of claimants falling within the conditions of the new means test increased to 825,000, subjecting millions to the humiliation and degradation of inquisition by the government means test investigators. By January 1932 the registered unemployed had soared past the 2,500,000 figure and 1,143,025 were in receipt of poor relief. It is significantly recorded that 15,795 persons entered the casual wards as tramps that year, a social tragedy.

People were poverty stricken by the million, deprived, helpless and frustrated. From time to time they fought back with mass fury, directing their anger towards the officials at local and government level who operated the unfeeling machinery of state.

Evidence (6c)

Comparing and evaluating historians' arguments
Source 12 and Extract 4 are two historians' accounts about the effects of the Depression.

1 Compare the two accounts above and identify factual statements or claims that they both agree upon. Make a list of these points.

2 Look carefully at how the historians use language. Do they both use equally cautious language in making their claims or is one more confident and assertive than the other? Is one, or both, of the historians over-claiming?

3 Historians select evidence in order to make their arguments. Look back in this chapter and find evidence to support the arguments of each historian.

4 Are both of the historical accounts equally credible or are there reasons to prefer one account more than the other?

ACTIVITY
SUMMARY

The impact of the slump and the Depression
1 How far did the Depression create regional differences in Britain?

2 Why was unemployment such a problem in the 1920s and 1930s?

3 What impact did the Depression have on British politics?

4 How successfully did the state deal with the problems generated by the Depression?

 WIDER READING

Aldcroft, D.H. *The British Economy between the Wars*, Philip Allan (1983)

Carnevali, F. and Strange, J. (eds) *20th Century Britain: Economic, Cultural and Social Change*, Longman (1994)

Constantine, S. *Unemployment in Britain between the Wars*, Longman (1980)

Harris, B. *The Origins of the British Welfare State*, Palgrave Macmillan (2004)

Mowat, C.L. *Britain between the Wars*, Methuen (1955)

Orwell, G. *The Road to Wigan Pier*, Penguin (1962)

Skidelsky, R. *Politicians and the Slump 1929-31*, Pelican (1970)

Wilkinson, E. *The Town that was Murdered*, Gollancz (1939)

Preparing for your A Level Paper 3 exam

Advance planning

Draw up a timetable for your revision and try to keep to it. Spend longer on topics that you have found difficult, and revise them several times. Aim to be confident about all aspects of your Paper 3 work, because this will ensure that you have a choice of questions in Sections B and C.

Paper 3 Overview

Paper 3	Time: 2 hours 15 minutes	
Section A	Answer 1 compulsory question for the option studied, assessing source analysis and evaluation skills.	20 marks
Section B	Answer 1 question from a choice of 2 on an aspect in depth for the option studied.	20 marks
Section C	Answer 1 question from a choice of 2 on an aspect in breadth for the option studied	20 marks
	Total marks =	60 marks

Section A questions

There is no choice of question in Section A. You will be referred to a source of about 350 words long, printed in a Sources Booklet. The source will be a primary source or one that is contemporary to the period you have studied, and will relate to one of the key topics in the Aspect of Depth. You will be expected to analyse and evaluate the source in its historical context. The question will ask you to assess the value of the source for revealing something specific about the period, and will expect you to explain your answer, using the source, the information given about its origin and your own knowledge about the historical context.

Section B questions

You will have a choice of one from two questions in Section B. They will aim to assess your understanding of one or more of the key topics in the Aspect of Depth you have studied. Questions may relate to a single, momentous year, but will normally cover longer periods. You will be required to write an essay evaluating an aspect of the period. You may be asked about change and continuity, similarity and difference, consequences, significance or causation, or you may be given a quotation and asked to explain how far you agree with it. All questions will require you to reach a substantiated judgement.

Section C questions

You will have a choice of one from two questions in Section C. Questions will relate to the themes of the Aspects of Breadth you have studied, and will aim to assess your understanding of change over time. They will cover a period of no less than 100 years and will relate either to the factors that brought about change, or the extent of change over the period, or patterns of change as demonstrated by turning points.

Use of time

- Do not write solidly for 45 minutes on each question. For Section B and C answers, you should spend a few minutes working out what the question is asking you to do, and drawing up a plan of your answer. This is especially important for Section C answers, which cover an extended period of time.

- For Section A, it is essential that you have a clear understanding of the content of the source and its historical context. Pay particular attention to the provenance: was the author in a position to know what he or she was writing about? Read it carefully and underline important points. You might decide to spend up to ten minutes reading the source and drawing up your plan, and 35 minutes writing your answer.

Preparing for your A Level exams

Paper 3: A Level sample answer with comments

Section A

These questions require you to analyse and evaluate source material with respect to its historical context.

For these questions remember to:

- look at the evidence given in the source and consider how the source could be used in differing ways to provide historical understanding
- use your knowledge of the historical context to discuss any limitations the source may have
- use your historical understanding to evaluate the source, considering how much weight you would give to its argument
- come to a judgement on the overall value of the source in respect to the question.

Study Source 12 (Chapter 4, page 104) before you answer this question.

Assess the value of the source for revealing the extent of opposition in the north of England and the problems facing the commissioners as they tried to implement the Poor Law Amendment Act.

Explain your answer, using the source, the information given about its origin and your own knowledge about the historical context. (20 marks)

Average student answer

The source is very useful because it gives us an authoritative account of what happened in Todmorden when the Poor Law commissioners tried to have the Poor Law Amendment Act implemented there. There was a great deal of opposition and the ringleaders of the opposition worked at the Fielden Mills. The mills shut in protest against the Act, and when two constables arrived to serve a warrant on the overseers for not implementing the Act, mill workers rang the factory bell to alert everyone and started a riot. The source is authoritative because it comes from an official report – the fourth report of the Poor Law Commission itself.

The source gives us an important insight into opposition in the north of England because it is linked to parliament. The MP for Todmorden was John Fielden, and he was the person who owned the mills and who was intent on keeping the new Poor Law out of the town. He had voted against the Poor Law Amendment Act in parliament. The Poor Law Amendment Act changed the old poor laws that were very much locality based and it was very much up to every parish how they treated their poor. The new Act tried to centralise everything, and tried to make all those who claimed relief go into a workhouse where they would be looked after, but where conditions had to be worse than those of the poorest person living outside the workhouse. It didn't really happen like this because more people were still getting outdoor relief than those that were getting relief inside the workhouse. Obviously, John Fielden didn't want workhouses to come to Todmorden.

> This is a weak opening paragraph, despite demonstrating an accurate understanding of the content of the source. It does not interrogate the source in relation to the question, nor does it set out the line of argument the answer will take.

> Although this paragraph contains information that is correct and is relevant to the period, contextualising the source, it is not made relevant to the question that is being asked. It is not specifically related to the north of England, nor to the problems facing the commissioners as they tried to implement the Act.

Edwin Chadwick, who was secretary to the commission, advised the commissioners not to start implementing the Act in the south. This was because it was always going to be easier to implement it there and the north was always going to be difficult because of cyclical unemployment. If the new Poor Law had been started off in the north when employment was high, there wouldn't have been any problem. But the commissioners didn't listen to Chadwick and by the time they got round to implementing the Act in the north, there was a fair amount of unemployment and so opposition. What happened in Todmorden is a good example of this.

The source is useful because of the insights it gives us into a northern town at the time the new Poor Law was implemented. However, it is not useful because of who wrote it and what the audience was. It is an official publication written for the government who had wanted the Act and set up the commissioners in the first place. The commissioners write an annual report and they aren't going to say anything the government doesn't want to hear in case they discredit themselves. This suggests that the report will be biased to what the government wants to hear and not to what was really happening. The authors of the report cast Fielden in a bad light, saying he was endangering the peace of the neighbourhood while at the same time praising the magistrates who were trying to uphold law and order. The commissioners who wrote the report would be using reports that came in to them, they wouldn't necessarily have visited Todmorden themselves. So there is danger of a double bias here: that of those reporting in to the commissioners, and those people would want to keep their jobs, and the spin the commissioners themselves put on the reports they received when preparing a more general one for publication.

Overall, the source is useful to a certain extent, because it is about implementing the new Poor Law in the north of England and does describe what happened in one town there when this was done. But it is not useful because it does not tell us anything about the rest of the country. We need to know from Fielden himself what was happening in Todmorden from his point of view before we can draw any balanced conclusions about the implementation of the new Poor Law in the north. From my own knowledge, I know that the south was peaceful when the new Poor Law was introduced and that cyclical unemployment made it very difficult to introduce a poor law based on workhouses.

> This paragraph is accurate with regard to Chadwick's advice and the order in which the commissioners set about implementing the Poor Law Amendment Act. It is beginning to get to the point about the problem of cyclical unemployment in the north of England, but doesn't develop this further to explain why cyclical unemployment created such problems for the commissioners. The paragraph touches on the relative ease with which the Act was implemented in the south, but, again, doesn't develop this to explain why this was.

> There is an attempt here at evaluation, but it is rather formulaic in approach. It suggests the commissioners were biased and that those reporting to them were biased, too. There is no evidence for this, only supposition. It would be better if the information about the provenance of the source was used to make informed judgements about its usefulness.

> This concluding paragraph is not strong. It repeats some of the undeveloped statements from earlier, and does not present a conclusion that relates to the actual question asked. Suggesting that alternative sources might be more useful, or could be used with the presented one, is not part of the question and should not form part of the final judgement.

Verdict

This is an average answer because:

- it does not always explicitly develop points or judgements
- it uses limited and imprecise evidence to expand, confirm or challenge points raised by the source
- it only superficially analyses the provenance of the source in a rather formulaic fashion.

Use the feedback on this essay to rewrite it, making as many improvements as you can.

Paper 3: A Level sample answer with comments

Section A

These questions require you to analyse and evaluate source material with respect to its historical context.

For these questions remember to:

- look at the evidence given in the source and consider how the source could be used in differing ways to provide historical understanding
- use your knowledge of the historical context to discuss any limitations the source may have
- use your historical understanding to evaluate the source, considering how much weight you would give to its argument
- come to a judgement on the overall value of the source in respect to the question.

Study Source 12 in Chapter 4 (page 104) before you answer this question.

Assess the value of the source for revealing the extent of opposition in the north of England and the problems facing the commissioners as they tried to implement the Poor Law Amendment Act.

Explain your answer, using the source, the information given about its origin and your own knowledge about the historical context. (20 marks)

Strong student answer

This source represents the crux of the problem faced by the Poor Law commissioners as they tried to enforce the provisions of the new Poor Law in the north of England. By beginning to implement the new Poor Law in the mainly agricultural south, the commissioners faced little opposition. Firm action by guardians and magistrates nipped any opposition in the bud, and the rural nature of the south of England prevented, by sheer geography, agricultural labourers from combining to oppose the Act. By the time the commissioners were able to turn their attention to the north of England, they were facing a very different situation. Cyclical unemployment, whereby the failure of the American cotton crop, for example, could lead to temporary unemployment, had hit factories and mills and thousands were temporarily unemployed. To build large workhouses capable of housing the maximum number of the unemployed likely to claim relief at any one time did not make economic sense and, furthermore, it would unnecessarily psychologically damage the workers who needed relief through no fault of their own. It should be noted that the Poor Law Amendment Act itself did not forbid outdoor relief. The source is therefore of value in showing the extent to which the commissioners themselves were intent on dogmatically implementing a rule rather than demonstrating an understanding of the realities of the economic situation and dealing with it appropriately.

> A detailed opening paragraph which appropriately and accurately contextualises the source, while at the same time maintaining a focus on the question.

It is possible, focusing on the source, to gauge the extent of the problem facing workers in the north. The source describes events in Todmorden, a town dominated by the cotton industry and by the Fielden works, owned by the MP John Fielden and his brother. The Fielden works was one of the largest textile companies in Britain. It is reasonable to assume that if cyclical unemployment hit the Fielden works in 1838, then it also hit all the other cotton mills in the north of England, making thousands of workers in need of temporary relief. The problems faced by the Todmorden cotton operatives would therefore be similar to those faced by other cotton operatives elsewhere in the north of England. Therefore, whilst the source can be taken as indicative of the problems faced by the operatives and the mill owners, it cannot be taken as indicative of the extent of opposition to the implementation of the Act. The very fact that Todmorden was singled out in the commissioners' report could mean that the nature of the opposition there was unique, or it could be being used as an example of what was common. We'll only know this by reading all the report, and maybe not even then.

> This paragraph makes sound inferences from the report about the likely extent of cyclical unemployment in the north, and draws a sensible conclusion about the weakness of the source with reference to the extent of opposition.

The source also reveals the ways in which the commissioners exercised their power. Guardians, overseers and magistrates worked together to ensure the clauses of the Act, as interpreted by the commissioners, were imposed. Overseers raised the money through the Poor Rate and sent it to the guardians who exercised their discretion in providing relief. In this, they were backed by the magistrates. In Todmorden, the overseers refused to supply the guardians with the necessary funds and so the guardians could not provide relief to the poor. The magistrates fined the overseers and when constables arrived to execute the warrant, they were set upon by the mob. Here, Fielden, the local MP as well as being a partner in the Fielden textile company, supported the overseers, closed the mills and paid relief out of his own pocket. This exemplifies the power local mill owners could exercise if they so wished.

> This paragraph goes beyond the surface features of the source to look at the unwitting testimony – what is there by implication. This adds to the utility of the source.

The source could be seen as being biased because it is reporting to the government that is wanting the Act to be implemented successfully, and is written by those who were appointed by the government to carry out the implementation of the Act. They could have been afraid for their jobs. The fact that the situation in Todmorden was highlighted was significant. Mill owner John Fielden was the local MP and he had voted consistently against the government at all stages of the Poor Law Amendment bill before it became legal as the Act. The commissioners could well wish to discredit him. Even so, the very fact that the report from which this source is an extract was published for all to read means that it could be challenged as far as accuracy is concerned. Overall, the source reveals much that is useful in understanding the extent nature of opposition to the implementation of the new Poor Law and the problems facing the commissioner in implementing it, particularly in the north of England.

> This is a strong conclusion. It deals with any potential bias within the source or by the report itself and has an interesting comment to make about the role of John Fielden, and reaches a substantiated judgement.

Verdict

This is a strong answer because:

- it uses well-selected, accurate evidence to interrogate the source
- it clearly points out areas of the source that are more valid and useful than others
- it reaches persuasive conclusions based on a range of well-substantiated points.

Paper 3: A Level sample answer with comments

Section B

These questions require you to show your understanding of a period in depth. They will ask you about a quite specific period of time and require you to make a substantiated judgement about a specific aspect you have studied.

For these questions remember to:

• organise your essay and communicate it in a manner that is clear and comprehensible
• use historical knowledge to analyse and evaluate the key aspect of the question
• make a balanced argument that weighs up differing opinions
• make a substantiated overall judgement on the question.

How accurate is it to say that the Liberal governments' welfare reforms (1906–14) succeeded in preventing pauperism? (20 marks)

Average student answer

The first Liberal government of the 20th century was elected in 1906 and immediately began a series of reforms that were aimed at helping the poor and keeping them out of the workhouse. In this way, the reforms stopped pauperism.

In 1909, parliament passed the Old Age Pensions Act. They were paid to men and women aged over 70, and they were paid through the Post Office, not via officers of the Poor Law, so there was no stigma attached. In order to be eligible for a pension, as well as being over 70 years old, a person had to be a British citizen and have lived here for at least 20 years. Pensions were non-contributory and were paid for from taxation, not from the poor rates. Around 600,000 elderly people claimed pensions, about the same number as would previously have claimed poor relief. They were so grateful that many old people called their pensions 'Lloyd Georges' after David Lloyd George who was the chancellor of the exchequer at the time and who introduced the Act into parliament. The Act prevented them from becoming paupers.

> This is a weak opening paragraph. It makes sweeping generalisations and doesn't indicate that there is any discussion or argument to be made.

> This paragraph is presenting accurate factual material, but with no development. There is no indication, for example, as to those who were excluded from claiming a pension, nor that they were paid on a sliding scale. A better answer would also point out that the government was side-stepping the structure of the Poor Law, but that the 'undeserving poor' would still need to use the processes and procedures of claiming relief from the Poor Law.

It wasn't only the elderly who needed to escape from pauperism. Throughout the 19th century, it had been necessary to pay poor relief to people who were unemployed. Sometimes this was given in the workhouse and sometimes by way of outdoor relief. Either way, there was a stigma attached to being a pauper. The Liberal government wanted to lift these people out of pauperism. In order to do this, they first had to help people to find work and then provide money for them if they fell ill or lost their jobs. The government therefore set up a series of employment exchanges across the country where employers listed job vacancies and unemployed people could see what was available. This saved jobless men tramping round different possible employers and speeded up the whole process. By 1914, there were over 450 labour exchanges throughout the country and they were a great success, and people who might have been thrust into pauperism through no fault of their own were helped to stand on their own feet. The Labour Exchanges Act was passed in 1909.

Closely linked to the Labour Exchanges Act was the National Insurance Act 1911. Some of the better-paid workers had tried to safeguard themselves against pauperism by paying into organisations like friendly societies, but only the better off could afford this. These societies paid out in case of illness or sometimes for unemployment. Trade unions did this too. The National Insurance Act was in two parts. Part 1 dealt with supporting the poor when illness struck. Employers contributed 4d, employers 3d and the state 2d, and for this workers received 10s a week for 13 weeks and then 5s a week for a further 13 weeks. Payments into the scheme were compulsory and applied to workers who earned less than £160 a year and to all manual workers. Part 2 of the Act applied to insurance against unemployment. Employers, employees and the state each contributed 2½d and the scheme paid out 7s a week for up to 15 weeks. This was compulsory and 2.25 million men were insured by the end of 1912. This ended the fear of pauperism if workers became ill and could not support their families.

> Both of these paragraphs contain a great deal of accurate information. However, it is not sufficiently directed at the question. There is the assumption that both of these Acts automatically ended pauperism. It says nothing about those who were not covered by the Acts and so 'How accurate...' in the question is not addressed. Furthermore, although each of the paragraphs deals with one Act, the information contained within them lacks organisation in places.

In conclusion, the Liberal government's reforms did go a long way to ending pauperism. Minimum standards were established, and for the first time the state was taking over responsibility for lifting people out of the need to slide into pauperism. This shows an important change in attitudes to poverty. Such Acts would not have been possible in the 19th century. However, the benefits the state was providing were not available to everyone. That was left to the welfare state that was set up after 1945.

> This is a weak conclusion because it does not provide a summary of the arguments made in the body of the response (there were no arguments) and so does not answer the question, which requires a substantiated judgement to be made. It hints that there were problems, but these should have been developed in the body of the answer.

Verdict

This is an average answer because:

- there is some attempt to link the key features of the period and the question, though an understanding of the conceptual demands of the question is insufficiently demonstrated
- mostly accurate and relevant knowledge is deployed, but it is not analysed in relation to the question
- points made tend to be assertions rather than being backed by evidence and there is little, if any, attempt to establish criteria by which judgements can be made
- the answer shows some organisation, but lacks coherence in places and little by way of argument is offered.

Use the feedback on this essay to rewrite it, making as many improvements as you can.

Paper 3: A Level sample answer with comments

Section B

These questions require you to show your understanding of a period in depth. They will ask you about a quite specific period of time and require you to make a substantiated judgement about a specific aspect you have studied.

For these questions remember to:

- organise your essay and communicate it in a manner that is clear and comprehensible
- use historical knowledge to analyse and evaluate the key aspect of the question
- make a balanced argument that weighs up differing opinions
- make a substantiated overall judgement on the question.

How accurate is it to say that the Liberal governments' welfare reforms (1906–14) succeeded in preventing pauperism? (20 marks)

Strong student answer

The Liberal Party, elected to government in 1906, embarked on a series of welfare reforms. These were not signalled in their election manifesto; they would seem to have resulted from the concern of leading politicians about the general state of the nation as referenced by the findings of Rowntree and Booth, as well as the general debate on national efficiency informed by the Fabian Society and the Inter-departmental Committee on Physical Deterioration. These welfare reforms focused on improving the position of the poorest in society and, in doing so, thousands were prevented from sliding into pauperism. However, the reforms were not universal and thousands more were still reliant on poor relief for survival and pauperism was not ended.

Two important welfare reforms concerned the provision of school meals and medical inspections for school children aimed at ensuring a healthy workforce in the future. However, it was the adult (usually male) breadwinner becoming too old to work, falling ill while in work or becoming unemployed that drove a family to seek relief from the Poor Law authorities and therefore to become paupers. It is government actions in these fields that impacted on pauperism.

The introduction of old age pensions in 1909 was a non-controversial issue in itself as it had been discussed for some time. The main arguments were over whether the pensions should be contributory or non-contributory, with one side fearing that the poor would not save for their old age if pensions were non-contributory, and the other side making the case that the poor were not able to save. In the event, the Liberal government decided that pensions would be non-contributory and would be paid for from taxation. They were available for men and women who were aged over 70, who had been British citizens for over 20 years and were means tested. This means that they were not universal. They were paid on a sliding scale to people who had incomes of less than 12s a week. Furthermore, no payments whatsoever were available for men or women who had been in prison anytime in the previous ten years, had continually failed to find work or who had been in receipt of poor relief in the previous two years. These clauses in the 1909 Act effectively removed the most vulnerable in society, forcing them to accept poor relief and pauperism.

> This is a strong introductory paragraph. It contextualises the Liberal reforms and indicates the shape the argument will take – that the reforms did not end pauperism. It sets up the criterion for making a judgement about the prevention of pauperism – universality.

> A brief paragraph that could, perhaps, have been part of the introductory one. However, it explains clearly why the focus of this response is going to be on sickness and unemployment.

> A good paragraph showing a clear understanding of the nature of old age pensions, and reaches a judgement based on the criterion of universality.

The Labour Exchanges Act, also passed through parliament in 1909, was equally non-controversial and by 1914 there were over 450 labour exchanges throughout Britain, finding work for 3,000 people every day. This did help those in the underclass, who would otherwise have tramped for hours looking for casual work. Labour exchanges were closely tied to national insurance: only by signing on at a labour exchange as proof that they were looking for work could people claim unemployment benefit. It was here that the government again failed to help all unemployed people. Part 2 of the National Insurance Act 1911 did not apply to all unemployed people, everywhere. Only those who worked in relatively high-paid industries but which were prone to seasonal unemployment, such as shipbuilding, were covered. The intention was to expand cover to a wider range of industries, but the First World War started before this could be properly rolled out. Thousands of workers and their families were still thrown into pauperism when they became unemployed. Part 1 of the National Insurance Act did cover far more workers, insuring them against ill-health. Contributions, as with unemployment benefit, were made by employer, employee and the state and benefits were paid out over a period of 26 weeks in any one year. The scheme applied to those earning under £160 a year and at first might seem generous. However, flat rate payments (which were compulsory) hit the lowest paid workers the hardest; furthermore, it was only the worker who was covered – there was no sliding scale relating to the size of the family. Thus, sick workers with large families would still need to turn to the Poor Law for relief.

This is a closely argued paragraph that analyses the impact of the Labour Exchanges and National Insurance Acts in relation to the question, and rigorously applies the universality criterion when reaching judgements as to whether the Liberal government prevented pauperism.

The social reforms of the Liberal governments in the years 1906–14 did result in a considerable number of people avoiding pauperism. But the Liberals did not abolish the poor laws as they could have done. It seems that they were providing a parallel structure that helped the poor, possibly in the expectation that the poor laws would eventually wither away. However, throughout this period it is clear that the Liberal governments did not end pauperism: poor relief and its accompaniment, pauperism, remained as the final safety net for the vulnerable.

This is a sound conclusion, summarising the findings of the body of the response and answering the question directly.

Verdict

This is a strong answer because:

- relevant key issues are explored by sustained analysis
- sufficient knowledge is deployed to demonstrate an understanding of the conceptual demands of the question
- valid criteria by which the question can be judged are established
- the answer is well organised and the arguments are coherent throughout.

Paper 3: A Level sample answer with comments

Section C

These questions require you to show your understanding of a subject over a considerable period of time. They will ask you to assess a long-term historical topic and its development over a period of at least 100 years, and they require you to make a substantiated judgement in relation to the question.

For these questions remember to:

- organise your essay and communicate it in a manner that is clear and comprehensible
- use historical knowledge to analyse and evaluate the key aspect of the question covering the entire period
- make a balanced argument that weighs up differing opinions
- make a substantiated overall judgement on the question.

How far would you agree that the key impetus behind public health reform in the years 1780–1939 was provided by central government? (20 marks)

Average student answer

In the years 1780–1939, the government provided the impetus for public health reforms by passing some significant Public Health Acts. These Acts set out what the reforms should be and they built on each other to provide a gradually changing and improving environment in which people could live and work.

> This is a weak introduction. It focuses only on government action and does not acknowledge that there are other factors driving change.

The Public Health Act 1848 was possibly the most important. It set up local boards of health and empowered them to take control of sewers and drains and all things in their locality that impacted on public health. The problem with this Act was that it was permissive, which means that cities and towns could only take it on if they wanted to. The only compulsion was if their death rate was higher than 23 per thousand living people. However, this Act did provide the impetus for some forward-looking local authorities to make a real start on public health reform. There were other Public Health Acts that also provided an impetus for reform. The next most important one was the Sanitary Act 1866, which gave local authorities the power to knock down slums if they wanted to and so prevent the spread of disease. They could also remove nuisances. However, the Act that was compulsory and that really made a difference to all local authorities was the one passed in 1875. This said that every part of the country had to have a public health authority and at least one medical officer of health. These public health authorities had to appoint a medical officer of health and a sanitary inspector and the local authorities also had powers to lay sewers and drains, build public lavatories and ensure that the public was kept healthy. So it was these Acts that really got public health under way and so were the key impetus.

> This paragraph summarises the main Acts and asserts that these were the key impetus behind public health reform. There is no suggestion that there could be other factors involved and no creation of an argument.

There were other factors that have to be considered, but none of them provides the key impetus. The second most important factor would have been the various reports from different towns and cities that described problems of public health. For example, in 1832, Dr James Kay reported on the state of the poorer areas of Manchester. He described damp, badly drained streets where there were piles of human and other refuse uncollected and houses that were hardly fit for human habitation. He said that typhus was common. Perhaps the most important report published in 1842 was that brought together by Edwin Chadwick and which he had to publish at his own expense because the Poor Law commissioners didn't like it. It covered the whole of the country and criticised just about everyone – water companies, local authorities and Poor Law commissioners, for example – for the poor state of public health. As well as reports from officials like Kay and Chadwick, there were ones that were privately organised, like the one from

> This paragraph introduces, with a reasonable degree of accuracy, an alternative factor – that of reports about the condition of the towns and cities. It makes no attempt to link these reports to any Public Health Acts, or to any other factors that could be seen to drive change.

the Bradford Woolcombers Sanatory Committee in 1845. This detailed appalling living and working conditions of the Bradford Woolcombers whose average age of death was 14 years.

Another factor that was important was the growth of population. Between 1801 and 1851, the population of Britain doubled. It didn't just double, it was on the move. In the 1820s, Bristol, for example, grew by 70 percent, Bradford by 66 percent and Leeds, Liverpool and Manchester by 46 percent. This rapid growth of the new industrial towns brought huge problems of public health. Houses were just thrown up by speculative builders without drainage or sanitation and hundreds of people were thrown together in overcrowded conditions where disease spread rapidly. These diseases were typhus and typhoid, cholera, diphtheria, tuberculosis and scarlet fever.

Thus, it will be seen that, although there were some factors that contributed to public health reform, it was the Acts of Parliament, which were provided by central government, that were key. Without them, local authorities would not be compelled to make the necessary changes to people's living conditions and public health would not change.

> Another factor is introduced here, but linkages to the various reports referred to in the third paragraph are only implied. Any argument relating population growth and movement to disease is undeveloped, and the opportunity to link the spread of disease with an understanding of the causes of disease is lost. Expression is occasionally clumsy.

> This is a weak conclusion. It asserts that the Acts were key to public health reform and again doesn't link parliamentary Acts to alternative factors. There is no sense of argument being brought to a substantiated conclusion.

Verdict

This is an average answer because:

- it does not cover the whole period 1780–1939
- mostly accurate and relevant knowledge is deployed, but it is limited and not analysed in relation to the question
- points made tend to be assertions rather than being backed by evidence
- the answer shows some organisation, but lacks coherence in places and little by way of argument is offered.

Use the feedback on this essay to rewrite it, making as many improvements as you can.

Paper 3: A Level sample answer with comments

Section C

These questions require you to show your understanding of a subject over a considerable period of time. They will ask you to assess a long-term historical topic and its development over a period of at least 100 years, and they require you to make a substantiated judgement in relation to the question.

For these questions remember to:

- organise your essay and communicate it in a manner that is clear and comprehensible
- use historical knowledge to analyse and evaluate the key aspect of the question covering the entire period
- make a balanced argument that weighs up differing opinions
- make a substantiated overall judgement on the question.

How far would you agree that the key impetus behind public health reform in the years 1780–1939 was provided by central government? (20 marks)

Strong student answer

Many factors contributed to public health reform in the years 1780–1939 and they were all interrelated to a greater or lesser extent. It is because of this interrelationship that to separate one out as being 'key' is very difficult because in many ways we are looking at a chain reaction. It would be too simplistic to fasten on central government, with their Acts of Parliament and directives, as being the key one that drove change. An Act of Parliament itself reflects a need for change that drove legislators to draw up a bill that would be acceptable to MPs. We need to consider what it was that drove the legislators to reform public health.

> A strong introductory paragraph, indicating that a range of factors need to be considered, and that these factors are linked.

Public health problems had been a worry to authorities since medieval times, but it only became a serious concern as a result of industrialisation. Between 1780 and 1850, the population of England and Wales grew from 7.5 million to 18.5 million, and people migrated, too, to the growing industrial towns of the north and Midlands. In 1851, 50 percent of the population lived in towns; by 1891 this had risen to 72 percent and over 80 percent by 1939. In the 1820s, for example, Leeds, Liverpool and Manchester grew by 46 percent and Bradford by 66 percent. Local authorities simply could not cope. It was not so much the fact of urban growth, but the rate of that growth. Industrialisation, for many millions of families, meant poor housing, lack of sanitation and clean water, disease and early death – all of the problems associated with poor public health. This did not go unnoticed. Various reports on the state of the towns were written and published. A good example is that of James Kay's 1832 report on the moral and physical condition of Manchester's working classes. This linked poor living conditions with the prevalence of contagious diseases. Probably the most influential report was Chadwick's 'Report on the Sanitary Condition of the Labouring Population of Great Britain', published in 1842. Chadwick had masterminded a nationwide survey and it reached very similar conclusions to those of James Kay. He found that existing water supplies, drainage and sewerage systems were woefully inadequate, and, importantly, he made the connection between overcrowding, disease and early death.

> This is a good second paragraph. It focuses on population growth and internal migration as factors, linking these to public health problems. It recognises the existence of reports on towns and hints at the linkage between poor living conditions and disease.

In order for public health reforms to be effective, there has to be an understanding about the causes of disease and the ways in which it is transmitted. While the provision of clean water and effective sanitation is important, improvements in public health will only be really effective if they are properly targeted. Despite the connection made by John Snow in 1849 that cholera was a waterborne disease, and the discovery by Louis Pasteur in the 1860s that microorganisms caused disease, it wasn't until the 1870s that the medical establishment finally abandoned the miasmic theory of disease. This meant that the implementation of what was probably the

> There is a lot covered in this paragraph and, given more time outside the time pressures of an exam, it could have been developed more. Nevertheless, linkages are made between key factors and there is a clear understanding that impetus for public health reforms was multifactorial.

most significant Public Health Act, that of 1875, was done with knowledge. It also meant that central government was able to target the mass prevention of specific diseases, for example in 1922 ordering the pasteurisation of milk so that tuberculosis would not be passed on to people from infected cows, and the campaign in the 1930s to provide vaccines for children to prevent diphtheria. It also meant that there was evidence to back up the slum clearances of the 1880s and 1930s.

The way in which government legislation moved from the permissive to the compulsory is indicative of the ways in which the different factors developed and impacted on the perceived need for public health reform. Until the first significant Act with national application, local authorities could apply for private Acts of Parliament to deal with public health concerns in their own areas. During 1831–32, for example, the City of Exeter obtained an Act of Parliament allowing officials to pave, light and cleanse the city. The Public Health Act 1848, allowing local boards of health to manage sewers and drains, wells and slaughterhouses, burial grounds, public baths and parks, was permissive and only those forward-looking local authorities were likely to buy in to it. It was, however, compulsory if ten percent of ratepayers overrode their local council and demanded it, or if the death rate rose above 23 per thousand inhabitants. Twenty-seven years later, a Public Health Act, allowing for the eradication of slum dwellings, the supply of sanitation to houses and the appointment of a medical officer of health, was compulsory, as was the Public Health Act 1936.

> A sound paragraph tracing the development of legislation across the period and showing an understanding that the change from individual to national, from permissive to compulsory, was dependent on the factors that drove change.

In conclusion, a number of different factors drove public health reforms across the period 1780–1939. Central government could be seen to be a key player in instigating legislation that provided for public health reform and, eventually, made it compulsory. Indeed, parliament was the only body that could do this. However, central government involvement in public health reform did not happen suddenly and would not have been successful had it not been for a number of contributory factors. Of these, probably comprehensive reports describing the state of towns and cities, coupled with increased understanding about the causes of diseases and the way in which infection was transmitted, are probably key. Central government involvement was in many ways the culmination of the contributory factors that combined to drive change.

> A strong concluding paragraph. It draws together the points made in the body of the response and reaches a sustained and supported conclusion that addresses the initial question directly.

Verdict

This is a strong answer because:

- key issues relevant to the question are explored by a sustained analysis
- sufficient knowledge has been deployed to demonstrate an understanding of the demands and conceptual focus of the question
- the relative significance of a range of factors is evaluated in the process of reaching and substantiating the overall judgement
- the answer is well organised, the argument logical and coherent and communicated well.

Index

Acknowledgements

The authors and publisher would like to thank the following individuals and organisations for permission to reproduce photographs and text in this book.

(Key: b-bottom; c-centre; l-left; r-right; t-top)

Alamy Images: Chronicle 24, Mary Evans Picture Library 137, National Geographic Image Collection 6, World History Archive 145; **Bridgeman Art Library Ltd:** Applicants for Admission to a Casual Ward, 1874 (oil on canvas), Fildes, Samuel Luke (1844-1927)/Royal Holloway, University of London 8, Cowpox pustule on the arm of Sarah Nelmes, from 'An Inquiry into the Causes and Effects of the Variolae Vaccinae' by Edward Jenner (1749-1823) engraved by Pearce, c.1800 (coloured engraving), Skelton, William (1763-1848) / Bibliotheque de la Faculte de Medecine, Paris, France / Archives Charmet 51, The Workhouse, St James, Parish, London from Ackermann›s 'Repository of Arts', 1809 (hand-coloured aquatint), Rowlandson, T. (1756–1827) & Pugin, A.C. (1762–1832)/Private Collection/The Stapleton Collection 72, Vaccination against Small Pox or Mercenary and Merciless Spreaders of Death and Devastation Driven Out of Society!, 1808 (colour etching), Cruikshank, Isaac (1756–1811)/Private Collection 44, Work, 1852–65 (oil on canvas), Brown, Ford Madox (1821–93)/Manchester Art Gallery, UK 122; **British Library Images Online:** Evanion Collection 118, The Penny Satirist, shelfmark MFM.M3599, No. 438, September 6 1845, vol 8 (front cover) 110; **Daily Express:** George Strube/Express Newspapers 171; **Fotolia. com:** camerawithlegs 59cl, fenlio 59tl; **Getty Images:** 'Blue Gate Fields', 1872. Artist: Héliodore Joseph Pisan, taken from *London: A Piligrimage* by Blanchard Jerrold and Gustave Doré. Museum of London/Heritage Images 27, Buyenlarge 131, George Cruikshank illustration for Charles Dickens' *Oliver Twist*, London, 1837–38. Engraving/Universal History Archive 127, Hulton Archive 96b, 149, Karl Hutton 154, Original Artwork: Engraved by Phiz Photo by Rischgitz 100, Popperfoto 120, Savill 160, The Conservative Party Archive 168, W. Brown/Otto Herschan 58; **Mary Evans Picture Library:** 15, 56, 73, Peter Higgenbotham 91, 94l, 94r, 96t; **National Archives:** Crown Copyright 12; **Richard Burton Archives, Swansea University:** With kind permission of National Union of Mineworkers (South Wales Area) 162; **Science Photo Library Ltd:** British Library 54; **TopFoto:** Balean 140; **West Yorkshire Archive Service:** Bradford Deposited Building Plan Number 78; A plan of eight houses to be built in Holme Top Street, Little Horton, Bradford 1852 14.

Cover image: akg-images Ltd: Imagno

All other images © Pearson Education

Picture research by: Susie Prescott

Text
Extract p.16 from *The First Industrial Nation: An Economic History of Britain 1700–1914* (Peter Mathias, 1969), p.207, by kind permission of Routledge Taylor & Francis Group; Extract p.22 from *Endangered Lives*, Dent (Wohl, A.S. 1983), p.147 The Orion Publishing Group, London; Extract p.33 from *The Origins of the British Welfare State: Social Welfare in England and Wales 1800–1945* (Harris, B. 2004) p.113, reproduced with permission of Palgrave Macmillan; Extract p.38 from *Victorian Cities*, Oldhams Press (Briggs, A. 1968) pp.210–11, Pelican Publishing Company, used by kind permission of The Estate of Lord Briggs; Extract p.44 from *Housing in Urban Britain 1780–1914*, Macmillan (Rodger, R. 1989) p.66, Cambridge University Press; Extract p.74 from *The Old Poor Law 1795–1834*, Macmillan (Marshall, J.D. 1968) pp.9–12, reproduced with permission of Palgrave Macmillan; Extract p.92 from *Victorian Social Reform*, Longman (Midwinter, E.C. 1968); Extract p.101 from *The Early Victorians 1832–51*, Panther (Harrison, J.F.C. 1973) p.109; Extract p.106 from *State Society and the Poor in Nineteenth Century England*, Macmillan (Kidd, A. 1999) p.30, reproduced with permission of Palgrave Macmillan; Extract p.111 from *Hansard 3rd Series, Vol XCII, 1847*, HMSO, Contains public sector information licensed under the Open Government Licence (OGL) v3.0.http://www.nationalarchives. gov.uk/doc/open-government-licence; Extract p.114, reproduced, with permission from Poor Rate Returns in sessional papers annually; Extract p.115 from *The Workhouse System*, Georgia (Crowther, M.A. 1982) p.80, by permission of Professor Margaret Anne Crowther; Extract p.121 from *Poverty and Welfare 1830–1914*, Hodder & Stoughton (Murray, P. 1999) p.76, reproduced by permission of

Hodder Education; Extract p.124 from *Society and the Poor in Nineteenth-century England*, Macmillan (Kidd, A. 1999) p.110, reproduced with permission of Palgrave Macmillan; Extract p.128 from *How the West Grew Rich*, Perseus, Basic Books, Inc. (Rosenberg & Birdzell 1986) p.175, CCC, © Copyright 1986, Rosenberg & Birdzell, reprinted by permission of the Perseus Books Group; Extract p.128 from *The First Industrial Nation: An Economic History of Britain 1700–1914*, Methuen (Mathias, P. 1969), by kind permission of Routledge Taylor & Francis Group; Extract p. 128 from *Industry and Empire: From 1750 to the Present Day* by E.J. Hobsbawm (Penguin Books 1968, third edition 1999). Copyright © E.J. Hobsbawm, 1968, 1969, 1999; Extract p.136 from *Poverty: A Study of Town Life*, Macmillan (Rowntree, B.S. 1901), reproduced with permission of Palgrave Macmillan; Extract p.137 from *Edwardian England 1901–15*, Larousse Harrup (Read, D. 1972) p.152, by kind permission of Donald Reed; Extract p.146 from *The Classic Slum* by Robert Roberts (Pelican Books 1978, Penguin Books 1990) Copyright © Robert Roberts, 1971; Extract p.147 from a speech by Winston Churchill, made in the House of Commons on 19 May 1909, contains public sector information licensed under the Open Government Licence (OGL) v3.0.http://www.nationalarchives.gov.uk/doc/open-government-licence; Extract p.148 from *The Rise of Labour, 1899–1951*, London Macmillan (Reekes, A. 1991) p.26, reproduced with permission of Palgrave Macmillan; Extract p.151 from *The Evolution of the Welfare State*, Macmillan (Fraser, D. 1973) pp.162–3, reproduced with permission of Palgrave Macmillan; Extract p.150 from *The Shaping of the Welfare State*, Longman (Birch, R.C. 1974); Extract p.151 from *The Origins of the British Welfare State*, Macmillan (Harris, B. 2004), reproduced with permission of Palgrave Macmillan; Extract p.156 from part of the budget speech made by Winston Churchill, Chancellor of the Exchequer, in the House of Commons on 28 April 1925. Contains public sector information licensed under the Open Government Licence (OGL) v3.0.http://www.nationalarchives.gov.uk/doc/open-government-licence; Extract p.163 from *Changing Horizons: Britain 1914–1980* by W.O. Simpson (Nelson Thornes 1986), p.252, copyright © W.O. Simpson 1986, reprinted by permission of the publishers, Oxford University Press; Extract p.165 from *20th-Century Britain: Economic, Social and Cultural Change*, Longman (Price, C. 1994) p.152, with permission of Routledge Taylor & Francis Group; Extract p.169 from *Brynmawr*, Allenson & Co Ltd (Jennings, H. 1934) pp.138–42, by permission, James Clarke and Co. Ltd/Lutterworth Press; Extract p.170 from *The Road to Wigan Pier*, Penguin (Orwell, G. 1962) p.70, from *The Complete Works of George Orwell* by George Orwell, published by Secker & Warburg. Reprinted by permission of The Random House Group Limited. Renewed 1986 by the Estate of Sonia B. Orwell. Used by permission of Houghton Mifflin Harcourt; Extract p.171 from Idle and Content, *Times*, 22/02/1938 (Davison. R.C.), Times Newspapers Ltd, News Syndication; Extract p.172 from *The Unemployed Man*, 1st ed., Nisbet & Co. Ltd (Wright Bakke, E. 1933) p.251, reproduced by permission, James Clarke and Co Ltd/Lutterworth Press.